BREAKING FEMINIST WAVES

Series Editors:

LINDA MARTÍN ALCOFF, Hunter College and CUNY Graduate Center
GILLIAN HOWIE, University of Liverpool

For the last twenty years, feminist theory has been presented as a series of ascending waves. This picture has had the effect of deemphasizing the diversity of past scholarship as well as constraining the way we understand and frame new work. The aim of this series is to attract original scholars who will offer unique interpretations of past scholarship and unearth neglected contributions to feminist theory. By breaking free from the constraints of the image of waves, this series will be able to provide a wider forum for dialogue and engage historical and interdisciplinary work to open up feminist theory to new audiences and markets.

LINDA MARTÍN ALCOFF is Professor of Philosophy at Hunter College and the City University of New York Graduate Center. Her books include *Visible Identities: Race, Gender and the Self* (2006); *The Blackwell Guide to Feminist Philosophy* (co-edited with Eva Kittay, 2006); *Identity Politics Reconsidered* (co-edited with Moya, Mohanty, and Hames-Garcia, Palgrave 2006); and *Singing in the Fire: Tales of Women in Philosophy* (2003).

GILLIAN HOWIE is Senior Lecturer in the Department of Philosophy at the University of Liverpool. Her previous work includes *Deleuze and Spinoza: Aura of Expressionism*; *Touching Transcendence: Women and the Divine* (edited with Jan Jobling); *Third Wave Feminism: A Critical Exploration* (edited with Stacy Gillis and Rebecca Munford); *Menstruation* (edited with Andrew Shail); and *Gender, Teaching and Research in Higher Education* (edited with Ashley Tauchert).

Titles to date:

RESONANCES OF SLAVERY IN RACE/GENDER RELATIONS

Shadow at the Heart of American Politics

Jane Flax

First published in 2010 by
PALGRAVE MACMILLAN®
in the United States—a division of St. Martin's Press LLC,
175 Fifth Avenue, New York, NY 10010.

Where this book is distributed in the UK, Europe and the rest of the
world, this is by Palgrave Macmillan, a division of Macmillan Publishers
Limited, registered in England, company number 785998, of Houndmills,
Basingstoke, Hampshire RG21 6XS.

Palgrave Macmillan is the global academic imprint of the above companies
and has companies and representatives throughout the world.

Palgrave® and Macmillan® are registered trademarks in the United States,
the United Kingdom, Europe and other countries.

ISBN: 978–0–230–10866–0

Library of Congress Cataloging-in-Publication Data

Flax, Jane.
    Resonances of slavery in race/gender relations : shadow at the heart of
American politics / Jane Flax.
        p. cm.—(Breaking feminist waves)
    Includes bibliographical references.
    ISBN 978–0–230–10866–0 (alk. paper)
    1. United States—Race relations—Philosophy. 2. Racism—United
States—Philosophy. 3. Race discrimination—United States. 4. Sex
discrimination against women—United States. 5. Slavery—United
States—Psychological aspects. 6. Slavery—Moral and ethical aspects—
United States. 7. Melancholy—Social aspects—United States. 8. United
States—Politics and government. 9. African Americans—Social conditions.
    I. Title.

E185.625.F 543 2010
305.800973—dc22   2010018769

A catalogue record of the book is available from the British Library.

Design by Newgen Imaging Systems (P) Ltd., Chennai, India.

First edition: December 2010

10 9 8 7 6 5 4 3 2 1

Printed in the United States of America.

This book is dedicated to the memory of Peter Lyman:
a much loved and much missed friend.

CONTENTS

Series Foreword

Breaking Feminist Waves is a series designed to rethink the conventional models of what feminism is today, its past and future trajectories. For more than a quarter of a century, feminist theory has been presented as a series of ascending waves, and this has come to represent generational divides and differences of political orientation as well as different formulations of goals. The imagery of waves, while connoting continuous movement, implies a singular trajectory with an inevitably progressive teleology. As such, it constrains the way we understand what feminism has been and where feminist thought has appeared, while simplifying the rich and nuanced political and philosophical diversity that has been characteristic of feminism throughout. Most disturbingly, it restricts the way we understand and frame new work.

This series provides a forum to reassess established constructions of feminism and of feminist theory. It provides a starting point to redefine feminism as a configuration of intersecting movements and concerns; with political commitment but, perhaps, without a singular centre or primary track. The generational divisions among women do not actually correlate to common interpretive frameworks shaped by shared historical circumstances, but rather to a diverse set of arguments, problems, and interests affected by differing historical contexts and locations. Often excluded from cultural access to dominant modes of communication and dissemination, feminisms have never been uniform nor yet in a comprehensive conversation. The generational division, then, cannot represent the dominant divide within feminism, nor a division between essentially coherent moments; there are always multiple conflicts and contradictions, as well as differences about the goals, strategies, founding concepts, and starting premises.

Nonetheless; the problems facing women, feminists, and feminisms are as acute and pressing today as ever. Featuring a variety of disciplinary and theoretical perspectives, *Breaking Feminist Waves* provides a forum for comparative, historical, and interdisciplinary work, with special attention to the problems of cultural differences, language and representation, embodiment, rights, violence, sexual economies, and political action. By rethinking feminisms' history as well as its present, and by unearthing neglected contributions to feminist theory, this series intends to unlock conversations between feminists and feminisms and to open up feminist theory and practice to new audiences.

—Linda Martín Alcoff and Gillian Howie

ACKNOWLEDGMENTS

This book gestated slowly. What evolved into the analysis of John Rawls's work in Chapter Four first emerged during a fall 1999 residency as a fellow at the Institute for the Human Sciences in Vienna. I am indebted to the staff and audiences there and also at the Freud Museum in Vienna for their inspiring attention. The Beatrice Bain Center at UC Berkeley provided six months of free time during which my thinking about unconscious process progressed. My "vertical community" compatriots, Barrie Thorne and Peter Lyman, provided many forms of sustenance. Responses to subsequent invited lectures at the following institutions and conferences were most helpful in refining my arguments: the Department of Political Science, UC Santa Cruz; the Department of Political Science, the University of Toronto; the Conference on Social and Political Thought (Canada); the McDowell Conference on Ethics, American University; the Annual Meeting of the American Psychoanalytic Association; the Annual Meeting, Psychology of Women, British Psychological Society; the International Conference on "Narratives for a New Millennium," Adelaide, Australia; the Conference on "Revisiting Dorothy Dinnerstein's *The Mermaid and the Minotaur*," the New School University; the Biannual Conference on Gender Studies, the Universidade Federal de Santa Catarina, Brazil; the Conference on "The *American Dilemma* Revisited," New York University; the 10th Biannual Conference, International Society for Theoretical Psychology, Istanbul; the Conference on "Deconstructing Feminist Mental Health Care: A South African Discussion," University of Stellenbosch, South Africa; AHRB Centre for Cultural Analysis, Theory and History, Leeds University; Institute for Gender and Development Studies, Nita Barrow Unit, University of the West Indies; and the "leaky pipe" project funded by the European Social Foundation Grant (European Union) and conducted at the University of Lund, Sweden. I am also grateful to the challenges and care provided by many people, often at just the right moment, without which this project would have died. These include Elisabeth Young-Bruehl,

Jennifer Nedelsky, Joseph Carens, Maureen MacGrogan, Ann Snitow, Griselda Pollock, Joan Cuffie, Toni Hetzler, Ann-Mari Sellerberg, Katarina Sjoberg, Lou-Marie Kruger, and Victor Wolfenstein. I am especially thankful to Linda Alcoff, Brigette Shull and Lee Norton for expediting the publishing process. To Eudine Barriteau I owe thanks for the special pleasures and support a former student's transformation into a respected colleague and friend provide. The comradery under difficult circumstance sustained by Rick Seltzer, Mervat Hatem, John Cotman, and Marilyn Lashley is much appreciated. For the deepening pleasures of his company, I am grateful to my son, Gabriel Flax Frankel. Ellen Feder's enthusiastic support and eagle eye editing were extraordinarily generous. Finally, I lament the impoverishment of current discourses of friendship. There is no language to convey what my relationships with Kirsten Dahl and Fred Risser mean and how they "keep me keeping on."

We Aren't There Yet

During a speech given in Philadelphia, on March 18, 2008, Barack Obama stated:

> Contrary to the claims of some of my critics, black and white, I have never been so naive as to believe we can get beyond our racial divisions in a single election cycle, or with a single candidacy—particularly a candidacy as imperfect as my own.[1]

Quoting William Faulkner, he reminded his audience that the "past isn't dead and buried. In fact, it isn't even past."[2] He told his listeners it is important to remember that "many of the disparities that exist in the African American community today can be directly traced to inequalities passed on from an earlier generation that suffered under the brutal legacy of slavery and Jim Crow."[3] The "legacy of discrimination—and current incidents of discrimination, while less overt than in the past—are real and must be addressed. Not just with words, but with deeds."[4] He characterized the relationship between the races as at a stalemate, with a "chasm of misunderstanding"[5] existing between them and delineated major differences in the narratives regarding race matters that black and white people tend to espouse. Referring to the nation's "original sin of slavery,"[6] he also suggested that if America is to move toward a more perfect union, major shifts in public discourse and policy are necessary.

In his autobiography, *Dreams from My Father*, Obama describes in more personal terms some of the effects on him of the legacy of America's original sin.[7] He weaves a narrative of his often painful attempts to negotiate the race/gender etiquette still pervasive within the United States. As a son of a white mother and a mostly absent black African father, with his mother's white parents often serving as his primary caretakers, he was forced to undergo a process of identity construction bounded by the simultaneously rigid and complexly fluid grammar of race/gender identities. "Away from my mother, away from my grandparents, I was engaged in a fitful interior struggle. I was trying to raise myself as a black man in America, and beyond the given of my appearance, no one around me seemed to know exactly what that meant."[8] Tormented throughout adolescence and early adulthood by the question of where he belonged, he slowly began to realize that the only solution to this American dilemma is to build a community in and through which America could redefine itself. By redeeming the American promise of a more perfect union, a community truly inclusive of all, Obama could finally answer the question, "where do I belong?"[9] By the time he finished law school Obama came to believe that only such a community could "admit the uniqueness of my own life."[10]

Adhering to such a vision is not the same as believing the dream has been realized. In his *The Audacity of Hope*, Obama denies that "we have arrived at a 'postracial politics' or that we already live in a color-blind society...To say that we are one people is not to suggest that race no longer matters—that the fight for equality has been won, or that the problems that minorities face in this country today are largely self-inflicted."[11] Furthermore, he warns, that while more "minorities may be living the American dream...their hold on that dream remains tenuous."[12]

Obama's election to the presidency evoked a tremendous surge of hope, legitimation, inclusion, and even redemption among many, perhaps especially, in the African American community. Despite Obama's disclaimer, some Americans are eager to insist that his election means we have finally achieved the dream as Dr. Martin Luther King so eloquently articulated it—that people will be judged on the content of their character, not their skin color. The realization of this dream means America is finally a "color-blind" society, and has thus entered a "postracial" state. However, as Obama himself suggests, there are ample reasons for caution in interpreting what his election means and might augur, particularly in regard to race/gender domination. American history is full of instances of raised hopes that at last the effects of our original sin of slavery will be expiated (e.g., the Reconstruction Era, passage of civil rights legislation in the 1960s, post-Katrina) followed by profound disillusionment as the legacy of race/gender domination reasserts its power. To investigate the possible meanings of his election, we must place it within the context of narratives and practices that deeply structure American political life. These include a particular version of individualism, complex grids of race/gender positioning, and what I call race/gender melancholia.

These processes undermine our ability to productively confront the effects of what Toni Morrison calls the "shadow at the heart" of the American dream—slavery.[13] Under the influence of our faith in individualism, Americans tend to overestimate the import of the singular instance and its representative power. Predominant race/gender grids were very apparent during the primaries, when the contest between Hilary Rodham Clinton and Barack Obama was categorized as a choice between an African American and a woman. This categorization reflects several dimensions of contemporary American practices of race/gendering, including the continuing effect of the "one drop rule"[14] and the conflating of woman and white and black and male. The erasure of black women is noticeable in some of these practices.

Perhaps most worrying to me is that Obama's election will strengthen the processes of denial, devaluation, and projection intrinsic to race/gender melancholia. Melancholia is a pathological response to loss. Rather than acknowledge the loss of a valued object (relationship, dream, etc.) the loss is either denied or the object is devalued so that the impact of its loss is minimized. Melancholic subjects are gripped by sometimes paralyzing wishes to magically erase the living past rather than engage in the arduous processes of realistically facing its effects and constructing practices to ameliorate them. I argue that as a society, America has never properly mourned the losses that would follow a serious grappling with the centrality of slavery in the development of our polity. There are at least two losses that such grappling would entail—a preferred narrative about the exceptional nature of American history and practices and a sense among dominant groups that their positioning is earned solely through individual effort and merit. As I will argue in chapter 6, proper mourning would entail numerous deeds, including publicly acknowledging and honoring the sacrifices enslaved persons made in the construction of a nation "dedicated" to freedom; initiating public and private discourse among and between members of various race/gender positions regarding the ongoing effects of the past's legacy; finding ways to reconstitute social relations so that existing practices of denigration, distrust, and ignorance are altered; and redistributing social goods and burdens to address contemporary, unearned asymmetries of wealth, power, and social respect and honor. Managing all this will require massive changes in the constituting practices of subjectivity, politics, and economics.

What would be sufficient evidence that America has shifted into a postracial state? I will argue that making such a case requires evidence that it is reasonable to anticipate that a person's life chances in areas deemed of value by that subject or their society will not be significantly affected by their race/gender location. Based on this criterion, it is premature for Americans to shout "free at last." I am certainly not claiming that, especially since the civil rights movements and legislation of the 1960s, no positive changes have occurred in our race/gender arrangements. Achievements such as ending legal segregation, enfranchising blacks so that they can register to vote without fearing for their lives, dismantling formal barriers to those in subordinate race/gender positions entering professions, and broadening access to important resources such as university education or buying real estate improve the lives of African Americans and all other citizens who care about justice. Reducing the horrible harms of the daily humiliations and fear inflicted on subordinates by white dominance is unambiguously good. Enjoyment of unearned privilege enables the dominant to organize themselves and the ways we live unjustly. Thus, any diminishing of dominance potentially enlarges the space for better practices that can generate more freedom and justice.

However, assuming that we have attained "postracial" nirvana is mistaken. It is reasonable to worry about the permanence of any improvement. There is little evidence for believing that history is unilinear and only moves in a progressive direction. As the unequal effects of the current recession illustrate, positive changes are fragile and subject to reversal. Instead, the post-Obama election flurry of discussion of achieving a "postracial" society turns out to be another manifestation of melancholic fantasy. Since he took office, a predictable repetition of the idealization/devaluation dynamic endemic to melancholia is manifest. What is unusual is that one person—Obama—is the object of both. Bestowing the Nobel Prize reflects, among other factors, an expression of idealization. The "birthers" who deny Obama is an American citizen and "Tea Party" members who by an overwhelmingly majority believe that Mr. Obama "does not share the values most Americans live by,"[15] express devaluation. Most importantly, I think that the typically American fantasy about the past, that it disappears without a trace and that therefore we can always start over again from scratch, has particularly pernicious effects on our ability to understand race/gender and its various dynamics and processes. As I will illustrate in various ways throughout this book, in regard to race/gender the effects of the past indeed are not past; instead its traces shape the distribution of valued goods, American political institutions, patterns of social relations, and what I call the political unconscious—powerful, culturally infused dynamics of fantasy and denial that structure American subjects. Understanding the operations of this political unconscious is not easy. As I will discuss more fully in the following chapters, it functions in and as that strange field anthropologists call the liminal. Liminal phenomena incorporate processes and material that a culture's practices treat as necessarily distinct and opposing. These phenomena transgress the normative boundaries and exclusionary categories cultures establish in organizing themselves. Their transgressive qualities enable liminal practices to do work cultures need to maintain the appearance of stability and coherence but also cannot acknowledge. The work cannot be acknowledged, because to do so would reveal how arbitrary and fragile cultures' modes of organization are and their practices' dependency on material they officially exclude or pronounce deviant, impossible, or nonexistent.

Despite the important work it does in American life, the operations and effects of the political unconscious are rarely explored. I hope that one of the major contributions of this book will be to highlight and address this malignant absence. As I will argue, failure to attend to unconscious processes and material is especially unfortunate in that it blinds us to many of the ways race/gender melancholia shapes our practices of subjectivity, citizenship, politics, and the distribution of valued resources. In contemporary American culture, the political unconscious transgresses boundaries of categories often treated as radically separate and distinct. These categories include psychic, material, personal, political, power, individual, social, thought, and feeling. The political unconscious is simultaneously idiosyncratic and widely shared. It is constituted through, as well as shapes and reflects, power relations, cultural and political practices, and affective states. It makes use of culturally available material to manage uniquely felt subjective dilemmas and so is deployed, experienced, and expressed differently by each subject. However, it also helps each subject carry out cultural demands (e.g., to locate oneself in particular race/gender grids) and in doing so makes use of widely available cultural and political information. Its processes are both limited and empowered by what is available for its use in any particular context, but it can remake practices of subjectivity and power relations in unpredictable and unexpected ways.[16]

In the rest of the book, I will develop and defend my claims regarding the existence, power, and effects of race/gender melancholia in contemporary American politics. In chapter 1, I will elaborate what I mean by race/gender melancholia and the political unconscious. I will also discuss the relationships between race/gender melancholia and race/gender domination. In chapter 2, I will introduce other concepts, especially race/gender, and discuss current distributions of valued goods to support the claim that Obama's election has not and cannot in the absence of profound changes signify the dawn of a post-race/gender era. Chapter 3 delves into the political unconscious, paying special attention to one of its most important modes, fantasy. I use three movies—*Monster's Ball*, *The Deep End*, and *Crash*—to explore some of the American political unconscious' contemporary content. I analyze the ways in which race/gender positioning and race/gender melancholia structure these movies' characters and plots. Each movie articulates different aspects of race/gender positioning and racial melancholia. Reading these enactments enables us to pay attention to dimensions of social practice and unconscious processes that we might consciously deny.

Individualism is the primary focus of chapter 4. Many variants of individualism exist, but I think it is fair to say that dominant American political culture has rarely strayed far from allegiance to some form of it. I will use the work of John Rawls to explore the work a particular kind of abstract individualism does to defend ourselves against race/gender melancholia. Rawls makes the best possible argument for a version of political liberalism grounded in such individualism, and thus I use his ideas as a case study to explore an important strand of American thought/practice. I will argue that, like all defensive processes, abstract individualism generates unintended and self-defeating effects. Tragically, in this case, it undermines the possibility of bringing about the result to which Rawls and so many others are deeply committed— the institution of a more just political framework. Therefore, generating more just political practices will require exploring alternatives.

I investigate alternatives in the last two chapters of the book. While chapter 4 focuses on rational constructions to reveal underlying fantasies, in the last two chapters I grapple with questions about how to weaken race/gender melancholia's grip. Chapter 5 is more abstract, considering different ways to think about subjectivity and congruent practices of citizenship. Chapter 6 suggests some public policies that offer leverage against the paralyzing and repetitive effects of race/gender melancholia and might reduce domination.

Initial discourses about the 2008 presidential election revealed a desire for the washing away of sin, a restoration of purity or the end of our enmeshment in history—longings that are understandable and recurring motifs in American thought and politics. However, as subsequent events suggest, unless we actively confront the race/gender melancholia that continually infuses the unmourned past into the present, wishes for a "more perfect union" will remain unrealizable for actual, socially constituted American subjects.

CHAPTER 1

Shadow at the Heart: Race/Gender Domination and the Melancholia of American Politics

What was distinctive in the New World was, first of all, its claim to freedom, and second, the presence of the unfree within the heart of the democratic experiment—the critical absence of democracy, its echo, shadow, and silent force in the political and intellectual activity of some not-Americans. The distinguishing features of the not-Americans were their slave status, their social status—and their color.[1]

Equality and freedom are central themes in the preferred narrative of America's founding and also our defining values.[2] In this context, the pervasive presence of the unfree—of slavery—is an irreconcilable paradox. David Brion Davis claims that "racial slavery became an intrinsic and indispensable part of New World settlement, not an accident or a marginal shortcoming of the American experience," and that we "must face the ultimate contradiction that our free and democratic society was made possible by massive slave labor."[3] While I agree with both these claims, I do not think that we have adequately confronted the consequences of this contradiction. The legalized practice of slavery, with its permanent relationships of domination and submission, as well as its creation of an utterly involuntary and fixed status, cannot be assimilated into the narrative of American exceptionalism—of a state uniquely born into and from freedom, destined to spread its essence beyond its own borders. We cannot resolve this contradiction, but we can devise better ways to deal with it, and proper mourning is one of the tools that can help us do that.

However, as Americans, we have not adequately confronted our history's contradictions and properly mourned their consequences. Instead, American politics and subjects suffer from untreated race/gender melancholia. In the ordinary process of mourning, we confront the loss of a valued object (a person, an ideal, an aspiration, etc.) and work it through. Going through this process enables the mourner to regain the lost object by creating a new relationship with it. In contrast, melancholia is a pathological form of mourning in which the subject does not acknowledge the loss of the object and hence remains unable to rework and reclaim his or her relationship with it. Race/gender melancholia stems from our collective failure as Americans to adequately mourn the centrality of slavery in the development of our nation's polity. This absence of mourning contributes to our persistent incapacity to constructively deal with slavery's legacy and its ongoing social, economic, and psychological effects. Instead, the influences of slavery on the constitution of American politics and citizenship and its profound effects on our current subjective practices remain insufficiently understood and acknowledged. The dominant attitude among most Americans, including academic writers is, as Paul Gilroy puts it, "If perceived as relevant at all, the history of slavery is somehow assigned to blacks. It becomes our special property rather than a part of the ethical and intellectual heritage of the West as a whole."[4] Or, even worse, in the periods of our history in which some people recognize slavery as "the dark side of the American dream" or the single sin marring national perfection, a "subtle psychological inversion" occurs, and the victims of slavery become the embodiments of the sin.[5] The failings and flaws of black people become the problem, the irresolvable American dilemma: "For two hundred years [with mixed success] African Americans have struggled against accepting or above all internalizing this prescribed identity, this psychological curse."[6] Imagining themselves outside this heritage, white Americans too often remain color-blind—that is, blind to our locations within race/gender dynamics and to the unearned benefits and advantages these locations generate.

Freud describes melancholia as a mental state in which "the shadow of the object fell upon the ego."[7] Toni Morrison describes "the presence of the unfree within the heart of the democratic experiment as its shadow."[8] Although it remains unacknowledged, this shadow has profoundly structured and continues to affect the heart of American subjects, institutions, and practices. Acknowledging this shadow is resisted because it would expose the gap between what many citizens would like the American polity to be and its actual practices. Of course, this gap is not unique to the United States; it is hard to identify any state in which ideals and practices perfectly coincide. However, as I will discuss in more detail in chapter 4, this gap is particularly problematic in the American context. States are complex social constructions. Their heterogeneous elements are rendered coherent through retrospective narratives about conscious intentions, founding moments and heroes, and a unique cultural identity.[9] In turn, such narratives become legitimating grounds, validating the state's claim to sovereignty and its citizens' loyalty. In the United States, these processes of social construction and narrative are unusually transparent. According to its dominant narrative, the United States originated in a particular discursive act—the writing and ratification of the Constitution. The fundamental ethical and political commitments of its soon-to-be citizens, especially freedom and equality, both necessitated and are reflected in this mode of origin. Given the freedom and equality of each individual, to be legitimate, any government must originate in and sustain the consent of its otherwise sovereign subjects. This founding of freedom and consent distinguished the United States from the Old World, mired as it was in relationships of status, ancestry, and caste.

Despite attempts to quarantine or marginalize them, the past and current effects of slavery are widespread: their traces exist in the Constitution; in the organization of labor and production of goods; in laws regulating subjectivity, property, citizenship, education, social interaction and marriage; and in patterns of child rearing and in sexual relationships. Slavery had been practiced prior to the founding of the United States, and it was not formally abolished for more than 200 years. Furthermore, while slavery in the United States was formally abolished in 1863, legalized race/gender domination was reinstated by post-Reconstruction Jim Crow laws. Even after formal emancipation, practices of peonage, psychological and physical terrorism (such as lynching and rape), political and economic exclusion, and cultural and social denigration and disrespect produced the functional equivalent of slavery. Children born today can still have grandparents who grew up in the reign of terror, deprivation, and entitlement that the Jim Crow laws enforced. Not until the passage of the Civil Rights Act of 1964 and the Voting Rights Act of 1965 did this formal legitimation end. However, actual practices, feelings, and unconscious fantasies have been even more resistant to change.[10]

The existence of the unfree is inextricably interwoven with race/gender. In addition to their status, slaves in the United States differed from most slave holders by their skin color. As I will discuss later, a complex discourse of race/gender developed to justify slavery or at least make it appear less incongruous with the stated principles of the free. White/male, free, and American emerged as mutually constituting terms. As Morrison claims, "deep within the word 'American' is its association with race...American means white."[11] "Whiteness," however, requires its reciprocal but degraded twin—"blackness"—to acquire meaning and effect. This interdependence produces an always potentially destabilizing paradox at the heart of American life:

> The Afro-American lies at the heart of Euro-America's conception of itself as a "race," as a culture, as a people, and as a nation. "Blackness" is the canvas against which "whiteness" paints itself, the mirror in which the collective eye sees itself.[12]

While it may no longer be politically correct to voice such feelings, even to oneself, legislation alone has not abolished them. It may even be the case, as Alexis de Tocqueville predicted, that the abolition of legal segregation increases "the repugnance for blacks felt by the white population."[13] Despite abolishing slavery, we have not destroyed three prejudices de Tocqueville describes as being "much more intangible and more tenacious than it: the prejudice of the master, the prejudice of race, and finally the prejudice of the white."[14] Instead, as Loury claims:

> Awareness of the racial "otherness" of blacks is embedded in the social consciousness of the American nation owing to the historical fact of slavery and its aftermath. This stigma even today exerts an inhibiting effect on the extent to which African Americans can realize their full potential.[15]

The reciprocal partner of the stigma, as I will discuss, is what Cheryl I. Harris calls a property in whiteness—an undeserved and often unconscious sense of entitlement that blinds some white people to the extent and effects of their undeserved advantages.[16]

As de Tocqueville predicted, the "remembrance of slavery dishonors the race, and race perpetuates the remembrance of slavery."[17] Intrinsic to race/gender melancholia is an inability to acknowledge and work through these memories. Instead, I will argue that denial and the splitting of responsibility shape dominant American political ideologies and ordinary practices of liberal citizenship. Admitting the constituting role of race/gender domination as enacted in slavery and in contemporary social relations disrupts dominant political-biographic narratives. Hence, it is either denied or its causes and effects are shifted to the raced/gendered other. Nonetheless, the "nation as a whole, and Afro-Americans in particular, are still paying the ethnocidal price of slavery and neo-dulotic Jim Crow system."[18] The silence, splitting of responsibility, and denial concerning such central practices defeat the possibility of better approximating the values of freedom, equality, and justice to which Americans pledge allegiance.[19] Denial poisons interracial relations and American politics. Domination and subordination are persistently reenacted, often in the very public and subjective practices and ideas that are said to be their opposite or remedy.

Facing this past and its enduring effects would inflict loss—loss of an idealized image that enables citizens to imagine that their ancestors constructed a shining "city on a hill," a city in which they now dwell. On an individual level, citizens would have to rework the dominant individualist narrative in which rewards or disadvantages are objectively determined solely by personal effort. We would confront our locations in complex networks of often unearned privilege and subordination and their distorting effects on all subjects. Instead, our failures to acknowledge and mourn the gaps between an idealized view of past and present America and the deep wounds inflicted by slavery and its ongoing consequences within our culture, political practices, social relations and subjectivities have left us in a suspended melancholic state. Whether consciously or unconsciously, Americans are "living with the ghost of the alien other within and living as the ghost in the gaze of another."[20] We cannot or do not face the enduring yet constantly mutating effects of our pasts. Instead, the power of the disavowed loss is endlessly renewed. American subjects are thus driven by a kind of compulsion to repeat in which they reiterate political narratives and practices and enactments of subjectivity that renew a melancholic attachment/denial of this shadow on its heart. Until we move from the pathological state of melancholia into more productive mourning, a sustained movement toward realizing usable American ideals such as freedom eludes us.

Race/gender melancholia serves as a way of simultaneously dealing with and defending against the acknowledgement of the effects of race/gender domination. Race/gender domination remains a structuring force in many aspects of American society and its subjects.[21] I purposely use the term race/gender domination rather than inequality. Domination signifies an illegitimate distribution of power in which neither the privileged nor subordinate positions are deserved. Exactly this sort of power generates and sustains our current race/gender arrangements. In chapter 2, I will support this claim with two kinds of arguments, one theoretical and the other empirical. The theoretical dimension is a "fabrication" approach to the construction of race/gender[22] and the empirical is an interpretation of an array of depressing facts regarding persisting patterns in the distribution of socially valued resources (wealth, power, social esteem) in the United States. These dimensions are connected because race/gender is fabricated partially through such differential distribution, and in turn race/gender functions to "naturalize" and sustain relations of privilege and subordination. The systematic asymmetries we can observe are a consequence of social relations and are therefore arbitrary since any subject's race/gender assignment (and its consequences) is a matter of luck or misfortune.[23] As Loury says, the "enduring and pronounced social disadvantage of African Americans is not the result of any purportedly unequal innate human capacities of the 'races.' Rather, this disparity is a social artifact—a product of the peculiar history, culture, and political economy of American society."[24] Neither the privileges of dominance nor the burdens of subordination are earned.

Many insightful works on race/gender dynamics within American politics are available. However, most lack consideration of the psychic processes—melancholia, fantasy, projection, identification, and abjection—that I will discuss here.[25] I am confident that the problem of race/gender domination persists and that part of the reason for this lies in the powerful effects of mostly unconscious processes, including race/gender melancholia, prevalent within contemporary American subjects. However, I believe it is wrong to claim that unconscious processes can provide a complete explanation for persistent social, political, and economic asymmetries. Nor do I think that shifting from melancholia to mourning is a sufficient remedy for race/gender domination.

In tracking race/gender melancholia I will make use of ideas such as fantasy, transitional space, and internalization. These are obviously tools taken from psychoanalytic discourses. In using them, I do not mean to imply that psychoanalysis is an unproblematic discourse for analyzing race/gender. Many of its bedrock assumptions would have to be undone for it to be fully useful to such a project. Psychoanalysis still remains primarily a narrative of white Western subjectivity, and its notions of subjectivity remain rooted in problematic notions of "sexual difference." Divorced from race, gendering is its privileged category of subjective development and embodiment. These narratives would look quite different if the denial and repression of racialization were undone.[26] As Abel and other authors argue, analysts could no longer assume the priority of gender in the constitution of the subject.[27] Subjects are inducted into the symbolic order of contemporary America, not only through what followers of psychoanalyst Jacques Lacan calls the "Father's no of the incest taboo and the phallic interjection of sexual difference," but also through the Law's demand for racial interpellation.[28] I was reminded of this when trying to convince my students of gender's pervasiveness. I had said, "when a baby is born, isn't the first question asked: is it a boy or a girl?" They replied, but also, and equally it might be asked, "How dark is it?" Gender, too, is conventionally constructed not only in relation to genitals but also skin color. As Cheng and the authors in *Female Subjects in Black and White* illuminate, intra- and interracial fantasies shape each subject's understanding of and affective relations with their socially assigned gender.[29] In contemporary American culture, idealized versions of white/male and white/female remain the norm; individual subjects are measured and ranked accordingly by others and often consciously or unconsciously by themselves.

What happens when what Sigmund Freud calls the "bedrock" of psychoanalysis—sexual difference—cracks open?[30] It turns out that, as Freud also knew, what is represented as solid rock is instead sedimented layers of unstable gravel, each filtered into the others and compressed by the force of social prohibition and power into an apparent solidity.[31] Comprising these intermingled layers are gender, heterosexuality, racial formations, identity, and ways of reading the body. The complex, polymorphous, sensuous bodily world is disaggregated and organized into a discrete, hierarchal scheme. Gender identity is assigned by reading bodies according to cultural conventions (which are racialized and historically and geographically specific). Raced, gendered, and contextually specific demands thus generate "sexual difference." Organs are assigned differential importance, meaning, and responsibility. The privileged few are the loci of identity and identification. The signification of organs articulates racial and gender relations; for example, in the context of the United States, it is necessary to incorporate the history of lynching and rape of black women into any thinking about the constitution of masculinity and femininity.

Psychoanalytic accounts of "sexual difference" normalize heterosexuality. In its prescriptive anticipation of future heterosexual coupling, the penis and vagina are paired—the vagina as the different to the penis/same. The "nature" of these privileged organs enables them to engage with their "opposites," and fortunately they have an "innate"—if mysterious—desire to do so. The raced/gendered reading of my body thus provides a narrative of identity. It enables organs to speak and tell me who I am. My core (gender) identity is secure when I internalize and consent to these normative readings. It is confirmed by verifying one's difference through desiring or being the desired object of a proper (gendered/ethnic/racial) other. My identity is confirmed and reinforced by the assigned race/gender of the object of my desire. I am female because a man desires or will desire me when I grow up. I am a male because I desire females and when I grow up I will get a woman to replace Mother. If I desire a woman, I am a lesbian. Being a lesbian is my core/true/authentic identity. Race shapes the constitution of appropriate object choice and the meanings and consequences of such choices. In the contemporary United States, object choices are enmeshed in race/gender power circuits. Access to women and control of sexuality have long been sites of domination and resistance. Subordinate others may signify a power move through laying claim to the same sexual access as enjoyed by a dominant group.[32] Relations among dominant and subordinate others remain fraught with their historical meanings and contexts.

Whether through fantasy, emotion, countervailing meaning schemes, "inappropriate" object choices, or political acts of race/gender rebellion, subjects also resist and remake the normative grids in which they find themselves. Resisting this circuit and detaching desire, organ, embodiment, identity, gender, race, and difference exposes the founding taboos structuring social relations and cultural formations. Psychoanalysis focuses on the incest taboo and its prohibitions related to kinship and desire, but in its narratives, desire is conflated with its heterosexual expression. As in its archetypical representation, the story of Oedipus, the incest taboo stipulates that desire must be turned from the "opposite sexed" kin to an exogamous opposite sexed object. However, this narrative obviously takes heterosexual desire as a given and obscures the law's function as another taboo—a taboo on other forms of desire and, as Butler points out, as a taboo on other forms of kinship.[33] Such kinship might include exogenous alliances between subjects socially assigned to the same gender position. As currently articulated, especially by Lacanian theory, such alliances remain outside the Law and hence are illegible as forms of kinship. As Butler puts it, when "the study of kinship was combined with the study of structural linguistics, kinship positions were elevated to the status of a certain order of linguistic positions without which no signification could proceed, no intelligibility could be possible."[34] Like all discourse, then, psychoanalysis generates its own prohibitions. If one questions

the privilege or the normalizing of (heterosexual) kinship and signification, the response is that it is the Law. The symbolic is founded on
the "Father's No." Without it, all is anarchy, the undifferentiated semi-
otic. In its normative accounts of subjectivity, psychoanalysis reinstalls
the repressions and categories (race, sexual difference) of the dominant
culture. Nonetheless, unlike many other discourses, psychoanalysis
requires and enables systematic attention to fantasy's power and effects.
Thus, it remains a necessary, flawed tool for those who seek to understand the political unconscious and the pervasive hold of race/gender
relations in contemporary American life.

Therefore, despite the limitations of the discursive formations
of which they are the subject and object, I will try to convince the
reader that attending to unconscious processes is a necessary part
of both analysis and treatment. Without analyzing its psychic regis-
ters, accounts of race/gender domination remain incomplete. Race/
gender relations remain so charged and obdurately malignant partially because they are simultaneously intra- and intersubjective. As
Cheng insists, "the politics of race has always spoken in the language
of psychology."[35] She advocates investigating the "roles that public
and private fantasies and desires play in historical formation of the
racial-ethnic subject."[36] I intend to undertake such an investigation,
extending it to practices of citizenship as well as subjectivity and
demonstrating through analysis that without theoretical and practical attention to these dynamics, enduring positive social change will
continue to elude us.

However, I do not think this proposition concerning race/gender
melancholia is subject to direct proof or disproof. Instead, by offering a "thick description" of a variety of contemporary subject formations, American political practices, political theories, and cultural
productions, I hope to convince the reader of its plausibility and of
the importance of acting as if this were the case. The need for acting
in this way has become even more urgent post 9/11. The dynamics,
power relations, and modes of thinking and subjectivity arising out
of and renewing race/gender domination do not remain contained
within their originary sites and ordinary domains. While the harm
done within their customary domains is bad enough, these practices
now inform the default response of both public officials and citizens
to many perceived threats (e.g., terrorism, the "aliens" within). As
they play out internationally, the possible scope of destruction mul-
tiplies in terrifying ways. Domestically, the fury and denigration of
the object intrinsic to melancholic processes fuels a search for culturally acceptable targets. Gay marriage, "illegal" immigrants, or deviant

"values" are constructed such that they can serve as recipients of such hateful projections.

Before entering the psychic register, I need to address an assumption that impedes comprehension of my use of psychoanalytic theory. Writers often assume that in discussing race/gender domination only two, mutually exclusive, alternatives are possible. These are either "prejudice" models that focus on individual beliefs or "structural/ materialist" approaches that analyze relationships of power. Within this dichotomy, it follows that paying attention to unconscious processes necessarily entails assuming that individual attitudes account for the persistence of race/gender domination. For example, Bonilla-Silva says (and I agree) that the prejudice paradigm interprets an "actor's racial views as *individual psychological* dispositions."[37] In contrast, materialist approaches focus on collective social structure and interpret racism as tied to differential, race-based distributions of costs and rewards. I certainly agree with the existence and importance of systemic, differential distributions of social goods and costs. Given the bias in American culture toward individualist accounts of social phenomena, it is especially important to avoid falling into this default. However, I think the structural/individual dichotomy does not exhaust the possible ways to analyse race/gender domination. It mistakenly postulates that attention to psychological processes such as feelings, fantasies, projection, and so on necessarily interprets a subject's psychic life as *individual psychological* dispositions. Her actions must therefore be the (agentic) consequence of an idiosyncratic inner world. The social world is simply the sum of the actions of its constituting individuals. The only alternative to this individualistic fallacy is to take the position that the race/gender domination is an effect of "structural/ materialist" forces such as class, power, or ethnicity in which "subjective" psychological processes play little if any role.

This dichotomy omits a third dimension—collective psychological dispositions, or what I call the political unconscious. Fantasy of the sort I discuss in this book reflects and enacts collective psychological dispositions. I believe such dispositions are themselves material. They inflict material harm and influence the distribution of material goods such as social esteem, status, and prestige.[38] Ignoring the existence and the effects of this dimension of social structure is a mistake for several reasons. First, to think of psychological dispositions as only "individual" presumes a problematic separation between subjects and the social structures in which they come to be. This is particularly odd for those like Bonilla-Silva, who profess to support a "social constructionist" view of subjectivity.[39] Second, it implies a sharp distinction between rational and irrational, mapping rational on group material interests and irrational on individual psychological dispositions. This ignores the possibility that group interests can be quite irrational, for example, in the instrumental sense of ultimately destructive to the group and its ability to attain its professed goals. Third, it suggests a highly impoverished view of material existence. Affects, dreams, fantasies, and other aspects of unconscious processes are intrinsic aspects of subjectivity. They are neither immune to nor unaffected by social structures of all sorts. In turn, subjectivity is partially constructed through these shared fantasies. One's social location generates emotionally saturated expectations regarding entitlements or disadvantages, or capacities or limits. The material benefits or costs of enhanced or devalued social worth are as socially real as augmented or diminished wealth. People will sometimes sacrifice potential economic benefits—or even life itself—for enhanced social esteem.[40] Furthermore, collective rage or hate can be as powerful a force in social and political life as class interest. For example, those in privileged social positions can be as terrified of falling into positions of the devalued other as they are of losing socioeconomic advantage. Among the disadvantaged, a shared sense of social disrespect can motivate relentless violence in the quest for intersubjective redemption.

D. W. Winnicott's notion of transitional space is particularly helpful in formulating and understanding the notion of a political unconscious.[41] Thinking in terms of such spaces enables one to resist the dichotomy of social construction/individualism in which discussion of race/gender is often trapped.[42] In transitional spaces (exemplified by a child lost in play) questions like, "is this real or not?" are suspended and irrelevant. Suspending the reality question or rejecting construing the objective/subjective as a binary enables us to hold in mind the complexity of race/gender. It is simultaneously a social fact, a socially constructed category, a possible site of intensely subjective fantasy, emotion and meaning construction, and an effect of power with differential and asymmetric consequences inherent to varying positions within its grid. Its salience varies within individual subjects and contexts, and race/gender is sometimes used as a defense against other psychic troubles.

Fantasy is the definitive mode within transitional spaces, and like Cheng, Morrison, Zizek,[43] and others, I think that understanding race/gender dominance requires close attention to this psychic register. Fantasy is neither ideology nor psychosis. Unlike in psychosis, consensual reality and fantasy are not confounded. Unlike ideology, meanings are not pregiven, and the subject is not simply inserted into a determining power/meaning structure. In transitional spaces, one remains in between; the social world is imaginatively made use of in the service of personal expression, meaning construction, and the constitution of subjectivity—it is not simply incorporated or imprinted upon us. Anchoring in the social world makes full expression of fantasy possible, since it protects one from being lost in a psychotic delusion. However, such anchoring also entails that the intra- and intersubjectivity are mutually constituting, and one is never extrinsic to the other.

Throughout this book, I make extensive use of Morrison's notion of the "Africanist presence."[44] The Africanist presence is an excellent example of a fantasy generated by the political unconscious. Morrison defines the Africanist presence as the fantasies white people develop about black people to secure their own sense of race/gender identity. She explores the material effects of this fantasy and then uses her analysis to resist its consequences. Moving the unfree's shadow from the margin to the center of the American political biography, Morrison dislodges racism from its framing as a "black" problem and instead locates it firmly within the subjectivities and political practices of white Americans. She shows how race derives from and expresses relational processes; the meanings of the interdependent subject positions it generates are a function of historically contingent and changing interactions. Through pursuing this analytic strategy, Morrison thus also undoes the positioning of African Americans as extrinsic to the supposedly pure and unmarked dominant subjects (pure/white Americans), destabilizing and reimagining the narratives that have previously passed for "mainstream" American history. In reconstructing collective memory, Morrison makes an important contribution to undoing race/gender melancholia.

BITTER FRUIT: RACE/GENDER MELANCHOLIA

In his essay "Mourning and Melancholia," Freud develops the distinction between these two processes.[45] Freud argues that the ego is constituted through internalization—the imaginative taking in of relations with other persons (objects). This process of internalization is usually unconscious, but it becomes evident when an object (or ideal) dies. The death of an object produces a painful internal rupture. The loss and consequent absence of an object makes us aware that it occupied an important place in our subjective world. Repair of this disturbance requires establishing a new kind of relationship with the object. To renew our relationship with the object or ideal we must remake it as memory. This is the work of grief and, paradoxically, only by accepting that the external object is lost can we undertake the process of remaking that will enable us to have it again. Of course, the object as taken is inflected with our own feelings, fantasies, and associations that have attached to or been evoked by the object, so internalization is never simply an eidetic data transfer. Internalization can occur absent a personal relationship or even any direct contact with an object. One's use of an object and construction of it can be quite independent of how that object might construct itself.

Processes of internalization and subjective organization continue throughout a subject's life. While our intimate relations offer rich possibilities for internalization, we make use of many objects and ideals. Our wider social and cultural worlds present many possible objects for psychic incorporation and transformation. As I will discuss more fully in the chapter 3, in the contemporary United States, both privileged and subordinate subjects satisfy psychic needs and manage anxieties by internalizing race/gender others. However, the psychic and social content and consequences of these processes differ. The privileged degrade the subordinate others and internalize this degraded object. They can then split off problematic aspects of themselves and imagine these feelings or qualities belong to the innate, essential nature of the other.[46] Fanon vividly describes these processes:

> In the remotest depth of the European unconscious an inordinately black hollow has been made in which the most immoral impulses, the most shameful desires lie dormant. And as every man climbs up towards whiteness and light, the European has tried to repudiate this uncivilized self, which has attempted to defend itself. When European civilization came into contact with the black world, with those savages, everyone agreed: Those Negroes were the principle of evil.[47]

Such splitting allows the privileged to project an idealized image of themselves. Merging long-standing representations of slaves as beasts with sin as black, the dehumanization of blacks anchors the superiority of whites.[48] Social arrangements permit the blurring of fantasy and consensual reality. The privileged can use their location in grids of power to make this idealization and degradation appear real. For example, feelings of insecurity about one's own skills can be turned into contempt for the supposed lacks of a whole group (e.g., "blacks just aren't as smart as white people"). This contempt informs social practices such as school tracking or providing insufficient resources to inner city schools, with the resulting poor performance confirming the imagined intellectual superiority of whites.

Subordinate others are in a double bind. They encounter an idealized image, an impossible perfection, as Cheng puts it, which is the privileged's self-created imago. This imago requires and incorporates denigrated representations of the subordinated. What is represented as perfection is actually a fantasy of the privileged, attainable for no actual subject (think of airbrushed models in fashion magazines). Rather than an effect of power and fantasy, perfection appears really attainable by some, but for the subordinated, perfection would require being what one is not. To accept the impossibility of perfection is a wound to one's pride, and it reinforces and lends credence to the internalized denigrated representation. This dilemma induces a loss that cannot be mourned—melancholia. Thus, for the subordinated subject, melancholia is "the condition of having to incorporate and encrypt both an impossible ideal and a denigrated self."[49] A profound sense of shame (—at desiring the denigrating other's esteem, of perpetually failing in their and hence one's own eyes) may be among the consequences of such incorporation. This shame may fuel intense self-hate, a hate then enacted in various forms of violence against the self or others perceived as the same.

The privileged have their own form of melancholia. For the privileged, Cheng points out, denigration can serve as a defense against guilt or shame—guilt for the historical context in which white subjects find themselves. There is a background sense of a people wronged in a systematic way, even if the privileged try to assign this wrong to the past (slavery). An honest accounting would require the acknowledgment of the internalized racial other and one's dependence on and incorporation of it within and as self, not other. Since full acknowledgment of the harm and the losses they inflicted would destabilize the privileged's psychic and social worlds, both the internalized other and the harm one has done to it (and actual subjects) is denied. If denial blocks access to what is lost, real grieving cannot occur. To ward off guilt, shame, and instability, subordinated subjects are situated as other and devalued and the cycle repeats. For the subordinated other, such denial of harm is simultaneously damaging and seductive. It provides some secondary gains. It protects these subjects from fully taking in the magnitude of their losses. For example, one can imagine that despite forcible transplant, one's roots remain undisturbed and that therefore relations with one's ancestral "home" or culture have not been irretrievably transformed. Such denial inflects Afrocentric ideas of returning to one's roots and other forms of racial "identity" with an almost unbearable but unspeakable melancholia.[50]

A consequence of denial is that grief is sublimated into, or confused and substituted with, grievance. Grievance specifies a particular harm and stipulates a reparative or at least compensatory action. However, even if a race/gender grievance is heard and remedy is offered, the result often feels unsatisfactory, at least to the subordinated. The remedy cannot address or salve the psychic wounds inflicted in subordinate subject formation. Furthermore, since the subordinate often must address the demands for remedy to the privileged who have inflicted these wounds, on a psychic level further wounding occurs. To some degree, for both groups the differential positions of addressor and addressee replicate and reinforce their devalued/idealized imagos. When demands are made by the subordinated it verifies for the privileged their own devalued imago of the subordinated.

Slavery as Psychological Trauma and Pathological Narcissism

Orlando Patterson articulates the general dynamics of slavery in ways that help us to understand why its psychological damage is so profound and long lasting.[51] Slavery entails the ultimate forms of disrespect and entitlement. Particular American practices such as the rarity of manumission and slavery's symbiotic relations with race/gender made its effects even worse. American slavery became "the ultimate form of inhuman bondage."[52] Patterson defines slavery as "the permanent, violent domination of natally alienated and generally dishonored persons."[53] These qualities—permanence, violence, natal alienation and dishonor—constitute the distinctive qualities of slavery. Conversely, the position of "master" entails the ultimate, godlike power of life and death, and also what I would call a socially sanctioned pathological narcissism. Creating and sustaining the relationship entails extreme, continuous violence. People must be transformed into slaves and any possibility of rebellion undermined. The slave's degradation and lack of power fuels the master's grandiosity. The master is great because his slave is nothing. The narcissist fantasizes that all the world is simply a mirror that reflects his grandeur, and slave systems permit a blending of consensual reality and unconscious imagination. Yet despite the narcissist's solipsism, mirroring and the need for it is a perverse form of social relation.[54] Part of what is so damaging about slavery is that it is a relationship between subjects, and often a quite intimate one. Being in such a relationship transforms the subjectivity of both master and slave.

The slave's "natal alienation" exacerbates his or her powerlessness. Patterson calls the slave a "socially dead person."[55] He or she is removed from all prior relations, rights, social existence, history, family, and heritage. Henceforth, she or he will only have life through the master, and this feeds the master's grandiosity. Slaves may have social ties with other slaves, but these have no binding force. The "slave was the ultimate human tool, as imprintable and as disposable as the master wished."[56] This natal alienation enables another important aspect of slavery. Unlike the position of a servant, slavery is permanent and inheritable. Only the master has a claim on the slave's children; no slave can free him or herself or children without his consent. This permanently bound quality of slavery informs the meaning of freedom. As the related opposite of slavery, freedom means the absence of constraint. Exercising absolute autonomy through degrading others shows what it is to be free. The master's freedom thus rests practically and psychologically on another's enslavement: "Those who most dishonor and constrain others are in the best position to appreciate what joy it is to possess what they deny."[57] Masters also gain a sense of honor through their position. Honor is a relational quality; it can only exist inasmuch as another being signifies that a person has value and is worthy of respect. Since slaves could have no power except through another, they could have no honor.[58] The master's sense of power is enhanced through the dishonor of his slave. Patterson points out that in many cultures, the honor of the master is a primary reason for acquiring slaves.[59]

While Patterson remarks that the slave is a "living embodiment of one's manhood and honor,"[60] he does not adequately explore the gendering dynamics of slavery.[61] Manhood is interwoven with multiple kinds of mastery, prowess, control, and freedom. The honor of mastership is intertwined with masculinity. Since historically in most cultures women are already dishonored persons, it would be difficult for the master to establish his superiority in relation to a female slave. Only other men are appropriate combatants in struggles for rank and esteem. Dominating other males demonstrates one's superiority. Free women and female slaves are often the territory through and over which men engage in their battles for dominance among themselves. Women are often objects used both for sexual gratification and to further dishonor male slaves. Only free men can exercise control over women. In treating female slaves as he wishes, the master further emasculates the male slave. Lacking this freedom himself, the male slave thus lacks manhood, and this is another source of his dishonor. Instead, he is seen by the master as a Sambo figure, child like and dependent on his master. Conversely, the master binds his honor to the ability to control "his" female kin. Any transgression of his rules, including by the women to whom he is kin, dishonors him, and the master can impose heavy sanctions against the transgressors. The master also lends honor to his female kin; as long as they glow in his reflected grandeur, their status is exalted. Hence, it is not surprising that slave societies are often marked by the "idealization and seclusion of women."[62]

Of course, female slaves were neither idealized nor secluded. The work of those more sensitive to race/gender intersections, especially black feminist writers, corrects Patterson's failure to attend to slavery's unique effects and consequences on those positioned as black/female.[63] Due to their gender and enslaved status, black women were especially vulnerable to the master's sexual predation. While black male slaves were not immune from sexual exploitation by white male or female slaveholders, dominant social norms condemned such behavior, and those whites engaging in it risked severe sanctions. White males faced no such risks from their sexual exploitation of black females. As it was fabricated in our history, whiteness required purity; it was a double negative, not-not white. This purity was anchored in white men's sexual control of white women and black men; until recently only maternity could be securely ascertained. The "policing of sexual boundaries—the defense against hybridity—is what keeps a racial group a racial group."[64] In relation to slavery, then, property right entailed not only control of labor power and the appropriation of value, but sexual access and domination. White men had access to women, black and white, and the power to refuse such access and control to black men.

Furthermore, the prevalent gendered division of labor meant that care of the slave holder's children would be assigned to black women. Since they give birth, women were considered children's "natural" care takers. However, under the coercive relations of slavery, the well-being of black women's own children and their relationships with them had no standing. Black mothers were forced to sacrifice these ties at the master's whim and to devote themselves to the slave holders' children. Under the perverse logic of domination in which the "other" becomes the problem, these coercive arrangements were transmuted into constructions of black female identity. These constructions include the hypersexed Jezebel and the asexual Mammy. The potential for compulsory liaisons with white men rendered the Jezebel's race and personal loyalties suspect, as did the Mammy's enforced tending to the master's children. As numerous writers have demonstrated, slavery's end did not eliminate such constructions of black/female. Intra-race struggles, public policy, law, divisions of labor, social relations, and dynamics of subjectivity still bear their traces.[65]

Despite the master's narcissistic fantasies and sense of entitlement to coerce, exploit, and control others, his own power is dependent on forces outside himself. Institutional power is necessary to secure the authority of the master, and the normative order of his culture must sanction it.[66] Without such social sanctions, slavery as a system of social relations could not exist. Slavery often anchors what Plato calls timocracies, systems in which honor is valued above all else and legitimates claims to rule or exercise power. Patterson calls the American slave-based South the most developed timocracy of modern times.[67] In America (and not only in the South), as in other slave societies, institutionalizing slavery benefits all free persons, even those who do not possess slaves. The extreme inequality of slavery moderates class conflict or resentment; in comparison to such disparity, differences among white men appear relatively small. The degradation of slaves enables all free persons to regard them as fitting object for abuse. Sharing a common object of degradation or contempt builds social solidarity and cements a shared sense of identity among the free. The master's sense of himself as a person of honor with its related values of manliness and chivalry and love of freedom diffuses to all free men. In turn, since only free men are honorable, their esteem further augments the master's honor. In contrast, the slave's dishonor further degrades him, as his loss of honor is often manifested as self-hate and blame or violence against the self. In chapter 3, I will explore in some detail how these dynamics of entitlement and dishonor continue to play out within and between contemporary American subjects.

Race/gender melancholia in the United States affects many aspects of contemporary practice, including thinking. Among the ways we can begin to undo race/gender melancholia is shifting habits of thought. Two particularly important areas requiring change are common sense understandings of race/gender and the popular belief that the United States is now a "post-racial" or "color-blind" society. Rather than enable us to confront loss and harm, these understandings and beliefs obscure the long term effects of social arrangements. They express longings rather than actual practices, and hence holding on to them undermines our capacity to narrow the gaps between ideal and present. In the next chapter I will discuss the common sense understanding of race/gender and why a "social fabrication" approach is more accurate. I will also discuss empirical data that illustrates why applying the term "post-racial" to the United States is, at best, an aspiration or wish, but in any case does not capture contemporary social arrangements.

CHAPTER 2

Melancholia: A Genealogy

THE SOCIAL FABRICATION OF RACE/GENDER

Acknowledging the complex social processes through which race/
gender is fabricated and renewed can contribute to shifting from melancholia to mourning. I use the term "fabrication" because it simultaneously connotes the double sense of made and made up. In regard
to race/gender, both meanings are accurate. Race/gender is made by
and through human action, and its making may entail deception or
selective representations. Like any form of social labor, race/gender
fabrication occurs under conditions that are not freely chosen, nor
are its conditions the product of a single individual's will. Such fabrication is not voluntary, and yet, as its conditions are heterogeneous
and variable, what is produced in any instance is not totally predetermined. To understand how race/gender is made and remade requires
tracking its social construction, and this analysis necessitates exploring the relationships between subjectivity, power, and history. Such
investigations can provide leverage against the melancholic denial of
the living presence of the past in the present. They may also recoup
the denied relationships between subjects and show how the meanings and effects of each subjective position depend on others.

Currently, the United States is an increasingly multiethnic (and
with current rates of intermarriage, a mixed race) society; the Census
Bureau estimates that by 2050 no one "race" will be a majority.
Conflicts over the meanings of race have again intensified as some
seek to expand, reorganize, or even undo racial categorization. For
example, some groups are pressing to incorporate "biracial" within
official census categories or to redefine the meaning of "Hispanic."
However, here, due to my interest in the ongoing effects of slavery, I
will focus on the race/gender relations among those marked "black"
and "white." Like many contemporary theorists, I refer to race/gen-
der rather than simply race, because in the United States the "social

construction of race is dependent on gender categorization and the social construction of gender is dependent on racial categorization."[1] Glenn identifies three shared features of race and gender: "(1) they are relational concepts whose construction involves (2) representation and material relations and (3) in which power is a constitutive element."[2] An additional common feature is that race and gender are the site and subject of intense, often unconscious, emotions and fantasies. Each of these features operate in the American context. From the beginning of American political history, race, gender, power, and sexuality have been intertwined.[3] Therefore, rather than try to isolate what is race and what is gender and then to see how they intersect or interact, I think it is more useful to assume that race/gender are invariably "interwoven or intermeshed or enmeshed."[4] The interesting and productive question is *how* race/gender is constituted and enacted in specific contexts.[5]

Like many contemporary writers, I posit that race/gender is not a natural fact. By this I mean that while common sense views it as a logical and necessary consequence of anatomy (genitals) and physiology (skin color), this is not the case.[6] Race/gender is a social, not a natural, fact. Social facts are the sedimented effects of human practices; they are artifacts with genealogies that are interpretable and subject to alteration. However, since we are social beings, social facts possess tremendous force and effect. They are not voluntary, a matter of individual choice or idiosyncratic whim. Try obtaining a driver's license without checking (one) "gender" box. In the contemporary United States, no ungendered, raced subject and no unraced, gendered subject can exist. As much as we may resist, every American finds his or herself located along preexisting grids of race/gender positions. We cannot be intelligible to ourselves or to others without doing so. Ask any child to state her race and gender, and most likely she will not find the question odd or puzzling. These positions appear as ordinary "facts" that everybody knows. Even hybrid positions such as bi- or multiracial or transgendered derive much of their meaning from the "commonsense" fixed ideas of race/gender. This observation may appear trivial, but I think we often do not do justice to its profound implications and consequences. Race/gender permeates American life in every dimension from psychological fantasy to constitutional law. It often structures and shapes practices that on the surface seem race/gender neutral or unrelated.

Thus, race/gender is best understood as a verb, not as a noun. It belongs to the class of things people do, not to the things they are. Treating race/gender as social fact requires focusing on the "processes by which racialization and engendering occur, rather than on characteristics of fixed race or gender categories."[7] Race/gender exists only in and through multiple kinds of human practices; it could not exist outside the practices that animate, replicate, and mutate it. Despite her inattention to the psychic register, Glenn usefully categorizes some of these practices, including representation ("the deployment of symbols, language, and images to express and convey race/gender meanings"); micro-interaction ("the application of race/gender norms, etiquette, and spatial rules to orchestrate interaction within and across race/gender boundaries"); and social structure ("rules regulating the allocation of power and resources along race/gender lines").[8] As I will discuss in the next chapter, additional practices include organizing a coherent and socially intelligible subjective identity and managing intrapsychic conflict.

Race/gender is inseparable from power relations. As we will see in chapter 5, in the contemporary West, it is a primary site of, and effect of, the modern forms of power that Foucault calls biopower and governmentality.[9] Race/gender and biopower colonize bodies and organize them into distinct, identifiable, and normalized social subjects. Race/gender effects the transformation of certain physical features into determining social facts, ideas, and subjective positions. Once these categories exist and regulate the lives of subjects, further expert knowledge emerges to justify them. The continuing operation of norms and regulation then reproduce race/gender. Since all subjects must live within their constituting knowledge/power networks, these categories are socially real. While subjects can resist or rework their normative meanings, we are thrown into a world where being positioned within these meanings is not voluntary. In being so positioned, the past, however transmuted or unconscious, shapes our present subjective and social practices.

Analyzing race/gender as processes helps us to escape the false concreteness of common ways of understanding. It is then evident that skin color does not compel the idea of race any more than genitals require an idea of gender. Instead, once we categorize race/gender as social fact, we can track the vicissitudes of its fabrication. While its constituting effects within American politics and subjectivities are never absent, the meanings of race/gender, its manifest and covert expressions (including in the political unconscious), the social positions generated, the intensity of struggle and resistance, and the criteria by which subjects are positioned within it vary.[10] For example, like "black," the meanings of "white" are unstable and highly contested.[11] "White" as a marker of subjective identity emerges in the

United States after about 1680.[12] Jacobson documents how, as immigration intensified between 1840 and 1920, whiteness fragmented from a unitary category of "free white persons" into "a hierarchically arranged series of distinct 'white races.'"[13] Irish, Jews, Italians, and other European immigrants had to struggle against their status as racially inferior to the "native" stock. Only in the mid-1920s were they incorporated into a new "natural" division of humanity—Caucasian. "Negro" simultaneously emerged as another such division; in the 1920 census, categories such as "mulatto," first seen in 1850, disappeared.[14] Assignment to one of these divisions came to be determined by the "one drop" rule. Any person with "one drop" of black blood was marked black.[15]

Treating race/gender as social fact and practices requires us to resist a dichotomy too prevalent in American thinking, that of autonomous individual versus determined object. Within American political discourse the claim is often made that if you do not assume people are unmarked individuals whose fate is determined solely by their own actions, then you are saying there is no freedom or responsibility. Both alternatives are inaccurate. Our embeddedness within socially constructed grids is what empowers us to act in socially intelligible ways and to resist norms.[16] Without cultural norms and power relations, we would have no framework of social intelligibility and shared meanings, no force vectors to appropriate and nothing to push against. Furthermore, as I will discuss in chapter 5, the fact that there are grids of power, resource distribution, and socially mandated identity coexists with the fact that for each individual subject these grids' effects are somewhat indeterminate. Depending on one's subject position and other contextual variables, the moves possible within grids will vary and change. A subject may find itself highly determined in one grid but able to move fairly creatively along another. The grids often intersect, sometimes in unpredictable ways, resulting in a more or less restricted range of moves. Our unconscious investments in and fantasies about various networks will vary, adding to the unpredictability of movement and systemic response. Individual subjects can thus resist some of the vectors of these grids or exploit slippage, conflict, or spaces within and between them. Conversely, the ability of some subjects to resist does not negate the power and ongoing effects of the grids. We cannot generalize from individual moves to social system any more than we can assume that any aspect of those grids will have a singular causal effect. An African American man may go to Harvard and be a well paid investment banker on Wall Street yet still experience racial profiling. He may be stopped in his expensive car by a police officer who suspects he stole it.

Failure to appreciate the coexistence of individuated action and structured frameworks or grids also informs a common objection to claims about systematic white privilege. People will object that their ancestors had nothing to do with slavery; they fled from places like Ireland, Ukraine, or Russia, where they themselves were subject to terrible oppression. While true, this view neglects other equally salient facts. Entering this country, immigrants encounter a preexisting set of social arrangements deeply sedimented with prior history. Like people born in the United States, immigrants must find ways to locate themselves within these arrangements. Some can (and, as Jacobson documents, do) vie for places of dominance while others, due to skin color and gender, are far less likely to succeed. Thus, while not necessarily of any individual subject's making, all American residents are incorporated into the prevailing schemes of benefits and burdens. Important for any subject is not only the geographic locations of their ancestry, but how current social arrangements mark their race/gender. In being marked, one enters into a more general history, social membership, and subjective formations and their concomitant benefits, burdens, and unconscious associations.

Removing the Blinders: The Ongoing Constraints of Race/Gender

One expression of race/gender melancholia is the recurrent claim that the United States is now a "post-racial" society. Whatever the past might have been, we have now moved beyond it into a present unmarked by its effects. The plausibility of this claim requires that we ignore the ongoing effects of the past on the present social, political, economic, and unconscious practices. Among these effects is the massive transfer of privilege to white males and, to a lesser extent, white females that has been documented by Ira Katznelson, Desmond King, Linda Williams, and others.[17] A critical review of our political history shows that "American social policy has consistently and cumulatively constructed and reinforced white privilege through the normal workings of American politics."[18] Benefits and burdens can accrue even from apparently progressive or race-neutral policies. For example, scholars have documented how the New Deal and Fair Deal legislation of the 1940s and 1950s, including social security, labor law, and the G.I. Bill, resulted in significant benefits for whites and disadvantages for blacks.[19] The power of Southern members of

Congress ensured that such legislation was written or administered in ways that minimized disrupting then-existing race/gender arrangements. The entrenched power of these members was itself partially a consequence of the Jim Crow laws. Due to the effective disenfranchisement and terrorizing of Southern blacks, white interests were overrepresented. Southern democrats' seats were safe, and under the seniority system they were guaranteed control of important committees. Incorporating their interests was essential, for they could effectively block passage of any legislation. Thus, domestics and farm workers (the predominant employment of most Southern blacks) were originally excluded from coverage under social security. Legislation specified that programs included within the G.I. Bill, such as grants for college education or vocational training and low cost mortgages, were to be administered locally, thus allowing for tremendous discretion (and prejudice) in determining who received such assistance. Deference to the Southerners (and the tacit sharing of their values or indifference to existing domination on the part of many of their fellow legislators) also insured that antidiscrimination language would be excluded from legislation establishing social welfare programs.

The result, as Katznelson puts it, was "a massive transfer of quite specific privileges to white Americans"[20] and significant, ongoing disadvantage for blacks. The asymmetric accumulation of social goods resulted in increasing inequality. By 1950, pre- New Deal gaps between blacks and whites—even veterans—in educational attainment, home ownership, and wealth had actually widened:

> at the very moment when a wide array of public policies were providing most white Americans with valuable tools to advance their social welfare—insure their old age, get good jobs, acquire economic security, build assets, and gain middle-class status—most black Americans were left behind or left out…And the effects…did not stop even after discriminatory codes were swept aside by aside by the civil rights movement and the legislation it inspired.[21]

Rather than facing these ongoing effects of the past, melancholic denial of them is enacted when a decline in consciously felt bias is equated with race/gender "neutrality" and the attainment of a "color-blind" society. Claims to the contrary are then treated as revealing the shortcomings of their makers. To bolster assertions of this arrival of "post-racial" society, some offer misleading claims about the representativeness of individual instances (e.g., the first African American president or Fortune 500 CEO) for the more complex

whole. Individual success is posited as proof of the absence of any systemic constraints. The following comment by Senator John Cornyn,
a Texas Republican, is typical of such moves; the "American ideal
is that justice should be colorblind...As we see people like Barack
Obama achieve the highest office in the land and Judge Sotomayor's
own nomination to the highest court, I think it is harder and harder to
see the justifications for race-conscious decisions across the board."[22]
Among the remarkable contradictions of such statements is the evoking of the idea of "colorblind" while simultaneously rendering highly
visible ("we see") the color of those meant to prove the irrelevance of
color. If we were truly a colorblind society, an individual's color would
be irrelevant to the narratives we posit about our system. Obama or
Sotomayor's color would not transform them into generalized bearers
of social meaning. Such statements employ a classic melancholic move
in which the person denies their own race consciousness (and race/
gender positioning) while making such consciousness a shortcoming
of those calling attention to race/gender inequities. As Neil Gotanda
puts it:

> nonrecognition may be considered a mode of repression. The claim
> that race is not recognized is an attempt to deny the reality of internally
> recognized social conflicts of race...the external world accommo-
> dates it by accepting and institutionalizing the repression rather than
> attempting to expose and alter the conditions of racial exploitation.[23]

A further reversal occurs when those who point out the effects of our
race/gender history and seek means to remedy them are now labeled
the "racists."[24]

While understandable as fantasies or longings, assertions that the
United States is now a "post-racial" society ignore the ways in which
past social relationships and grids of social, political, psychological,
and economic power shape our current social, political, economic, and
unconscious practices. The effects continue in part because the kinds
of social goods that have been transferred unequally—education,
home ownership, employment, social respect, and honor—are correlated with the well-being of one's children and their own likelihood
of success. Advantages tend to be transferred across time. Thus, like
quantum mechanics, looking at power networks can inform us about
probabilities. What the constitution of such networks suggests, as
Linda Williams puts it, is that race/gender still generates constraints.
Within these constraints, subjects assigned to certain positions are
more likely to benefit from existing social relations while others will

be burdened by these relations. If we assume, as I do, that capacities are randomly distributed among individuals, this systematic maldistribution of benefits and burdens poses serious issues of social justice.

One way to ascertain if systematic relations of domination persist is to ask what a society's socially valued goods are and then see how they are distributed over time. I think it is fair to say that in the contemporary United States, wealth, power, and social esteem or respect are among the most highly valued social goods. We can also look at the distribution of social disfavored burdens. As I will discuss in chapter 5, sacrifice is necessarily endemic in any democracy. In systems based on majority rule, the winning outcome of any dispute, election, or contested policy may reflect the preferences of only a marginal majority of the contestants or affected parties. The losers must sacrifice goods ranging from a preferred policy outcome to—in the case of a contested war for example— life itself. However, the distribution of such sacrifices can vary. If patterns of systematic, unequal distribution of sacrifice to some groups and of benefits to others persist, then it is reasonable to suspect the existence of relations of domination. While social esteem or respect is harder to measure, persistent race/gender skewing in the distribution of wealth and power is unambiguous. Never since the founding of the United State have white males been systematically disadvantaged in the distribution of such goods. Despite improvements in the conditions of some blacks, white males still continue to enjoy disparate privileges. The fragility of these improvements under economic stress is illustrated by the differential effects of the current recession.[25] One's location along race/gender grids sharply affects one's risk of disadvantage. Those positioned as black/female are least likely to enjoy advantages. The persistently asymmetric distribution of its benefits and disadvantages suggests that race/gender domination remains intrinsic to the United State's basic social arrangements. Economic disadvantage is unequally distributed. Black females are more than twice as likely as white males to be poor. Similarly, black families have the lowest median income of any segment of the American population. In 2006, 26.2 percent of black females had incomes below the poverty level. This contrasts with a rate of 11.4 percent for white females, 22.0 percent for black males, and 9.1 percent for white males. In constant (2006) dollars, the median money income of all American families was $58,407. For white families it was $61,280 while for black ones it was $38,269. The disparity of $23,000 in median family income of black and white families has remained constant since 1990, when (in constant 2006 dollars), black family income was $32,037 and white family income was $55,205.[26]

While those situated in the position of black/female face the greatest risk of poverty, those marked white and male are most likely to occupy remunerative and powerful economic positions. For example, in April 2006, only four blacks (all male) were CEOs of a Fortune 500 company and in August 2006, only ten women (all white) occupied this position. In May 2009, the first black female was chosen as the CEO of a Fortune 500 company (IBM). Among the current leaders of large Wall Street investment firms, only one is a black male. "In 2005, women held 16.4% of corporate officer positions...up just 0.7 percentage points from 2002." The representation of women of color "increased only 0.3 percentage points from 2002 (1.8 percent) to 2005 (2.1 percent.) If this pace continues, it would take forty years to reach gender parity in such positions."[27] In 2005, lawyers of color accounted for just 4.63 percent of the partners of major American law firms.[28] According to the American Association of American Medical Schools, in 2008, 389 black men and 720 black women graduated from medical school. For whites, the number was 5492 men and 4867 women. Further compounding the lack of accessibility of medical training, in 2000, only 6 percent of those attending medical school came from families with a household income of under $50,000.[29]

Comparing possession of tangible assets across households provides another measure of the distribution of economic goods. According to the U.S. Census Bureau, in 2000, 71.1 percent of white, non-Hispanic, households owned interest-earning assets at financial institutions, but only 41.6 percent of black households did. Of white, non-Hispanic households, 29.7 percent owned stocks and shares in mutual funds, as contrasted to 10.2 percent of black households. Approximately 73 percent of white, non-Hispanic households owned their home, but only 46.8 percent of black households did. Of white, non-Hispanic households, 27.5 percent owned an IRA or Keogh account, while only 6.5 percent of black households did.[30] These disparities reinforce Ira Katznelson's and Linda Williams' claims about the ongoing effects of public policy. They also help account for the gap in median household net worth. According to the Census Bureau, in 2000, the median net worth of non-Hispanic white households was $79,400 while for black households it was $7,500.[31] These disparities have important implications for the future; the higher the net worth of a household, the more likely their children will stay in school and graduate from college. In turn, college graduates will earn far more over their lifetimes than others, and so race/gender disparities are likely to be replicated. Since, relative to their percentage of the population, black people are overrepresented among the poor and whites are over-represented among the rich, the general trend toward greater income inequality is likely to further reinforce these disparities. Today the wealthiest 10 percent receive 40 percent of the nation's total income. "Not since World War II have the top 10 percent of earners had such a large share of total income."[32] Comparing households with any asset holdings show wide disparities in wealth distribution among racial positions. In 2007, the median net worth for families with holdings was $171,200 for white, non-Hispanic families and $28,300 for nonwhite or Hispanic families. The net worth of white families went up by 10.6 percent between 2004 and 2007, while that of nonwhite families increased by 4 percent.[33]

Perhaps even more troubling than these inequalities is the current status of black youth. After all, they represent our future citizens, and given their present situation, it is unlikely a "post-racial" future is on our horizon, much less already here. According to the U.S. Census Bureau, in 2006 33 percent of black children lived in poverty, as con-trasted to 13.6 percent of white children.[34] Poverty increases chil-dren's risk of poor health and poor education, which in turn place them at further risk for future poverty. Race/gender disparities in college enrollment are equally alarming. In 2006, the Census Bureau reports that 29.9 percent of black males and 41.9 percent of black females were in college. College enrollment rates among whites were 42.5 percent for white males and 51.6 percent for white females.[35]

Political power is also unequally distributed. Until Barack Obama's election in 2008, only white men had held the U.S. presidency. One hundred and twelve people have served as U.S. Supreme Court jus-tices. However, of these, only two black men, three white women, and one Latina have held the position of justice. Of the 1,885 women and men who have served in the U.S. Senate since the country's found-ing, only five have been African American (and two of these were elected from Mississippi during Reconstruction; one of these, Hiram Revels served only a few weeks in 1870, the other, Blanche K. Bruce, male, served from 1875 to 1881). Only one of the African American Senators, Carol Moseley Braun, was female. Currently one black male serves in the U.S. Senate.

Conversely, blacks are overrepresented among the powerless. Prisoners are among the most disenfranchised of American subjects, and in some cases their disenfranchisement persists after imprison-ment. Although laws vary concerning the duration of disenfranchise-ment and procedures to undo it, many states bar convicted felons from voting. Felons are also permanently barred from many kinds of jobs and often find obtaining any steady employment after their release extremely difficult. On a per capita basis, the United States has the world's highest incarceration rate, approximately 750 per every 100,000 adults. In 2007, 2.3 million Americans were in prison, and about an additional 5 million were on probation or parole. These Americans are disproportionately people of color. While one in 30 men between the ages of 20 and 34 is behind bars, for black males in that age group the figure is one in nine. Men still are roughly 10 times more likely to be in jail or prison, but the female population is burgeoning at a far more rapid pace. For black women in their mid- to late-30s, the incarceration rate also has hit the "1-in-100" mark. If current incarceration rates continue, 32.2 percent of black boys born in 2001 will go to prison.[36] According to the U.S. Justice Department, at midyear 2008 there were 4,777 black male inmates per 100,000 black males held in state and federal prisons and local jails, compared to 1,760 Hispanic male inmates per 100,000 Hispanic males and 727 white male inmates per 100,000 white males. Of the total prison population of 2,103,500, the race/gender breakdown was 712,500 white males, 846,000 black males, 427,000 Hispanic males; 94,500 white females, 67,800 black females and 33,400 Hispanic females.[37] Even life itself (without which, as Thomas Hobbes stresses, no power is possible) is unequally distributed. According to the U.S. Center for Disease Control, in 2005 median age at death was 75.7 years for white males, 80.8 for white females, 76.5 for black females, and 69.5 for black males. Conversely, mortality rates at birth were higher for black children—15.20 per 1,000 births for black males and 12.32 for black females. Among whites, the rates per 1,000 births were 6.33 for white males and 5.11 for white females.[38] Blacks are also over repre- sented among those without health insurance. At the end of 2007, 10.4 percent of whites were uninsured compared to 19.2 percent of blacks.[39]

Social respect or esteem is harder to measure. However, numer- ous experiments have demonstrated that unconsciously, "everyone— white, black, men, women—think the white man is more valuable."[40] Conversely, in a survey of 2,864 people reported by The Washington Post on Sunday, June 4, 2006,[41] 76 percent of black men said being respected by others was important to them, while only 59 percent of white men said it was a priority. This suggests that respect is some- thing many black men feel is fragile or lacking. Black men are also more likely to report false arrests and be subject to racial profiling. While the Jim Crow laws have been repealed, public spaces can still seem dangerous for black people. Black parents admonish their sons never to run from police officers and, should they be stopped, to keep their hands visible at all times. They warn daughters about social stereotypes regarding sexually "loose" black women and offer strategies to deal with their possible ramifications.[42] Black people often encounter embarrassing or humiliating "microaggressions."[43] These include being followed in a store, not being able to get a taxi, watching white women grab their purses as one approaches, observing white people moving away in the elevator as a black person enters, receiving disrespectful or slow service in stores and restaurants, listening to people express surprise when one speaks excellent standard English, and encountering skepticism about one's competence or intelligence in school or employment settings. Equally as demoralizing, as I will discuss in the next chapter, this lack of respect is also enacted intrasubjectively and within black relationships. Domestic violence, intraracial homicide, and self-destructive habits are partially reflections of internalized disrespect.

Conversely, occupying positions of dominance enables subjects to sustain an often unconscious but enabling and empowering sense of entitlement.[44] Although her focus was on gender, no one has conveyed the psychological benefits of such entitlement better than Virginia Woolf. In *A Room of Her Own*, Woolf writes:

> Women have served all these centuries as looking-glasses possessing the magic and delicious power of reflecting the figure of man at twice its natural size...Under the spell of that illusion, half the people...start the day confident, braced...they say to themselves...I am the superior of half the people here, and it is thus that they speak with that self-confidence, that self-assurance, which have had such profound consequences in public life and lead to such curious notes in the margin of the private mind.[45]

Among these curious notes is a deep and self-reinforcing belief in one's own abilities and desert. One of the paradoxes of entitlement is that it blinds one to the effects of systematic arrangements of power. The privileged are often buoyed by an unquestioned and sometimes unconscious sense of simply deserving their good fortune. They do not recognize one of the benefits of domination: in already occupying positions of power, social resources to augment and perpetuate advantage or disadvantage are readily available to them. Unlike those located in other race/gender locations (who bear the burden of being an instance or representative of their race/gender position), the privileged can see themselves as "individuals." In this self-representation what is obscured is that privilege enables one to occupy the "unmarked" position. One can imagine oneself existing outside of the race/gender grids and not see that these grids function to erase one's own social fabrication. Instead, the privileged attribute their successes solely to their unique individual qualities; the benefits flowing from power are reimagined as natural consequences of innate superior capacities. These benefits are deserved reflections of one's individual worth. This absence of doubt about one's own capacities and the rightness of one's rewards frees up an enormous amount of psychological energy. The energy is available to pour into making further use of one's systematic advantages. Furthermore, if one expects to do well at something, one is more likely to do so. Thus, both in subjective and systematic practices, domination tends to be self-replicating.[46]

BEYOND DENIAL

Violence, social death, honor: when these circulate through grids of race/gender the fruits are bitter indeed. The American polity now confronts an inescapable situation with which it is ill suited to cope.[47] Our problems extend beyond melancholic denial of the constituting forms of domination in American institutions. Race/gender domination cannot be remedied by ignoring its psychic and intersubjective power. Yet, even if melancholic denial, repression, and splitting ended, we would lack the discursive and political spaces for thinking about forms of responsibility appropriate to socially constructed and fantasizing subjects. As I will argue in chapter 4, a dominant approach—attempting to attain equality by articulating abstract principles of justice such as Rawls's "least advantaged" principle—will not destroy the domination required to reproduce race/gender. The categories and practices retain their constituting effects. Organization of subjects through these categories remains problematic. Appeals to deploy abstract reason are ineffective because no individual, reasoning subject can adequately control the political unconscious's race/gender enactments. Until race/gender ceases to construct political subjects, there is no one available who can devise or implement color-blind policies. Therefore, prescribing "blindness" to color and gender can only mean a failure to see the existing relations of inequality, privilege, and denigration. Instead, collective discussion of contingent determination in devising basic principles and approximating justice is required. An entire network of practices must be dismantled, not to create a "race blind" society but one in which these categories cease to operate.[48] This deconstruction cannot occur without admitting that a particular set of relations was constructed. We cannot just pretend that race/gender does not shape us, that we can operate simply as (rational) "color blind" individuals. All the effects of race/gender on American subjects and our institutions must be actively confronted and reworked.

As I will discuss in chapter 6, affirmative action is one of the practices through which such confrontations can occur. The lingering effects of race/gender domination and our melancholic denial of the past in the present necessitate affirmative action to benefit the least advantaged. However, these same effects help explain why it is the site of so much anger and resistance, especially among the privileged.[49] Affirmative action policies provoke controversy in part because they work against melancholic denial. They not only threaten privileged access to economic goods but disrupt emotionally fraught narratives about subjective identities and power.[50] No defense can be mounted of such policies without explicit reference to a history that many Americans would like to declare irrelevant or being without contemporary consequences. Affirmative action policies force us to confront the fact that the constituting subjects of America are not, never were, and cannot be abstract or perfected individuals. Affirmative action for the disadvantaged acknowledges that every American subject is located within race/gender grids and that such positioning has consequences, including its effects on one's possession of, access to, and control over socially valued goods. Domination is not only in the past, but it at least partially accounts for the present distribution of privilege and subordination. Rather than perpetuating discrimination, affirmative action policies attempt to counteract the long-term effects of race/gender domination, including the accrual of advantages among the dominant. Recognizing that unequal race/gender relations shape many of our institutions, such policies attempt to undo these inequities. Twisting recognition of forces that shape American subjects and institutions into "reverse racism" or "reverse discrimination" has to be one of the most perverse expressions of race/gender melancholia. In an amazing act of fantasy, the powerful are transformed into the victims of the subjected, and the powerful deny their own entitlement, displacing their privilege onto the disadvantaged. Despite all evidence to the contrary, the privileged assert that, not only has the playing field been leveled, but it is now also tilted in the subordinated's favor.

The strategy of denying the constituting effects of race/gender on all contemporary American subjects is not only futile but malignant.

Repeated attempts to rescue the fantasies that produce American citizens nurture the politics of hate. We do not often think of communities as being bonded through hate. Indeed, even the recent resurgence of "communitarian" writings ignores these bonds altogether.[51] Yet, throughout American history, hate has provided important resources for and bases of solidarity. Hate ties people to others in ways they cannot consciously acknowledge. Rather than facing the impossibility of subjective perfection and neutral or pure political spaces, motives, principles, or actors, it is less frightening to find others to hate and to charge with undermining (our) order/culture. Their differences and inadequacies, not asymmetric social relations and the unjust privileges of the powerful, again become the problem.

As I will discuss in chapter 4, rationalistic individualism, one of the preferred modes of subjectivity within American practices, including political theory and constitutional law, can render subjects vulnerable to hate. Rather than ground justice, rationalistic individualism often requires its denied, devalued other to function and thus necessitates the development of sadomasochistic relationships within and between subjects. Sustaining this subjective mode requires a category of the abject, onto whom all heterogeneous determination can be projected and blamed. Subordinate others may partially incorporate these projections into their own subjectivities. They too violate themselves and develop powerful feelings of hate for themselves and the others.[52] One hates oneself for being mutilated by one's own actions and the actions of others. Identification with or dependence on the wounding other is equally painful and shaming.[53] It generates a desire to destroy the other who so unrelentingly affects one's own fate, or, as Cheng argues, to participate in their fantasized perfection through identification with them and self-denigration. However longed for, no amount of intersubjective or social retribution or reparation seems sufficient to repair such intrapsychic and intersubjective damage. Rage erupts and produces some of the violence that is so pervasive in contemporary intra- and inter-race/gender relations. Unfortunately, as Fairbairn argues, such bonds are among the most difficult to break.[54]

I do not think justice is served by assuring the abjected that they too can be abstracted individuals "like us," or that even though we feel no need to listen to any particular voice, properly located subjects can articulate principles that are good for all through feats of reason. This fantasy assumes that one can know an other without listening to her. It also assumes that there is nothing in the "comprehending" subject shaping her reception and representation of the other. Assuming that a (color-blind) neutral "view from nowhere" is possible obviates a basic problem in contemporary America, "that blacks and whites often bring radically different understandings of the social world, with radically different sets of political vocabularies and radically different understandings of central political and events to political conflicts and debates."[55] These differences often stem from the ongoing effects of the past on the present. Race/gender melancholia renders productive discussion of such differences impossible. Instead, it often leads the privileged to deny our embeddedness in local networks of power, to assign race/gender positioning only to the subordinated and then use such positioning as evidence for their inferiority. These displacements reflect blindness to a felt entitlement to one's privilege and to the effects of the political unconscious. Instead, all subjects—but especially dominant ones—must render identities, subjective processes and felt experience, socioeconomic locations, access to power and resources, and moral categories problematic to ourselves and in conversation with others. The dependence of privilege on subordination, the constitution of dominant subjects in and through denigration and negation of subordinated others, and the consequences of such denigration on both subordinated and dominant subjects should be explored. Without such deconstruction, subordinates have every reason to expect the privileged will act in bad faith and cannot be trusted. The paralyzing effects of race/gender melancholia will remain undone. Contributing to such undoing is the purpose of the rest of this book.

I turn first to further exploration of the psychic register, especially of the political unconscious and some of its predominant and recurring fantasies, then to a more extensive critique of rationalistic individualism as a mode of subjectivity and a grounding for justice. Subsequent chapters will offer an alternative way to think about and practice subjectivity and some practical policy recommendations that might contribute to the undoing of race/gender melancholia and relations of domination.

CHAPTER 3

Fabricating Subjectivity:
Monster's Ball, *The Deep End*, and *Crash* as Enactments of Race/Gender in the Contemporary United States

In the first chapter, I argue that contemporary American subjects suffer from untreated race/gender melancholia. Unable or unwilling to confront the gaps between an idealized view of our history, culture, and subjective organizations and the more complex realities of our wounded present, dominant and subordinate groups remain imprisoned within this affective state and its pathological dynamics. We have yet to learn and put into practice the crucial difference between "burying the dead" (mourning) and "burying the past" (melancholia).[1] Burying the past does not obliterate the dead; they return to haunt us. Without properly mourning the dead, we cannot make productive use of the past. In chapter 2, I claim that race/gender is a social, not a natural, fact, and that it is fabricated and sustained through a wide variety of political, cultural, economic, and unconscious processes. In this and the following chapter, I try to render these claims more plausible by analyzing certain local sites in which race/gender melancholia and the fabrication of race/gender are enacted. In this chapter, I pay close attention to how race/gender domination shapes our subjectivity and how as individual subjects we both live and resist these relations. In the following chapter, I look at the constitution of American citizenship and how it is both formed by these relations and by conflicting wishes to deny and undo them. In closely analyzing these sites, I undertake the task Walton urges of conducting investigations "in very specific and detailed ways, (of) local constructions of racialized identification and desire."[2] Such projects provide rich material for delineating the psychic and political work race/gender performs in the contemporary United States. I hope that they might increase subjects' awareness of our multiple locations on race/gender grids and of some of the ways in which we are constituted by and could confront them.

The local sites I discuss in this chapter are three films, *Monster's Ball* (2001), *The Deep End* (2001), and *Crash* (2005). Through detailed analysis of scenes in these films, I explore the often painful practices our current race/gender grids demand. In their actions and interactions, characters in each film illuminate the powers, constraints, and possible points of resistance their race/gender position affords. In his or her own way, each finds themselves enmeshed in circumstances in which intention and agency are certainly not meaningless, but neither are they the sole determinants of the narrative. Enactments of race/gender melancholia and the political unconscious generate outcomes that are sometimes tragic and occasionally hopeful. I chose films rather than another medium because movies' fluid and visual qualities render them effective modes of transmitting or activating unconscious fantasy. The information conveyed and emotions stimulated far exceed the screenplay. It is often easier to analyze someone else's subjectivity than our own, but empathic identification with characters can simultaneously provide insight into our own fabrication. Also, unlike novels or plays, movies more frequently have a domestic and international mass audience, and those who act in them occupy an important place in many Americans' imagination. Film makers can use movies to affect as well as reflect the beliefs, emotions, and desires of their viewers. The unique qualities of films and their place in American culture render them a significant index to social fantasies and preoccupations. Therefore, analyzing films can provide access to the political unconscious' content and processes.

This is the case for these three movies. On the surface, the films differ greatly, yet each offers many insights into the pervasive and intertwining effects of race, gender, and power. In each film, racialized gender positions, patriarchal power, racialized maternity, and racially specific relations between fathers and sons are enacted as the characters and stories unfold. *Monster's Ball* directly confronts the sickness of contemporary race/gender positions and the intra-and intersubjective violence required to maintain them. *The Deep End* reveals the work required to sustain the facade of white, heterosexual, bourgeois normalcy and domesticity and the desires that animate its perpetuation. *Crash* explores all these themes and also blows apart the false assumption that the emergence of increasingly "multicultural" societies necessarily entails the elimination of race/gender domination.

MONSTER'S BALL

Monster's Ball offers an exemplary portrayal of race/gender melancholia. All its characters are gripped by an aspect of melancholia that Cheng underemphasizes—a pathological combination of psychic numbness and rage. In the movie, numbness is signaled by the characters' lack of and craving for sensation; the craving is often expressed through an obsessive search for stimulation, especially eating, drinking, smoking, and sex, none of which appear to provide any pleasure or relief. The movie begins with a shot of a dim room, flashing light, a rumbled bed, and someone vomiting. That person is Hank, a guard at the local prison, who is soon to participate in another execution. Like all the major characters in the film, Hank tries to counter his numbness with some sort of oral gratification, in his case chocolate ice cream, which he can only eat with a plastic spoon (metal may remind him of what is put into the prisoner's mouth in preparation for electrocution). Hank's father, Buck, has emphysema, from smoking, and the main female character, Leticia, also smokes incessantly. Her son, who is grossly overweight, sneaks candy and eats it compulsively. Hank and his son joylessly engage the services of a prostitute. Hank, his father, and son (Sonny), are white; all these men are (or in Hank's father's case, were) prison guards. Leticia, her son, and her soon to be executed husband (and the son's father) are black. Race/gender is registered almost immediately in the film when Hank's father sees two young black boys in his yard and launches into a tirade about their proximity, how they used to know their place, and "there was none of this mixing going on." Hank, the good son, goes out and shoots his shotgun to scare the boys away. It turns out the boys are friends of Hank's son, and foreshadow the mixing to come. Hank and his father are bound by racial hatred, which deflects and is fed by the hatred between them, and the father claims Hank's mother hated "niggers" too. Hank hates Sonny, but he and Sonny are bound by the violence of the prison, as we see them practicing what will be his son's first execution. Masculine pride is affirmed by taking on such work, and Hank is enraged when his son messes up the practice, for Sonny's inadequacies reflect badly on Hank and his capacity to induct his son into this world.

The prison reflects the complexity of contemporary race/gender relations. Hank's squad is integrated; it includes one white woman and a black man. Yet, as discussed in chapter 2, we know that prisons are disproportionately populated by black men, and they are more likely to receive the death penalty. This disproportion is reflected later in the movie when we see several shots of a chain gang from Hank's prison, all black men. It is hard not to think about the judicial system, particularly our draconian and unevenly enforced drug laws and extraordinary rates of incarceration, as new forms of Jim Crow. According to the U.S. Department of Justice, in 2002 there were an estimated 624,900 state prisoners serving time for a violent offense. State prisons also held an estimated 253,000 property offenders and 265,000 drug offenders. Thus, 21 percent of all state prisoners were sentenced on drug charges. In 2000, 82 percent of all drug users were white, compared to 16.9 percent who were black. Yet blacks accounted for 37.3 percent of all drug arrests and were five times more likely than whites to be arrested on drug-related charges.[3] In 2008, more than 2.3 million people were in American prisons. The United States had the highest rates of incarceration—750 persons per 100,000—in the world. Our rate far exceeded that of the next two highest countries—Russia and South Africa—and was eight times that of any European country.[4] If present practices continue, enormous numbers of black men (and increasingly, black women) will spend some portion of their lives segregated from the free population. The consequences for them and those connected to them, as we see with Leticia and her son, are dire.

We first see Leticia with her son in her battered car, heading to the prison on their last visit before her husband's execution. What can this father pass on to his son? A warning not to be him ("I'm a bad man," he says) and the drawings he has made in prison. His relationship with Leticia is full of hate and humiliation. He cannot play the normative male role of protector; he cannot take care of her.[5] She is alone, lacking the protection expected by some in her gender position (particularly, privileged white women). Located as poor, black, female, resistance is difficult; she is losing her house because she cannot afford to pay for it. After a painful parting, the guards deny her husband his final phone call, and we see Leticia and her son desperately watching television, she smoking, he sneaking candy. Leticia turns her rage on her son, beating him for the candy and being fat; humiliating him by making him weigh himself. Leticia's abuse of her son is an all too common experience among his cohort. The rate of child abuse in black families is at least double that of other groups.[6] Longstanding use of violence as a tool of race/gender domination is now incorporated within relationships among the subordinated.[7] These actions can also be interpreted as toxic effects of race/gender melancholia; hate and denigration are turned inward and toward one's closest relations. Her son's fat may wound Leticia's narcissism;

taken to reflect her failure as a mother, that she is that much further from any fantasy of perfection. Her rage must also be fueled by a sense of powerlessness; she later tries to frame her attack as a form of protection, saying that a black man can't be fat in America. Yet, as a subject positioned as a poor, black woman, what access could she provide her son to power networks of normative masculinity? At the moment of her husband's death, Leticia is brushing her teeth, but no oral consolation is to be had.

Sonny vomits as the prisoner is walking to the electric chair. (Hank vomits most mornings at home.) Afterward Hank turns on him and beats him for messing up the man's last walk. Sonny's behavior violates normative white/male practices, hence Sonny must be located in another subject position. Hank tries to humiliate Sonny by calling him a "pussy," a woman, just like his mother, who left Hank and evidently was also hated by him. When a fellow officer tries to restrain Hank, he calls him a "nigger," reminding us again of the not so repressed presence of the past. Shamed by a black/male witnessing this failure of his son (and by implication, Hank's paternal practices) to conform to race/gender norms, Hank needs to denigrate the officer as well. He regains his dominant position by warning the officer to never again touch a superior and makes him shout "yes, sir" to signify his subordination.

At their house, Sonny points a gun at Hank, tries to humiliate him, says Hank always hated him but that he loved Hank; then Sonny sits down, turns the gun on himself, and kills himself. One could say his is a social suicide, or both a failed and successful interpellation. Interpellation fails, because Sonny cannot locate himself within his father's and grandfather's practices. Yet it succeeds because Sonny feels like a failure because he cannot do so. His love for his father and his wish that his father recognize him disable effective resistance or subjective remaking. Suicide is a way out of this impossible double bind. Buck is sitting in the room. His interpretation of events differs; he dismisses the suicide by saying Sonny was weak, like his mother. Although Hank cleans up the blood and locks Sonny's possessions away in his former room, something snaps. He resigns from the prison and burns his uniform; his father attacks him for letting him down, as Hank's mother did. Buck calls her a shit; he denigrates her because she committed suicide, which Buck terms a betrayal, a failure to meet his expectations and desires. Later Buck says the same about Hank because he leaves the prison, rejecting his father's identity, and buys a gas station.

Meanwhile, Leticia is fired from her waitress job; she gets another one at the restaurant Hank patronizes; her car dies, and as she is

walking home with her son, he is hit by a car. Hank happens by and
takes them to the hospital where the son dies; more filial blood, this
time on Hank's backseat. The hospital too reflects the complexity of
contemporary race/gender relations. It is no longer segregated, and
Leticia is comforted by a white nurse who holds her, violating previous racial taboos. However, the son died because his mother, a poor,
black woman could not afford to repair her car. Hank awkwardly tries
to express sympathy, but Leticia says that, despite what Hank says, no
one will try to find the killer of a black boy. What follows is a painful unfolding of a relationship between Leticia and Hank, as each
confronts the death of their son and their inability to feel grief, or to
feel anything at all. Each reconstructs the narrative of their parental
history, resituating their children as "good" sons so as to reconcile
with loss and their own failures. Hank says that since his son died, he
feels like he cannot breathe; he cannot get out from inside himself.
Sex between them is an almost brutal, avaricious attempt to escape
the claustrophobic imprisonment of each within their own, inarticu-
late worlds. Leticia repeatedly begs Hank to "make me feel, make me
feel good." They connect around loss and need, a form of the long-
postponed grieving Cheng discusses. After making love, each says to
the other, "I needed you."

When Leticia goes to Hank's house to give him a present, she
and his father have an ugly conversation in which the father discusses
his own taste for "nigger juice," and its connection with manhood.
Leticia flees in rage and horror from this blunt reminder of the often
violent and predatory history of sexual power relations between white
men and black women. Buck tries to reestablish the primacy of his
claim on Hank and their shared race/gender position by first asking
him "what's the problem?" and then asserting "we're family after all."
Leticia also tests the nature of her relationship with Hank; she only
reconciles with him after he puts his father in a nursing home. Doing
so is another, ambivalent move toward differentiation for Hank; when
the intake worker says he must love his father very much, Hank says
he does not, but he's my father and there it is. At the home Buck says
he is stuck now, and Hank says he is too. Ties and histories can be
reworked, but not erased.

After Leticia is evicted, she comes to live with Hank in his redeco-
rated house; there they have a tender scene in which Hank says he
wants to take care of her and Leticia says she needs it. When Hank
goes to get ice cream, she finds the drawings her husband did of
Sonny and Hank, and she realizes what he did (he made the connection before they first have sex). It may seem implausible that Leticia

could be unaware that Hank worked in the prison; she went there many times and they live in a small town. However, I take her lack of (conscious) awareness as a metaphor for the (unconsciously) willed blindness that dominant and subordinate groups must acquire to avoid confronting our intersecting histories and their consequences. Without speaking, we watch her face as she tries to connect these parts; the man who was so tender, the executioner, the white prison guard. Hank embodies the best and worst of American race/gender relations; he has perpetuated its most hateful aspects, yet comes to hate his own complicity. She is shaking and literally speechless, gripped by emotions and desires unrepresentable in language. Hank comes back; they sit outside while he feeds her ice cream, still with a plastic spoon. Although the camera slowly pans out to the star filled sky, it first lingers on the three gravestones of Hank's kin. No matter how large our perspective, the memories of violence and the histories in our present cannot disappear. His last words are, "I think we are going to be alright."

The film strikes me as both despairing and hopeful. Hopeful because, as Cheng argues, through grieving the appalling violence of the history in which they are both enmeshed and participants, Hank and Leticia reduce the grip of melancholia. Furthermore, the relationship between them is necessary for each to tolerate their own emotional work and attempts to change. As each says to the other, after their first lovemaking, "I needed you so much." This intra- and intersubjective work opens new perspectives outside the compulsive, claustrophobic repetition of the same, as Hank and Leticia contemplate the alternative universes the stars suggest. The film is also despairing because it suggests that race/gender domination can be resisted only under extreme circumstances of loss, personal disloca- tion, and the somewhat involuntary stripping of desires that fasten us to privilege. It graphically conveys the depths of hatred and rage; the passing on of white masculine identity through the power of life and death over others (primarily, in this case, black prisoners) and through a shared denigration of women and racialized others. The helplessness and inability of black people to protect those they love or themselves from the internalization of race/gender denigration and its concom- itant self-hatred and intra- and intersubjective violence is painfully evident. Instead, that denigration, hatred, and its accompanying rage is destructively expressed both inwardly and outwardly. The social compact between white fathers and sons is equally violent—hate who I hate, or I will turn my rage on you. Any reduction of privilege or race/gender boundary crossing is perceived as a threat to one's property and hence the target of justifiable attack. Women are dangerous, untrustworthy creatures, for whom it is threatening to have any tenderness, and white masculinity is a fragile accomplishment, requiring constant, hateful toughening up. Femininity is constricted in its range of possibilities. Leticia's felt choices are to be taken care of by a white male protector or to be utterly on her own and hence vulnerable to the risks of her subordinated subject positions (black female).

Her assessment of her alternatives is not unrealistic; as recent Census Bureau statistics show, compared to black or white males and white females, black women have the lowest rates of marriage. Furthermore, Leticia's alliance with Hank is unusual in that black females have very low rates of out group marriage. On the basis of 1990 Census Bureau data, Orlando Patterson calculates that 98.8 percent of married black women had black husbands. African American men are more likely to engage in out group marriage; according to the Census Bureau, in 2000, in 73 percent of black-white couples, the husband was black and wife was white. This means that African American men had white wives 2.65 times more often than black women had white husbands. This 2.65 ratio is similar to the 2.54 ratio in 1990. Furthermore, this interracial gender gap is even sharper among black-white couples who cohabit without being married. Five times as many black men live with white women as white men live with black women.[8]

What makes it possible for Hank and Leticia to resist historic patterns of hateful bonds and reduce inner- and intersubjective violence? The film is vague on this point, as Hank's motivation for moving away from his old practices is never clear. My ingrained analytic suspicion leads me to speculate that Leticia's subordinated subject positions may make it easier for him to sustain a relationship with her. His dominance is not challenged and so she represents less threat to his subjective stability. Leticia's position also remains ambiguous. She acknowledges her desire to be taken care of, and Hank promises her a "privilege" usually restricted to some white women—that is, the protection and care of a white male. Yet, to what degree does her shift of position represent empowerment, or is it another ratification of white male dominance? It is not clear whether Leticia's desire stems from awareness of her vulnerability in a largely unchanged world or an increased self-respect. Although Hank makes her partner in the gas station he purchases and names after her, it is unclear whether her agency is significantly increased. Perhaps she takes the best deal available within the existing power relations, but it is by the grace of white/male attachment, historically a rather precarious position. What the film does make clear is the desperate circumstances of all its characters, which I take as a metaphor for our current race/gender positions. If unmourned and unaltered, they poison us, imprison us, and make us ill, violent, and deadly to ourselves and to others.

THE DEEP END

While *The Deep End* opens with its main character, Margaret, knocking on the door of a seedy bar, its primary location could not appear more different than the world of *Monster's Ball*. A recipient of those differentially beneficial public policies discussed by Ira Katznelson, Desmond King, and Linda F. Williams, Margaret lives with her family in a beautiful house on Lake Tahoe, a lake renowned for its deep blue color (the blue of Renaissance Madonnas) and purity. Given current household income and family composition, far more white than black households would find this suburban haven accessible. In 2001, the U.S. Census Bureau reports that the proportion of non-Hispanic whites among the highest earning households was far higher than that of blacks. Furthermore, since white women are more likely to be married (and to be married to higher-earning white males) than black women, they are also more likely to be situated in those highest earning households.

Surrounded by pine trees and an intensely clear blue sky and inhabited by healthy-looking, prosperous white people, the fantasized impossible perfection of what Cheng calls racial idealization seems actualized. This perfection as always requires its flawed twin, in this case the city of Reno, the location of the bar. Reno is the abjected urban other to the pristine country, a common American figuration. On film it appears dirty, the air smudged. It is the mirror opposite of normalized, family-centered, suburban innocence. Gambling is legal there, and it is a place people come to drink and "sin." The bar Margaret visits is called The Deep End, and this name is meant to evoke a colloquial phrase; to go off the deep end means to go crazy. Margaret is intensely blond, as are two of her three children, and the actress who plays her (Tilda Swinton) is almost translucently white. Her family's name is Hall, as WASP and vanilla as one can imagine. Hers is a world of full-time domesticity, of car pools, children's music and ballet lessons, sports, and the errands of daily life. Margaret's husband is in the navy, and he is frequently absent for long periods of time. Yet Margaret does not lack for male surveillance; her husband's father, Jack, lives with them, and her husband is very much present in his absence as armed protector of the home front and as the ultimate, intimidating sovereign. Margaret's intense anxiety about pleasing her husband is soon quite evident; her job is to keep the home front operating smoothly. The central organizing principle of their family life is that nothing must occur that would disturb or anger her husband. The military protects the home front, but it relies on the home front to anchor and free the protector.

However, Margaret's anxious efforts to maintain the placidity and respectability of the domestic surface are undermined by her oldest son, Beau, a high school senior. His age is significant, for it means that Beau is in the middle of a ritual essential to the replication of race/gender privilege, applying to college. The timing raises the stakes for failures to act normally and intensifies Margaret's anxiety regarding her responsibility to ensure his conformity to regulatory norms. It also reminds us of the fear intrinsic to hierarchal social relations—that without conformity, one can lose one's place. Even for many dominant subjects, no guaranteed positions exist. This anxiety translates into the expenditure of an enormous amount of resources, material and psychological, among those who have them to spend. Such work is both motivated by and expresses the fear of falling into the position of the abjected other.

Nonetheless, Beau acts out the always-lurking potential sources of masculine disorder that are white women's responsibility to domesticate—that is, sexuality and the reckless pursuit of pleasure. First Beau has a car accident while driving drunk; he is accompanied by an older white man. Later, we briefly glimpse another potential symptom of resistance to expected race/gender behavior. Beau is a musician, but his chosen fields appears to be jazz (the archetypical "black" music), for he is shown recording an audition tape for his college applications. He plays a bit of Miles Davis' "Sketches of Spain," and there in this scene is the only, brief, sighting of a person of color in the film; one of the recording engineers is a black man. The person with Beau in the car is Darby Reese, and he is the man Margaret confronts in the bar. He is obviously gay. In a disturbing foreshadowing of current American politics, in this film homosexuality occupies the place of the denigrated but dangerous other. It threatens "family values" and "our way" of life, potentially undermining Beau's ability to occupy and enact his subject positions and carry on the work of the fathers and proper (heterosexual) domesticity.

Margaret tells him to stay away from her son, but Darby does not comply. He comes at night to her house to visit Beau; they end up in a fight, and Darby dies in ambiguous circumstances (he falls off their launch dock with a boat anchor in his chest; appropriate for someone portrayed as a sexual vampire). Beau and Darby have been having a sexual relationship; they kiss before the fight, but Beau becomes enraged when Darby says Margaret offered him money to stay away. When Beau returns to the house, Margaret sees his bruised face and asks him what happened. Their stilted conversation is interrupted by Jack, and then Margaret covers for Beau, protecting his place within the patriarchy. In the morning Margaret finds Darby's body, puts it on their boat and dumps it in the lake. Darby has a piece of Beau's shirt in his hand, which Margaret buries in the trash. Returning, she notices his car, has to go back to the submerged body, take his car keys, and drive his car to a Reno parking lot. Even this car, an expensive racing model with a "deep end" vanity licence plate, signifies flamboyant excess. All the other characters drive that icon of American suburban domesticity, the SUV, or modest sedans. Margaret never directly questions Beau about what happens. Fearful that she could not maintain the relationship, like Leticia with Hank, she never directly confronts her son with what she thinks she knows. Margaret simply assumes he killed Darby, and that she must cover up the crime. When Beau asks her not to say anything about the previous night to his father, Margaret agrees, purposely leaving ambiguous what "last night" means.

A different embodiment of deviant male danger now appears in the form of Alex, the blackmailer. In a further foreshadowing of current American politics, Alex has a foreign accent and looks Mediterranean. He is the foreigner within, ready to wreak violence, undermine homeland security, destroy innocence, and destabilize the good and the right. His boss, Nagel, sees Beau's affair with Darby as a business opportunity and sends Alex to demand a payoff. Alex forces Margaret to watch a video of Darby and Beau having sex. Beau is the "bottom," clearly enthralled by erotic submission to Darby. Margaret cannot bear directly confronting her son's position—literally and metaphorically in the grips of a man, subordinated to a denigrated other, beyond her normalizing reach, and outside the regulative practices of domesticity and normative heterosexual white masculinity. Alex demands $50,000 to destroy the video and protect Beau from exposure, as a homosexual and, by implication, killer. Their encounter is interrupted by her younger son Dylan and then Jack, complaining about his dry cleaning. Fortified by these reminders of her normal context, she demands Alex stay away from her family and agrees to meet him the next day in town. Margaret and her sons then hurry off to her daughter's ballet recital, a portion of Swan Lake. The blackness of blackmail starkly contrasts to the traditional connotations of ballet, that fantasy of perfection and embodiment of normative femininity—female innocence and virginity, purified romantic love, the all white swans, the idealized female form and the blue lake.

Now Margaret is confronted with the powerlessness of her protected race/gender position. Without her husband's signature she cannot borrow money on the house, and he is unavailable at sea. Even Alex, however, is not immune from the seductions of affluent white domesticity. He looks at Dylan as he arrives home from school attired in a baseball uniform with naked and intense longing. His desire to be that son, or to have had that childhood, is palpable. After Margaret misses him in town, he returns to the house. Jack has a heart attack and Alex helps Margaret perform CPR; while she accompanies Jack to the hospital, Alex looks around her house. He sees a picture of Margaret with her three children, and something shifts for him. Alex, too, however, is constrained by white male power; he is working for Nagel who demands the money. He returns to tell Margaret he will give up his share, but she must get $25,000 for Nagel. Alex and Margaret have an intense scene in which she details the demands of domesticity and accuses him of being heartless for disturbing it; he asks whether she ever gets away from her family. Through the emotions her face expresses, we see a fleeting glimpse of the wishes Margaret must repress to enact her position. Alex touches a forbidden desire for pleasure and subjective practices outside the circuit of domesticity. Margaret has also projected onto Alex the submerged needs frustrated within her marriage. She uses him as an idealized object; she fantasizes him as everything her husband is not—empathetic, tender, available, and attentive.

Margaret comes up with part of the money, but this is not enough for Nagel. In contrast to Alex, Nagel is the personification of the completely undomesticated male. Lacking any vulnerability to sentimental appeals, he is a violent monster. Nagel comes to Margaret's house, takes her to the boat shack where Darby and Beau fought and begins to hit her. Alex shows up and confronts Nagel. Nagel tries to regain control over Alex by appealing to constitutive masculine anxieties—that he is weak, that she is making a fool of him (she is not to be trusted), and that he must be "fucking her" (and hence in thrall to Margaret's sexual powers). Alex resists these appeals and kills Nagel while Margaret watches. Once again protected, Margaret helps Alex with Nagel's body. He tells her to go back to her family and forget any of this ever happened. Alex ratifies the supreme importance of sustaining the fantasy of perfection. She must keep her family together and not let them see the effort this costs. Margaret must ensure they stay in their house, their safe domestic shell, and away from its windows while Alex drives away with Nagel's body. Even murder is not too high a price to pay to protect this illusion of perfection and thus forestall the need to abandon the wishes animating it, including an assumed right to entitlement and privilege.

Margaret decides to follow him but cannot drive Alex's car (it has a stick shift). She asks Beau to help her. Unlike her daughter, who despite her interest in car repair, earlier in the film could not fix Margaret's when it would not start, Beau can exercise instrumental (masculine) mastery. They find Alex in Nagel's crashed car, dying. She does not want to leave him there, but he says she must. She cannot be muddied by his imperfection. Alex helps her retrieve the money and video, apologizes, and then dies. The last scene is between Beau and Margaret; she is crying, he comes into comfort her; while he incorrectly suspects Alex and Margaret were lovers, he says he does not need to know. Like Margaret, he would rather submerge doubts and secrets rather than confront events that might destroy the possibility of sustaining desired illusions. We see a pieta-like image of Beau and Margaret on the bed in a symbiotic embrace, holding each other as the camera pans to Margaret's wedding ring, through the well-ordered house with its many domestic objects, out the shiny window to the starry dark outside. While this panning shot is similar to the ending scene of *Monster's Ball*, the difference in its framing is appropriate. Here the home, the site of domesticity, remains the focal point. Hank and Leticia sit outside, but Margaret and Beau are inside, looking out. The idealized domesticity Margaret preserves sustains its normalizing power; Hank and Leticia's household could never assume its place in our contemporary race/gender grids. Then Dylan says his father is calling and asks Margaret to pick up the phone. We know Margaret will indeed pick up and go on. Disenchantment and a potential void have been contained by masculine protection and the white/feminine work of re-knitting illusion, including the belief in its unambiguous goodness.

Margaret personifies a particular form of the subject position, (idealized) white femininity. This position is generally inaccessible to women of color, for it entails fantasies of an asexual maternity it is assumed they lack. Madonnas must be white; women of color are either Sapphires (sexy, tough, emasculating, domineering, independent, dangerous) or Jemimas (earthy, embodied, domestic servants). Lacking access to dominant masculine subjectivity, black men cannot fully enact protective practices. Hence within our current race/gender fabrications, among black people aggression and domesticity cannot be readily split along gender positions. Insufficiently domesticated, black women cannot domesticate their men, and both genders are imagined by dominant subjects as dangerously prone to transgressing regulative norms. Black women are imagined as inadequate mothers and emasculating heterosexual partners while fantasies about black men center around their alleged hypersexuality and proclivities for violence and irresponsibility.[9]

While Margaret devotes her life to the care of others and preserving domestic order, she feels entitled to male protection in return. However, to sustain this exchange, she must curb male violence and sexuality, submerge any desires (including her own) that exceed the regulatory practices of domesticity, and please or appease male power. As with her son, she must also maintain a willful blindness to or denial of certain masculine practices and deny the violence that sustains their power, even over her. Women like Margaret are highly competent in their sphere and can muster great ingenuity when domesticity is threatened. Nonetheless, they are represented as essentially lacking. They require protection because they lack the prowess required by the larger world. Margaret cannot save Alex, although he can rescue her. This representation is reenacted and passed onto Margaret's children as well. While she appears to break gender expectations by fixing cars, her daughter Paige more competently performs stereotypical female roles; at a crucial moment, she is unable to get her mother's car started. Paige is far more in her element dressed all in white, elegantly dancing a part in Swan Lake with her white female cohort. In contrast, all the normalized males assist Margaret in restoring domestic order and proper race/gender hierarchies. Although Jack is older and requires more caretaking, she respects him as her husband's stand in. Beau will go to college in the fall. Alex kills the threat to domestic normalcy and by retrieving the money and video tape enables Margaret to act as if absolutely no regulatory norms were violated. Even Dylan helps her by calling 911 when Jack has his heart attack.

Margaret can enlist men to discipline other men, for all those who are redeemable are deeply invested in the fantasies of idealized domesticity and maternal, constrained femininity. Most people want the caretaking mother but do not want to see the effort or costs of what is provided. The more heartless the world, the more people crave their imagined haven from it. The fantasy of a clean place, of a home front to return to, sustains men at war and cleanses white men of their violence. Despite the cost to her, Margaret remains within her normative race/gender position. Perpetuating race/gender stereotypes, unlike Leticia, she is never shown as a sexual being. She thus remains available as the object of maternal fantasies. When she strips to her underwear to retrieve Darby's keys, it is simple, utilitarian white cotton. What she allows herself to crave from Alex is empathy, not sexual pleasure. Yet, she is not a helpless victim. Eager to enable her son to benefit from white masculinity, she enacts our culture's homophobia and demands that he fit into the normative grids of his race/gender position. In so doing, she is not merely her husband's agent. She is animated by her own desires to retain her and her family's privileged positions and to exercise the passive-aggressive pleasures of caretaking while seeing herself as weak and needing protection. Enfolding Beau in her embrace at the end, she reinserts him into domesticity and ensures herself future care, the privileges of masculine protection, and the cover of white/male dominance. Representing herself as in need of care and as a caretaker allows her to escape responsibility and deny her own aggression, sexuality, and desire. Aggression and sexuality are located outside, as male prerogative and danger. Somehow her complicity in violence does not count, because her actions are in the service of preserving and protecting her family and that sphere of imagined innocence. Here, her race enables a splitting and denial that is unavailable to Leticia. Leticia knows she can never pass for a Madonna; that position in our race/gender grids is unavailable to her. She also knows that Hank's history is intrinsic to his character, as her history is to hers; she takes the full weight of it and, partially out of an unromanticized necessity, goes on. Margaret, as Cheng argues, projects badness outward, and she too goes on, leaving the lovely blue surface unmarred by its deep end.

CRASH

"You can check out, but you can never leave."

(The Eagles, "Hotel California")

Set in Los Angeles, *Crash* follows the interwoven stories of its characters over a thirty-six-hour period. Fragmented and episodic, the movie reflects its location, a sprawling metropolis lacking an identifiable center. As the movie unfolds, it undermines any illusion that increasing ethnic diversity inevitably erases race/gender domination and its pathological melancholic dynamics. As in *Monster's Ball*, its characters are gripped by various forms of the psychic numbness and the rage that race/gender melancholy engenders. Like *Deep End* and *Monster's Ball*, themes of protection, power, and the fragility of perfection weave through *Crash*. *Crash* also provides many illuminating examples of the simultaneously determinant and indeterminate character of contemporary American power grids. In it, we watch subordinated subjects enable domination's perpetuation and privileged persons resist it. Plot lines and characters' actions also clearly show how the effects of relations of power can exceed or subvert individual subjects' conscious intentions. The race/gender position of subjects within these relations of power does not necessary alter their operation, and whatever effect individual subjects may generate cannot be readily deduced from a simplistic logic of identity politics. Many viewers have recognized the film's potent depiction of the interplay of race, gender, class and power; for example, in July 2006, after Inspector Andy Solberg of the Washington, D.C. police made a racist remark, his chief of police, Charles H. Ramsey, ordered him to develop a lesson plan for the police academy based on the film.

The illusion—or perhaps defensive rationalization—that diversity necessarily eradicates or signals the end of domination is both dangerous and apparently fairly widespread. It provides a rationalization for denying the many remaining asymmetries of power and resources and enables a perverse reversal in which one can appear progressive while actually supporting domination. Under the cover of diversity, concern about domination is transformed into a pathetic inability to recognize a transformed present or, even worse, a regressive desire to return to the bad old days of racial politics. A report in *The New York Times* concerning an appeal recently decided by the U.S. Supreme Court exemplifies this fantasy's dangers. A group of parents sued to overturn a Louisville, Kentucky school desegregation policy. Their lawyer, Teddy B. Gordon, concedes that if the policy is overturned, the schools will rapidly resegregate. However, he says this is not a problem, because we're "a diverse society, a multiethnic society, a colorblind society...race is history."[10] Perhaps Gordon's statement is made in good faith and is not, at least consciously, meant to rationalize a desire to undo whatever lessening of race/gender domination has occurred. However, his serene assumption that the mere existence of multiple ethnicities necessarily entails color-blindness—or justice—is questionable. Highly diverse societies, for example caste-based ones such as pre-independence India, are often organized hierarchically and marked by stark disparities in the distribution of social goods. Apartheid South Africa was also simultaneously ethnically diverse and racially tyrannical. Mr. Gordon's lack of puzzlement about why, if society is diverse and colorblind and race is without meaning or consequence, the schools would rapidly resegregate is odd. If race is truly "history" in his sense, wouldn't people be fairly randomly dispersed? Equally puzzling is his assumption that resegregation would not undermine diversity or colorblindness. Most problematic, as *Crash* so clearly illustrates, is his claim that history does not affect the present.

The mere existence of diversity exercises no magic erasure of long-standing relations of dominance, denigration, and subordination. In *Crash*, like Hank's prison staff, the Los Angeles police department is diverse, yet everyone, including black officers Detective Waters and Lieutenant Dixon, acknowledges that obdurate race/gender domination pervades its daily practices. Instead, as in the film, diversity may evoke anxiety and a phobic desire to avoid contamination, as dominant groups seek to avoid contact with denigrated others. It is as if they fear that contact with lesser others will degrade them or infect them with the subordinates' inferiority. Several recent studies support this view.[11] According to this research, rather than intensify multicultural interaction, increasing diversity results in higher levels of isolation, including intensified residential and school segregation. Whites tend to perceive integration as a threat to their social status and well being and therefore prefer low levels of integration. They associate increasing numbers of blacks with a decline in the quality of their neighborhoods and schools.[12] When the percentage of blacks in a neighborhood rises to around 20 percent, a dramatic increase in white flight occurs. Those "who wish, even unconsciously, to maintain the psychological security that comes from being a member of the permanent majority have to limit the ambit of their own movements. To keep their sense of well-being, they have to set themselves apart."[13] One consequence of white flight is that schools today are more segregated than they were twenty years ago. By 1986, the proportion of African American students in intensely segregated (90 to 100 percent students of color) schools started to climb, as did those attending schools with student of color majorities. By 1991, that proportion returned to the same level as in 1971, when the Supreme Court issued its first school desegregation busing decision. Currently, 63 percent of all white students go to schools that are 90 percent to 100 percent white.[14]

If power grids and unconscious processes remain intact, increasing diversity also may not encourage tolerance; instead, it can provide more opportunities for hate. The preexisting grammar of race/gender superiority and denigration can incorporate multiple ethnicities and subject positions. As in *The Deep End*, where homosexuals and darker-skinned foreigners occupy the denigrated position, this grammar is flexible enough to allow substitutions and replacements. Its adaptability is illustrated in *Crash*. As in our contemporary power grids, all the characters in the film are linked to others and their narratives intertwine. While their partners shift, almost always the relationships are asymmetric. Often one character connects with another to restore some form of superiority (psychic, political, etc.) at the other's expense. Koreans denigrate blacks; whites denigrate Hispanics, Koreans, Iranians, and blacks; and blacks express contempt for whites and Hispanics. Even intimate contact provides no magic escape from this oppressive grammar—much less color-blindness. In *Crash*, Ria, the girlfriend and police partner of Graham Waters, a black detective, is Hispanic, but this does not prevent him from making a racist comment about Hispanics right after they make love.

As in *Crash*, diversity does not automatically melt the numbness of race/gender melancholy, stimulate a productive process of mourning or eliminate the repetition of old patterns. Like *Monster's Ball*, *Crash* opens with a darkened screen. We see lights flashing and white blurs; these turn out to be headlights and flakes of snow. The opening lines, spoken by Graham Waters, express the feelings of psychic numbness and isolation that are often symptoms of melancholia. He says, "It's the sense of touch. Any real city, you walk, you're bumped, brush past people. In LA, no one touches you...We're always behind metal and glass. Think we miss that touch so much, we crash into each other just to feel something." Throughout the film, phobias and fantasies about race/gender reinstall this isolation and its related misrecognitions, sometimes with near-fatal effects. It is appropriate that a locksmith, Daniel, is one of the film's central characters; everyone wants to lock themselves in and someone else out—or at least keep them at bay. No matter what the actual circumstances or subjectivity of an individual, the dominant race/gender grid often determines how one character sees another. The effects of such preconceptions are sometimes disastrous and always hurtful. Graham and Ria are stopped at the site of a car crash, and in one of many misunderstandings based on race/gender assumptions, at first are not recognized as police officers. A white woman sees a tattoo on the back of the (Hispanic) locksmith's head who is replacing their door locks, assumes he is a gang member who will sell the keys to his "homies," and lauches into an angry tirade against her husband for putting their family at risk. An Iranian immigrant, Farhad, goes to buy a gun and the white clerk initially refuses to sell one to him, calling him Osama; later Farhad's store is trashed and defaced with anti-Arab graffiti. In a hospital, a distraught Korean woman runs down the hall yelling an unfamiliar phrase. The white nurse screams at her to speak English, that she is in America now. The woman answers perfectly in English that she speaks the language, but she is searching for her husband, Choi, who has just been admitted after an accident; the phrase is his full name. Although he is just looking out for his well-being, Farhad assumes that Daniel is trying to cheat him when the locksmith tells him his shop needs a new door. After the shop is trashed, due to this defective door, his insurance company refuses to compensate Farhad. He channels his rage into an attempt to shoot Daniel whose daughter comes between them. (Luckily, Farhad's daughter had inadvertently bought blank bullets.) The two carjackers see an expensive SUV and, assuming it belongs to a white person, move to steal it; they discover the driver is black. Since they pride themselves on never stealing from other blacks, they are about to flee when the police spot them. One flees, but the other and the driver are almost killed in a tense interracial scene with the police. A white policeman, Officer Hansen, who had earlier tried to report Officer Ryan, a white man and his police partner, for racist and sexist behavior, picks up a black hitchhiker, Peter, Detective Water's brother. After a testy interchange in which Hansen believes Peter is making fun of him, Peter reaches in his pocket. Convinced he is pulling out a gun, Hansen shoots and kills him. The object in Peter's hand is the saint's statue he always carries and meant to show Hansen; Hansen has an identical one on his dashboard.

After Graham is allowed to join the investigation at the crash site, he discovers one running shoe. We return to this scene at the movie's end, when Graham discovers that the shoe belongs to his just murdered brother. Peter is one of the carjackers who, with Anthony, his partner in crime, appear in several important episodes. Graham's discovery foreshadows another of the film's central themes, protection— who expects it, who hopes to provide it, the forces that frustrate these wishes, and the consequences of such disappointments. Despite his police powers, Graham cannot protect his brother, and his mother, a crack addict, while resenting his professional achievements and escape from poverty, hates him for his failure. Graham cannot protect his mother, as she repeatedly returns to her crack habit and its self-destructive consequences, or himself from the emotional impact of her toxic contempt. Instead he lashes out at Ria by denigrating Hispanics. The District Attorney, Rick Cabot, cannot protect his wife, Jean Cabot, and himself from crime; they are the victims of a carjacking Anthony and Peter perpetrate. Jean takes her anger out by verbally attacking her Hispanic housekeeper and David, the locksmith. Ryan cannot protect his suffering father from the heartlessness and inequitable provision of the current American health care system. He denigrates Shaniqua, the black female insurance case manager, and sexually assaults Christine, a black woman. Farhad, the Persian immigrant, cannot protect his shop from the attackers who mistake him for an Arab or his family from the consequences of his losses. He hunts Daniel down and tries to kill him. Daniel cannot protect his own daughter from Farhad's shooting attempt. In one of the film's most tender scenes, Daniel returns from work to find her hiding under the bed, terrified of gun shots. To increase her feeling of safety in their violence-ridden barrio, he pretends to give her a protective magic cloak but later her belief in this fantasy results in her potentially fatal attempt to protect him from Farhad's gun. Cameron, a successful black television director, cannot protect his wife Christine or himself from the race/gender humiliation Ryan inflicts after he pulls their car over. He later turns his rage on Anthony, who attempts to carjack him.

The scene with Ryan, Christine, Cameron and Hansen vividly illustrates the profound error of assuming "the past is history," because all its participants are aware that their present actions derive much of their meaning and effects from the historical relationships between white men, black men, and black women. The scene's—and the movie's—impact on the audience also depends upon the reverberating presence of this past. The scene encapsulates 400 years of race/gender domination in which there is "abundant evidence that many slaveowners, sons of slaveowners and overseers took black mistresses or in effect raped the wives and daughters of slave families...the ubiquity of such sexual exploitation was sufficient to deeply scar and humiliate black women, to instill rage in black men, and to arouse both shame and bitterness in white women."[15] The terrorizing regime of Jim Crow and Northern black women's (especially those working as domestics) lack of power and employment alternatives enabled such patterns of abuse to continue after slavery's formal abolition.

The scene begins as, sitting in a diner, Ryan hears the report of the Cabots' carjacking. He and Hansen leave the diner and cruising down a street, they see a black Navigator. Hansen says that since neither the plate nor the driver match the crime description, it is not the stolen one. A woman pops up in the passenger seat and, in the headlights, her face looks white. Saying they were doing something, Ryan turns on the police flasher and pulls them over anyway. Christine, who is a light skinned black woman, and Cameron, a black man, are in the car. They are returning from a rewards dinner, elegantly dressed up, and Christine had been giving Cameron oral sex. Ryan puts his hand on his gun and asks Cameron for his license and registration; he tells him to keep his hands in sight. He then asks Cameron to get out of the car for a sobriety test. Christine, perhaps enacting her background knowledge of the potential dangers in any situation in which a white man with a gun confronts a black man, attempts to intervene. She protests that he is a Buddhist (hence, implicitly, nonviolent) and does not drink. As the test proceeds, Christine steps out of the car, and Ryan calls her "ma'am" and tells her to get back in it. She explodes and, explicitly evoking the past in the present, says, "Don't you Ma'am me, I'm not your fucking mammy." He orders both her and Cameron to face the car for a search. As Cameron protests, Ryan shoves him against the car, tells Hansen to search him, and then while she continues to protest Ryan brutally pushes Christine against the car. Ryan says, "that's quite a mouth you have," and turning to Cameron says, "course, you know that." Furious, Christine says, "Fuck you. That's why you're doing this, isn't it? You thought you saw a white woman blowing a black man and that just drove your little cracker ass crazy." As Ryan slides his hands down her body, pretending to search for weapons, Cameron tries to quiet Christine. Gazing at Cameron while he does so, Ryan continues, moving his hands up the inside of her legs and then inside her crotch. All the while Ryan is asking Cameron what to do, saying he could arrest him for endangerment, a felony, and Christine for lewd conduct. Like the master, to establish his own honor and masculinity, Ryan needs to dominate another male. In posing his questions to Cameron, Ryan is conveying a double message. He acknowledges that potentially Cameron could be another male; he might share his subject position with its rightful claim to masculine authority. Simultaneously he asserts that only he possesses the privilege to determine who can fully occupy this position and deploys his authority to deny it to Cameron; he emasculates Cameron. Ryan's actions say, "I'm puncturing your pretensions, cutting you down to proper size; despite your money and professional success, you can never be a real man as I am. You can't even control your own woman." Cameron and Ryan share an understanding of masculinity's historical meaning; it includes the control and possession of women and the regulation of sexuality. Abusing Christine reasserts the white/patriarchal order; Ryan demonstrates his mastery and superiority and humiliates and emasculates Cameron through reducing Christine to his sexualized object. As his hand moves up her thighs, Christine's anger turns to humiliation; her gaze turns beseechingly to Cameron, her face and body language signal disgust, degradation, shame, and helplessness. Cameron clearly feels enraged but humiliated and helpless; he understands the historical salience of this sexual abuse and knows that he is also its target. Their locked gaze conveys recognition of a shared, yet differentiated, history. She, like so many black women, experiences a white man's sexualization and forcible rape; her body is the direct target, but the attack, as always, is meant to demean her subjectivity and her husband and his feelings about himself and her. As for many other black American men and women, this history generates a deep sense of solidarity, but also, as subsequent scenes (and the low marriage and domestic partnership and high divorce rates among black men and women) illustrate, it tears them apart and undermines empathy between them. Finally, Ryan says that since they are a block from home he will let them go, and sarcastically reminds them to drive safely now.

In two subsequent scenes Cameron and Christine discuss this episode. In the first, immediately after, Christine explodes at Cameron, saying she needed a husband who would not just stand there while she was being molested. She turns her frustrated aggression and fury at all Ryan's actions represent against Cameron. Attempting to salve her own humiliation, she denigrates him as Leticia does her son. Wielding the past as a weapon, she accuses him of shucking and jiving. Evoking the stereotype of the emasculated, shuffling male servant, she shifts into a "folk" accent and says, "Let me hear it again. Thank you master po-lice man. You sure is mighty kind to us poor black folk. You be sure to let me know, next time you wanna finger-fuck my wife." Cameron defends himself, saying he was afraid of being shot. Ironically in the circumstances, they trade the demeaning accusation sometimes made by other blacks against people of their class and accomplishments. Each accuses the other of not being "black enough," of failing as black subjects, unable to act black, and ignorant about its real meaning. She accuses him of sacrificing her to maintain his professional image; she asserts that he feared an accusation of lewd conduct would remind his co-workers that he really was just another black man (implicitly, a man unable to control himself or his oversexed Jezebel). Later she visits him at his studio to apologize for attacking him. However, she says she still can't believe he let Ryan molest her; she felt humiliated for him and that she "couldn't stand to see that man take away your dignity." Cameron walks away from her, the matter unresolved between them. Relations between them, as for many black women and men, remain conflicted.

At this subjective level, no resolution is possible. Ryan, Cameron, and Christine are enacting long-standing dynamics of race/gender domination. Ryan asserts his dominance by using Christine as a

means to humiliate Cameron. Like a slave master, through asserting his sexual prerogatives, he marks his mastery and his masculinity,
simultaneously emasculating Cameron and reducing Christine to an
object for his use. Flaunting his power, he reminds Cameron of his
place. Despite his fancy clothes, career, car, and elegant light-skinned
wife, Ryan's actions say that Cameron is just another "nigger" and
his woman is a whore. Neither have any honor, nor are they worthy
of respect. Although Cameron and Christine resist such denigration,
they understand the constraints of their situation. Ryan could have
shot Cameron; as a later scene shows, as a black man Cameron's professional status is fragile and contingent on the support of and approval
by white/male power. Despite their class privileges, Cameron cannot reliably deliver to Christine a benefit intrinsic to the position of
white women such as Margaret: protection, even against other men's
aggression. Race/gender dominance renders each subject to acts
of denigration—humiliation, emasculation, and sexualized attack.
While Cameron and Christine understand the historical forces playing out between them and between each of them and Ryan, as individual subjects, they lack the power to alter them. The best they can
do is to resist internalizing denigration and turning its subsequent
rage and shame against their relationship or into self-destructive acts.
Christine's attack on Cameron and the behavior of other characters
in the film exemplify how difficult it is to sustain these forms of resistance.[16] Despite his fondness for the ideas of 1960s black power advocates, for example, Anthony turns to carjacking. He rationalizes his
choice by explaining that he purposely restricts his activities to white
targets. This, he claims, proves that, unlike most black people, he is
not afraid of whites. However he rationalizes it, though, Anthony's
choice puts him at terrible risk; its potential consequences are far
more harmful to himself than to his white victims; he may end up in
prison or dead.

   Turning denigration against similarly denigrated others occurs all
too frequently in contemporary social relations, and it is sometimes
deadly. In 2005, black men were six times as likely as white men to
be victims of a homicide, and in 94 percent of the cases, the assailant
was also a black man.[17] The homicide rate per 100,000 people was
3.3 for white men and 20.6 for black men. Approximately 79 percent
of all murder victims were male. In 2005, the rate of violent crimes
against blacks was 13.6 per 1,000 people and for whites 6.5, and the
perpetrators of most of these crimes were members of the same racial
group. 82 percent of the perpetrators of crimes committed against
black men were other black men. The rate of intraracial crime among

white men was 71 percent. Rates of domestic violence are also much higher for black women; for the period 1993–1998, the rate was approximately 12 per 1,000 for black women and 9 for white women; comparable rates for men were around 3 for black men and 2 for white men.[18] Since, as we have seen, most black women's domestic partners are black men, such abuse is mostly intraracial. Cameron himself is almost the victim and then the perpetrator of such intraracial violence. When Anthony and Peter attempt to jack his car, Cameron explodes in rage. As Peter runs off, he turns on Anthony and begins beating him. Anthony calls him a "nigger," further enraging Cameron who escalates the fight. Only the arrival of some police who suspect the car is stolen causes him to tell Anthony to get back in the car. After the police leave, Cameron drives Anthony back to his neighborhood and says, "you embarrass me; you embarrass yourself." As Cameron's statement indicates, he cannot escape the power grids that shape how he lives out his subjective position. Despite his professional success, he cannot prevent others from seeing him as just another violent, black criminal. By acting out this stereotype, Anthony demeans Cameron and himself. Nor is Ryan the only white man to whom Cameron must submit. He must defer also to his white producer. In one scene, this producer even asserts his superior knowledge of "blackness." He tells Cameron to reshoot a scene because the black actor in it uses standard English. While the producer acknowledges it "might seem a strange thing for a white guy to say," he asserts the actor is "talking less black" and is therefore not credible.

However, no one else can escape the effects of race/gender domination, either. One of the most pernicious of these is equating power and domination. If expectations of power are shaped by the absolute dominion exercised by a master, when their power is circumscribed, those in positions of dominance are bound to suffer disappointment. In contemporary America, where many relations of power are local, not absolute, such delimited forms of control are common. Those exercising such power are likely to be disappointed in the relatively meager payoff of their positions. Often, the response to such disappointment is to blame or victimize someone in a subordinated position. Several scenes with Ryan show both the effects of such expectations and the consequences of confounding local with other power relations. In his position as policeman, Ryan might wield almost unlimited force, but neither his authority nor his gun translates into any power over a managed health care system. When we see Ryan in the diner prior to stopping Cameron and Christine, he has just finished a frustrating conversation with an administrator at his father's managed care plan. Unlike Hank, Ryan appears to deeply love his father. His father is in terrible recurring pain, and Ryan believes he is the victim of poor medical care. The suffering that Ryan's inability to alleviate his father's plight causes him is evident in their interactions and in this phone encounter. Despite his efforts, the administrator tells him there is nothing she can do for him; the father must make an appointment to return to the clinic and the doctor who Ryan believes is mistreating him. At the end of the heated discussion Ryan demands to speak to the administrator's supervisor. She replies she is her supervisor. He asks her name, and she replies Shaniqua Johnson; he responds, "big fucking surprise that is," and she hangs up on him.

Insulting Shaniqua, sexually molesting Christine, and humiliating Cameron do nothing to ameliorate his father's pain or augment his power over the health care system, so later Ryan barges into Ms. Johnson's office. A dialogue ensues, pervaded by the beliefs and misapprehensions endemic to our current race/gender arrangements. Ryan says that his father was a janitor who managed to build a company providing cleaning services for the city. According to him, all the eventual 23 of his employees were black, and Ryan's father worked with them and paid them equal wages when no other employer did so. Then the city council decided to give contracting preference to minority-owned firms and overnight his father "lost everything"— his business, his savings, his wife, and his health insurance. Now Ryan says, he looks at Shaniqua and can't help but think of those "five or six better qualified white men" whose job she took. She ought to be grateful for the help she may have received and be similarly generous to his father by granting him permission to see an out-of-plan physician who will provide adequate care. Shaniqua looks at him coldly and says that his father "sounds like a good man," and for his sake it is "a real shame" that his son, rather than he, showed up in her office. If it had been the father, she would have granted the request but refuses to do so for the son. She calls security and orders him out of the office.

No one wins in this confrontation. As Shaniqua refuses Ryan's request, her face and body language convey a multitude of emotions. These include revenge, as one can glimpse the memories of many past instances in which she, like Christine, had to helplessly endure the humiliations inflicted upon her by whites. There is a flicker of triumph and the pleasure of exercising a bit of power over a usually dominant white male. She is certainly exasperated, as Ryan's tirade repeats denigrating assumptions with which she is probably all too familiar. As his narrative indicates, Ryan is quite willing to accord the status of individual to his father. He attributes his father's success solely to his own merits. In any fair system, Ryan assumes, his father would win the contract. His winning proves the system's fairness, and his loss means the system is no longer just. He does not consider the possibility that his father initially won the contract in an unfair system, one from which on account of their race/gender many competitors were automatically excluded. Perhaps, had these competitors participated initially, his father would have never won the work or enjoyed the resulting seventeen good years. While he valorizes his father, Ryan is unwilling to accord Shaniqua any such respect or honor. He enacts the grammar of race/gender domination in which subordinates are reduced to mere undifferentiated instances of a homogenous class. He assumes Shaniqua achieved her position not due to her own merits, but simply because she is a black woman. She is a representative of her denigrated group and nothing more. Cameron's producer treats him similarly. Before overruling his judgment and requiring him to reshoot the scene, he says Cameron is "the expert." This statement suggests that the producer assumes blackness is a homogenous essence, known naturally (if inadequately) by all of its instances.

Despite her pleasure in a momentary reversal of the ordinary dynamics, however, Shaniqua's face also conveys a twinge of regret. In her temporary triumph she knowingly inflicts harm on a "good man." A recipient of injustice, Shaniqua has now contributed her own tiny portion to the enormous sum. Ryan loses as well. His father remains without adequate health care, and blaming Shaniqua will get him no closer to it. The logic of race/gender domination blinds Ryan to a relevant broader question: why doesn't his father have adequate health care? Why should job loss mean anyone loses everything? Why isn't there, unlike every other Western country, an adequate safety net for people like his father? This absence is certainly not Shaniqua's doing, nor does she have the power to change the situation. Ironically, Ryan's father may be suffering the unintended collateral damage of race/gender domination. Some scholars argue that, since its beginnings, race/gender domination has encouraged white solidarity at the cost of perpetuating intra- as well as interracial inequalities. Whites' fear that the "undeserving" (poor, black) would benefit from a more robust system of social support partially accounts for its absence in the United States.[19] This is another instance of the past's perverse, present power. Whites in less-privileged positions may gain honor, but this does not inevitably translate into an adequate provision of other social goods.

Crash is a heartbreaking and terrifying film. Its structure mirrors the situation it represents. The ending occurs at the beginning; the story loops into itself. This compulsive, deadening repetition of the same is commonly found in melancholia. Nothing new can emerge without confronting what is desperately split off or denied. The inability to mourn, to productively rework the losses incurred and to acknowledge the harms inflicted, results in stasis. No one is better off at the film's end; the system, while endlessly reproducing itself, in some ways works for no one. Merely inserting a person of color—Shaniqua, Lt. Dixon, Detective Waters, Cameron—does not significantly alter its operation. It would require far more radical interventions and resistant practices to redirect its forces and grids. The system seems to confound even its well-intended subjects. Hansen acts like the racist cops he deplores; he kills Peter and then covers up his crime. Shaniqua enjoys her exercise of power while knowingly incurring its ethical costs. Waters and Rick Cabot will advance in their careers by participating in a cover up of police corruption. Lt. Dixon humiliates Hansen for reporting Ryan's treatment of Christine; he fears such a report would undermine his fragile authority as their unit's supervisor. There are a few redemptive moments. Jean Cabot realizes after her carjacking that she wakes up every morning angry, and she does not know why. Even occupying a place of fantasized perfection, with her beautiful house, successful husband, and domestic staff, does not relieve her discontent. She finally acknowledges that, while she tries to blame them, her anger is not caused by the flaws she attributes to the denigrated others who serve her. Her position cannot deliver what it promises; fantasy and everyday practice will never coincide. Ryan heroically rescues Christine from a burning car and afterward their faces convey a momentary, startled, raw knowledge of the other. Anthony steals Choi's van; he discovers chained Asians in the back. They have been smuggled into this country by the ring of which Choi is a part of for sale into a modern form of slavery. We watch Anthony's face as he internally struggles with conflicting desire for monetary gain, empathic identification with the Asians' plight, and a wish to do the right thing. He declines to sell them, gives them some money, and lets them free in L.A.'s Chinatown. Yet one does not have the sense that these acts have any systemic effect. Just as the story loops back to its beginning, the awful dynamics of melancholia persist. Despite the almost miraculous, beautiful snowflakes swirling without favor over what Joni Mitchell (in "Court and Spark") calls the "city of the fallen angels," it remains an apt representation of our melancholic state.

CHAPTER 4

Paradise Lost: Race/Gender
Melancholia and the Limits of
Political Liberalism

We assume that slavery should have nothing to do with freedom; that a man who holds freedom dearly should not hold slaves without discomfort; that a culture which invented democracy or produced a Jefferson should not be based on slavery. But such an assumption is unfounded...slavery and freedom are intimately connected....Once we understand the essence and the dynamics of slavery, we immediately realize why there is nothing in the least anomalous about the fact that an Aristotle or Jefferson owned slaves. Our embarrassment springs from our ignorance of the true nature of slavery and of freedom.[1]

Citizenship and other political practices could offer promising sites for the project of undoing race/gender melancholia. However, I will argue, as currently constituted in the contemporary United States, their utility is limited. In this chapter, I track the interdependence of race/gender domination and American practices of citizenship. I also explore the usefulness of constitutional and formal legislative remedies for diminishing such domination and undoing race/gender melancholia. As we saw in the previous chapters, while the results of such remedies are not inconsequential, so far they have been disappointing. Although I do not believe that psychic processes alone can account for these failures or provide a complete basis for eliminating race/gender domination, the persistence of such domination, despite the often bloody struggles for legal remedies and the formal attainment of rights by the previously disenfranchised, suggests a need to consider their influence. Rather than providing public spaces and techniques to undo race/gender melancholia, existing practices often disable us from doing so. The persistence of race/gender melancholia blocks our capacity to adequately grasp the nature of our problems and to develop better remedies for them. The resulting inadequacies of political practices then contribute to the persistence of race/gender domination.

Existing institutional remedies for race/gender asymmetries are embedded in a broader context of political discourse and social practices, and their meaning and logic are dependent upon this context. Broadly speaking, this context fits within the complex set of beliefs and practices called political liberalism. While there are many variants of this ideology, most share assumptions about the possible neutrality of law, the priority of individual rights, and consent as the legitimating principle of the state. Other commonly held tenets include that in some sense all individuals are equal, that freedom is our "natural" state, and that the capacity to exercise autonomy is an innate human/ individual trait. Autonomy is understood as the opposite of being determined or constrained; it exists to the extent that an individual can engage in freely chosen or undetermined thought or action. This ideological context ensures our "ignorance of the true nature of slavery and freedom" because, as I briefly discussed in chapter 2, such ignorance arises in part from a false dichotomy (subject/ networks or grids) that structures American liberal political discourses. As Glenn puts it:

> ...the very tenets of republican and democratic ideology, which proclaim universal equality while simultaneously assuming exclusion and hierarchy, have helped obscure the existence of institutionalized systems of inequality. To the extent that Americans believe in independence and free choice, they deny interdependence and are blind to institutional constraints on choice.[2]

These tenets both depend upon and reproduce a distorted view of subjectivity. To work, this view splits off or denies important aspects of our subjectivity, including unconscious processes and their effects. Doing so obscures but does not negate the influence of interdependence, contextual constraint, and the political unconscious. Instead, obscuring or denying their existence undercuts our ability to recognize these forces and to devise better political practices that take them into account. Furthermore, as we will see below, holding on to problematic assumptions about subjectivity can serve as a dangerous defense against recognizing our inextricable fabrication through and embeddedness in contexts that necessarily exceed our conscious knowledge and intents, including race/gender and asymmetric relations of power. This unconscious defense enables a misguided innocence that can generate enormous, if unintended, harm. One of the unfortunate consequences of unconscious defenses is that they can undermine our best and most admirable conscious intentions and commitments; their deployment may even ensure that the outcome of our practices is the opposite of what we intend. Such, I will argue, occurs to one of the most influential contemporary arguments for political liberalism, the work of John Rawls. Despite his deep commitment to justice, his recommended practices disable resources necessary to undo race/gender melancholia and adequately confront race/gender domination. This unintended outcome is due in part to Rawls's misguided theory of subjectivity, which among other problems is completely blind to the operations of the political unconscious.[3]

In this chapter, I will argue that Rawls is correct in saying that acting on unconstrained self-interest is problematic, especially when asymmetries of power ensure that the more powerful will be able to act more effectively on such interests and therefore reproduce their privilege and systemic inequalities. However, his cure for the problem (acting as if we don't know what our situation and self-interest is) won't work. This is so because (1) even if some procedure worked to render us unaware of our particular situation, it won't solve the problem of the effects of unconscious processes. Ignorance of unconscious motives doesn't keep us from acting on them. (2) Offering hope that ignorance equals neutrality inadvertently permits the continuing shift of blame to those who point out the effects of such acting out—"we can transcend or control for our particularity, why can't they?" (and often those who object to acting out are the ones most disadvantaged by it). (3) Our best hope for controlling unconscious material is to cultivate practices that require us to continually seek it out. Such practices require interaction with others, since nobody can have full access to their own unconscious. To be effective, such interaction requires all participants acknowledge and take responsibility for their social positioning and that others can call them on possible enactments of their positioning. Furthermore, recognizing that subjects are differently situated helps us see the peculiarities of our own, and also potentially helps us to be more careful about mistaking its enactments as neutral or universal. (4) While knowledge of our own positioning can lead to harm if we simply act ruthlessly in our immediate self-interest, requiring us to act as purely rational deliberators also disables us from calling on other resources that subjects can cultivate—for example, empathy, practical wisdom, and humility.

These are important resources for imagining more just practices. The dangers of our passions, fantasies, and desires require active management practices, not ignorance.

Thus, analysis of one of the most powerful cases for political liberalism suggests that undoing race/gender melancholia will require different theories and practices of subjectivity and citizenship. In particular, we need more attention than is generally found in liberal theories to the power/knowledge circuits through which citizens are fabricated. Furthermore, due to its prevalent bias toward individualist and rationalist accounts of subjectivity, liberal theorizing often does not explore the ways in which citizenship can serve as a site for the enactment of unconscious fantasy and emotions such as envy, as well as for the preservation of race/gender asymmetries.

As I will argue below, if our goal is less domination, even holding onto the idea of a detached legislator as a normative ideal is counterproductive. We cannot possibly control all the effects of the unconscious. Rights or any other human construct are ambiguous tools because there is no magic force capable of erasing the effects of how their makers are constituted. As long as legislating subjects come to be through race/gender grids, these race/gender processes will be endogenous, not extrinsic, to rights and law. As Patterson says, "contrary to our atomistic prejudices it is indeed reasonable that those who denied freedom, as well as those to whom it was most denied, were the very persons most alive to it."[4] These grids animate a certain kind of willing subject who, to secure their own freedom, can readily deny it to others and simultaneously deny that they are doing so or rationalize their acts. Thus, while investment in the emancipatory powers of rights and other liberal remedies remains strong, such hopes require chastening through recognizing their shaping by and location within practices that also actively enable and reconfigure race/gender domination.[5]

FOUNDING SUBJECTS

The traditional story of America's founding, as the expression of freely willed acts of rational, contracting subjects resulting in the bringing into being of a historically unique realm of freedom, is incomplete and inaccurate.[6] The origin and history of rights discourses are interwoven with "the hierarchy of race"[7] and gender. By 1787, when Congress passed the Articles of Confederation, "the idea of citizenship had become thoroughly entwined with the idea of 'whiteness' (and maleness) because what a citizen really was, at bottom, was someone who could help put down a slave rebellion or participated in Indian wars."[8] The United States is the only modern liberal-democratic state that wrote slavery into its founding, legitimating document (the Constitution). Debates over slavery shaped the American constitution in many direct and indirect ways. Although slavery is not explicitly mentioned in the Constitution until its abolition was ratified by Amendment XIII, its traces are evident in numerous clauses of the original document. These include Article 1, Section 2, which specifies that for purposes of apportioning representatives and direct taxes the population of each state shall be determined by adding the number of free persons, and "excluding Indians not taxed, three fifths of all other persons." (Among other political issues, the three-fifths clause represented an attempt to solve one of the Southern representatives' dilemmas. This problem was how to maximize their population for purposes of determining representation in Congress without opening up the possibility that slaves could count as "persons" and hence be entitled to rights.)

Furthermore, the Constitution reveals an anxious awareness of the potential of the slave holders' property to exert human-like will. As Davis points out, the "framers definitely had slave uprisings in mind."[9] Several articles signal anxiety about handling possible internal insurrection, including Article I, Section 8 and Article IV, Section 4. Article I, Section 9 forbids Congress to prohibit the "importation" of persons (e.g., the slave trade) prior to 1808. While a tax or duty not exceeding ten dollars per person "may be imposed on such Importation," the same section prohibits any taxation of interstate commerce that would include the domestic slave trade. Article IV, Section 2 stipulates that no state can discharge a person "held to service or labour," in another. It requires instead that such persons be "delivered up on Claim of the Party to whom such Service or Labour may be due." This would require states that had outlawed slavery to ensure that escaped slaves were returned to their "owners." Article V, concerning amendments, explicitly excluded only the first and ninth Section of the first Article from any amendment prior to 1808. It also permanently enshrines the rule that all states shall have equal suffrage in the Senate—that is, despite population differences each state must forever have the identical number of senators. This issue was of particular concern to the Southern founders; the arrangement eventually enabled their disproportionate power in that body. Amendment X, which reserves to the states or to the people the powers "not delegated to the United States by the Constitution, nor prohibited by it to the States," also enabled Southerners to protect "their way of life" from outside meddling.

Slavery was abolished less than 150 years ago. It was barely more than that when the Supreme Court declared in the Dred Scott decision (1857) that black men had no rights that white men were obliged to respect. Despite resistance in many forms, in the 1850s, women of any race lacked legitimated political existence. In 1868, while the ratification of Article XIV of the Constitution guaranteed citizenship rights to all "male inhabitants," it simultaneously reconfirmed women's exclusion. The right to vote was not extended to American women until 1920. The most recent wave of legal challenges to race/gender dominance began less than 50 years ago, and it is barely 30 years since attempting to vote could be a life-threatening exercise for many black people. Congress did not fully eliminate its 1790 limitation of naturalized citizenship to "white persons" until after World War II. For most of its history, therefore, citizenship in the United States entailed not what Carol Pateman calls a sexual contract—that is, agreements among men concerning the disposition of women—but a race/gender one.[10] The contract stipulated the distribution of full political rights, which were simultaneously and identically rights of white heterosexual masculinity, and these were allocated by and reinforced race/gender subject positioning.[11] Paradoxically, as Holland argues, by making this always tacit arrangement visible, the constitutional amendments adopted during Reconstruction "fundamentally altered the nature of the American political imagination."[12] The Fifteenth Amendment for the first time explicitly introduces the terms "race" and "color" into the Constitution and, by referring to "male inhabitants," the Fourteenth Amendment inserts gender. The extension of rights does not necessarily disembody subjects; rather, these "Amendments made the body visible, and they recast its meaning: once a figure of the suppressed past of political life, the raced and gendered body became a symbol of its future."[13]

Slavery is also intrinsic to the construction of one of the most important of the liberal subject's rights—property. Consider John Locke's account of natural rights. (While his own position on slavery was ambiguous, Locke's writings on rights and government influenced the Englishmen who wrote our Constitution.) The inalienable possession of rights, including property, is an essential aspect of Locke's definition of the individual.[14] Authors such as C. B. Macpherson usefully interpret Locke's emphasis on property by locating it within his historical context, specifically the problematic posed by wage labor and early market capitalism.[15] However, while Macpherson provides a rich account of the emergence of commodities and market society, this classic political economic understanding of the connection of labor, value, and property is incomplete. While Macpherson is not unique in omitting slavery from his narrative, ignoring the impact of the slave trade is wrong. It is not accidental that in his *Second Treatise of Government*, Locke's chapter on property (chapter 5) is preceded by one on slavery. Slavery provided not only labor and wealth but the defining limit against which the modern European subject could comprehend his own freedom. The first form of property is labor—property in one's body and its products. One marker of freedom and a defining attribute of "the individual" is its interdependent opposite—slavery, the lack of property in one's own person. "Nothing highlighted freedom—if it did not in fact create it—like slavery."[16] A central purpose of rights is to provide a defense against the actual historical possibility that free males could literally cease to be through suffering the social death Patterson describes. They could lose property in themselves; they could be enslaved and cease to be individuals. Once slaves, subjects are not individuals; consequently, the problem of their rights is irrelevant.[17] Only individuals possess rights, but not all persons are individuals. Euro-American women had no property in their person either, but total gender conversion appears to have been outside the cultural imagination of the time. Males could make other men slaves, but while they might "unman" others, they could not make them female.

In American politics, citizenship was interwoven with the right to property, not only in one's own person, but literally in the possession of other persons as property. According to the terms of the founding American contract, ownership of human beings was among the forms of property that the state was obligated to protect. Race/gender determined the most basic form of property—who had property in their own person and to what degree. Slaves were property and, while considered human beings, married white women were incorporated within the person of their husbands. Neither white women nor slaves existed as autonomous political agents. Their political status was as subjects, not citizens. Individuals have a right to own property, but no subject can be property and remain an individual. Slavery also grounds the adult male wage earner's belief in his own freedom. Unlike a slave, he is free, because his labor is his own property; others (a parent, spouse or master) have no claim to it. In post-Reconstruction America, this distinction between slave and male wage earner changes. New distinctions emerge between workers, who are white and male, from race/gender others.[18] Blacks were excluded from the full benefits of "free labor," including membership in labor unions and secure property ownership. Although the franchise long-remained an empty promise for many black men, all black women were excluded from voting until passage of the Nineteenth Amendment.

Once modern grids of race/gender emerge, subordinated persons are seen as radically other than dominant subjects. However, this belief masks an equally strong dependence. The characteristics of the new American citizen—"autonomy, authority, newness and difference, absolute power"—are each "made possible by, shaped by, activated by a complex awareness and employment of a constituted Africanism."[19] One of the expressions of race/gender melancholia is denial of such dependence. In turn, this denial underwrites a dominant set of claims regarding the transformative potential of American liberal practices. The recent and influential arguments of Rogers Smith illustrate what happens when such dependence is denied. He claims that what he calls the ascriptive aspect of American citizenship, (its race/gender-based inclusions and exclusions) is an independent, third dimension of American political practices.[20] He also argues that "American politics has historically been constituted in part by two evolving but linked 'racial institutional orders.'"[21] One of these orders is "white supremacist," but the other offers a "competing set of 'transformative egalitarian'" practices. Honig's assertion that such an argument is "tautological" is probably accurate. She points out that Smith "defines liberal values as egalitarian (which is the question, not the answer), and then everywhere he finds egalitarianism he claims to have found liberalism and only liberalism, and he never finds liberalism anywhere else."[22] However, I think it is more interesting to interpret Smith's claims as effects of the processes of splitting and denial intrinsic to race/gender melancholia. Such processes are unconsciously activated to preserve the "purity" of the self-understanding of the liberal subject. There is the "good citizen" within a "transformative order" who can institute and sustain freedom and equality for all and a separate prejudiced one. Simply detach the bad part, and all will be well.

However, if this "ascriptive" aspect is internal, not extrinsic, to individualism and democratic republicanism[23] then our narrative of American politics, including the diagnosis of the problem of race/gender domination and remedies for it, becomes much more complex. Then there is no intrinsic contradiction between commitments to traditions of liberal and democratic republican ideologies and inequalitarian ascriptive ones.[24] Faith in an unconstrained transformative order is problematic; it expresses a longing or fantasy, not social fact. The failures of liberalism to mitigate systemic inequalities cannot be solely attributed to its "bad" ascriptive strand, nor can we simply assume that a purified version will perform its transformative magic.[25] As Gunnar

Myrdal argues, not only is there no necessary contradiction between ascriptive beliefs and practices and commitment to equality, but racism may enable one to manage the gaps between commitments to equality and inequalitarian beliefs or even to deny that such a gap exists.[26] The problem of equality only emerges if a group is considered worthy of it, and there is little evidence that dominant American political practices have ever consistently extended full individualism to all race/gender subject formations. Rather than different strands, from the beginning the modal American citizen, the liberal individual, was white and male. His sense of equality, equal entitlement, and social solidarity rested upon the privileges guaranteed to all in his race/gender position. This image and history remains active within our political unconscious. Splitting enables Smith (and others) to circumvent these concerns. Such approaches obscure the need for the unfree to define freedom, for exclusion to produce inclusion, or for inequality to propagate equality. Furthermore, we do not have to consider the affective and unconscious dimensions of subjectivity and belief systems that operate even within "transformative" liberal practices and subjects. Denying our collective fabrication through race/gender grids may express race/gender melancholia, but it will not enable us to undo it.

THE LAW OF THE SHADOW

Current constitutional law proscribes many traditional exclusionary practices. However, such changes have not eliminated the need for race/gender dominance or its pervasive effects on American politics. The political unconscious retains its force. Although it arises from a somewhat different set of problematics, the Africanist presence (white subjects' fantasies about black ones) is no less necessary than at the American founding. It helps to manage what would otherwise be a profoundly disorganizing recognition of the shadow at the heart of the American dream. Despite the ubiquity of such social positioning and processes, the persistence of systematic race/gender domination cannot be integrated as a social fact without radically disrupting our dominant political narrative and the subjects who have woven it into their particular senses of place and entitlement. As Myrdal points out, the centrality of equality to the American creed necessitates cognitive dissonance in regard to the simultaneous existence of its shadow. As he puts it:

> The race dogma is nearly the only way out for a people so moralistically equalitarian, if it is not prepared to live up to its faith. A nation

less fervently committed to democracy could, probably, live happily in a caste system with a somewhat less intensive belief in the biological inferiority of the subordinate group. *The need for race prejudice is, from this point of view, a need for defense on the part of the Americans against their own national creed, against their own most cherished ideals.* And race prejudice is, in this sense a function of equalitarianism.[27]

While perhaps rendering them less "politically correct," legislation alone cannot eliminate the melancholic dynamics of denigration and grandiosity. De Tocqueville's chilling prediction that, "the abolition of slavery in the South will increase the repugnance for blacks felt by the white population,"[28] appears all too accurate.[29] Projecting all flaws on to the race/gendered other enables one to live comfortably with what otherwise might be a felt contradiction between that repugnance and egalitarian commitments. To sustain fantasies of perfection, entitlement, and innocence and comfort with the denigration these fantasies require, the privileged even turn race/gender dominance into the subordinated's fault. In David Brion Davis's memorable phrase, in the United States, the race problem is formulated so that the "so-called Negro—and the historically negative connotations of the word are crucial for an understanding of my point" is identified as the "GREAT AMERICAN PROBLEM. The road would be clear, everything would be perfect, if it were not for his or her presence."[30]

Another essential function of the Africanist presence for whites is to protect the illusion that white subjects and our political spaces are unraced, although this unraced status plays out differently along gender and class lines. Blacks are "the race"; race is extrinsic to whites; just as women are "the sex" and gender is understood as "the woman problem." These unraced/ungendered spaces, whether in the form of abstract individualism, democratic republicanism, or John Rawls's "original position," ground the legitimacy of American political practices and law. In the dominant American narrative of its founding (as in Smith's "transformative strand"), the central actors are unmarked, rational individuals. The legitimacy of what they created (the constitution, political institutions, law, etc) requires the autonomy and disembodiment of the creators. They act as agents of impersonal and universal principle, not as embodied socially generated subjects. What they institute is extrinsic to any social location. Hence, to suggest that the constitution of privilege and unfreedom is intrinsic to the democratic experiment and that the meanings of freedom and citizenship require its shadow calls into question the legitimacy and foundations of the founding.[31]

Despite the persistence of Africanist fantasies, the gradual undermining of legally legitimated race/gender domination in the United States that began in 1863 with the Emancipation Proclamation does produce disruptive effects. These changes restrict existing political practices' (including citizenship's) capacity to enact race/gender melancholia, but they have not provided sufficient new tools for undoing it. When what Julia Kristeva calls the abject (shame-inducing or denigrated aspects of subjectivity)[32] cannot so readily be projected outward, dominant political subjects are unsettled. As I will argue in the next chapter, another transformation further exacerbates this unsettling. In this same period, two new modes of power acquire more force and gradually extend their influence. Michel Foucault calls these biopower and govermentality.[33] Biopower entails productive networks of power that generate new objects or subjects that then serve as additional sites for its exercise. Unlike older modes of power that prohibit or punish certain kinds of behavior, biopower incites subjects to act, and especially to do so by organizing their subjectivity in particular ways. One way this mode of power works is to posit and then claim to treat (often newly "discovered") diseases within the body politic, at both the micro (individual subjects) and the macro (public health) levels. The federal government's recent funding of programs to teach "marriage skills" as a remedy for poverty is a good example of this mode of power. Under the cover of "public health," such initiatives are meant to encourage subjects to organize themselves only within a particular kind of socially constructed relationship (heterosexual marriage). These initiatives redefine problems in the social distribution of resources as pathologies of subjective behavior for which professionals with the right expertise know and are authorized to administer the appropriate remedy.[34] Governmentality installs a perpetual demand for subjects to participate in their own disciplining and management. It teaches practices which then enable subjects to take up certain positions or roles "freely"—that is, without apparent external coercion or surveillance. The U.S. government's preferential funding for programs that support sexual abstinence as a means to avoid AIDS or unwanted pregnancy and the subsequent invention by "private" subjects of "chastity rings" and ceremonies is a good example of governmentality.

These processes of subjection proceed alongside the continuing cultural valorization of individualism.[35] The American norm of subjectivity—the self-made, self-directed, atomistic and autonomous individual—directly conflicts with the practices in which modern subjects frequently find ourselves. Projecting unfreedom onto the denigrated other, overt race/gender domination provides a way to manage this tension. However, when domination is no longer sanctioned through law, fantasy loses some of its social sanction. The less overt race/gender dominance can function to ward off or compensate for the consequences of modern subjection, the more politically unstable American society becomes.[36] The absence of a compelling single state-based international enemy such as the former U.S.S.R., additionally undermines possibilities of coherent organization through hatred of a common object. Even that once promising substitute, terrorism, seems to have destabilized rather than unified the American polity. Its indeterminant qualities—being everywhere and nowhere at once—exemplifies the other's elusive presence and frustrates our wish for a fixed object to hate.

The disruptive effects of changes in formal law and the increasing force of biopower and governmentality in the constitution of modern subjectivity are further intensified by the gradual diminishing of citizenship as a mark of social standing. I take the notion of citizenship as social standing from Judith Shklar.[37] She argues that originally American citizenship functioned as a marker for and an instrument of social standing. When the dominant political ideology claims all humans are equals, the status of citizen is a mark of respect. The absence of the status brands one as inferior, not fully human and lacking. Thus, citizenship is most appreciated by those who lack it and is most valued as long as some are excluded from it. Once citizenship becomes truly universal, it can no longer function as such a marker. Despite its location within a discourse of equality, its connection with privilege gave citizenship much of its value and psychological rewards.[38] Fully inclusive citizenship loses status and much of its social salience.

Shklar suggests that as citizenship ceases to mark social status in the United States, income emerges as the primary determinant of worth and respect. This shift accelerates citizens' withdrawal from public life and intensifies the emphasis on individualism, earning, and consumption that are such distinctive aspects of American culture. The belief that wealth signifies worth and that the worthy will gain enables Americans to tolerate features of social life, such as sharp inequalities in the distribution of income and wealth and the absence of an extensive network of social welfare programs that other democratic cultures find more problematic. This process also further undermines the possibilities for constructive engagement in the public sphere, as citizenship devolves into a means for protecting private material interests. Stark economic inequalities corrode any sense of a life in common or of a shared public world, producing a vicious circle of deepening estrangement and privatization.

I think there are additional consequences of these shifts in social standing and citizenship. The ability of a few to go from "rags to riches" reinforces the mythology of individualism. Individualism teaches us that social locations such as race/gender are purely contingent or matters of luck. They can be surmounted by any worthy person. Inability to do so signals personal failure; no systemic barriers to success or systematic asymmetries of power can exist.[39] Since personal qualities must account for failure, this mythology permits a covert moral blaming along ascriptive, race/gender lines. In addition, citizenship retains a tie to social standing, but now a defensive one. Citizenship permits the public expression and subjective management of envy[40]; it becomes a stage for what Nietzsche calls ressentiment.[41] It serves as an anxious site from which to monitor and control the status or claims of others.[42] Under the guise of a commitment to equality, it is used to ward off perceived threats to the current distribution of status. For example, as I discussed in chapter 2, many of the same people who enjoyed their superiority during the denial of equality to others are now the first to assert their unequivocal support of absolute equality. In the name of this equality, they oppose affirmative action, calling it reverse discrimination.

Another function of contemporary American citizenship is its role as a form of manic defense. Manic defenses enable the subject to ward off aspects of subjectivity that produce anxiety or disorganize identity. They are frantic internal responses to conflict that require tremendous energy to retain and renew. These defenses work by enlisting anxiety in the service of psychic processes such as projecting disturbing material outward, splitting it off from consciousness, or denying its existence. By employing manic defenses, the subject can construct a fantasy about its situation that keeps underlying anxiety at bay. This defense enables a subject to identify with or as an idealized object but at a terrible cost. The disparate aspects of any object—person, institution, culture or idea—are split in two. Some aspects are categorized as good, and these are assigned to a now idealized version of the object. Others are categorized as bad, and these are projected outward onto a "now externalized threat" to the good: "the nation against the foreigner; the demos against the outsider...the good citizen against the bad immigrant."[43] Just as the good object is idealized to an unreal perfection, the bad is demonized beyond redemption. The belief that as citizens, persons exist apart from their race/gender locations is an example of such a defense. Acknowledgment of such locations would undermine the subject's claim to abstract individualism. Only as a being outside of such concrete social determinations can one can be an abstract individual. Only such individuals can legitimately exercise power. In turn, imagining citizens as abstract individuals permits some subjects to disavow their race/gender positions, assert their legitimacy as public actors, and claim their unearned entitlement as merited rewards. Denigrated others are imagined as the containers of all the disavowed aspects of the privileged's subjectivity—race, gender, and social determination.

The universalizing of citizenship undermines its potency to function in this way. It leaves an enormous amount of material related to race/gender—including power, identity, status, place, entitlement, and devaluation—floating and unmanaged. The marked others can now claim to be us. However, the histories and daily practices of unmarked citizens do not vaporize. If their effects cannot be projected onto the marked others, where can the social collective allocate them? Smith is wrong to attribute contemporary American political discontents to the absence within liberalism of any gripping account of civic identity.[44] The problem rather, is that the ascriptive (white/male) material internal to individualism, citizenship and civic identity can no longer be publicly named and made use of. Civic identity is thus temporarily without a coherent narrative organization or recognizable, homogeneous agent.[45] This absence creates an anxious, almost hysterical need to identify, control, and eliminate disruptive internal differences so that an idealized purity might be restored. Such anxiety is expressed in the frantic attempts to censor art, circumscribe immigration, eliminate teaching evolutionary theories, make welfare recipients work, "protect marriage and family values," and so on. Alongside hysteria, other common responses to the collapse of manic defenses emerge: paranoia, enacted in various conspiracy theories, survivalist cults, terrorist groups, and so on and sheer, often randomly murderous, rage. The shrinkage of mass political spaces intrinsic to modern liberal practices, while meant to contain and neutralize disruptions, may instead make the United States increasingly vulnerable to them. The desiccation of the public sphere leaves Americans few positive outlets for the will to power and thus ample space for politics of ressentiment—a frightening conjunction of events. None of the variants of liberalism offered within the narrow spectrum of dominant American political theory—individualist liberalism, rational choice, communitarianism—have resources adequate to confront, contain, or channel these energies.

READING RAWLS:
PARADISE LOST AND NOT REFOUND(ED)

One could say then, as a general rule, that white misunderstanding, misrepresentation, evasion and self-deception on matters related to race *are among the most pervasive mental phenomena of the past few hundred years, a cognitive and moral economy psychically required for conquest, colonization, and enslavement. And these phenomena are in no way* accidental, *but* prescribed *by the terms of the Racial Contract, which requires a certain schedule of structured blindnesses and opacities in order to establish and maintain the white polity.*[46]

In this section, I support my claims that American political liberalism lacks sufficient resources to undo race/gender melancholia and that race/gender is internal to democratic practices and subjectivities. I do so by analyzing John Rawls's account of how just principles regulating the basic political structure should be established.[47] It would be equally appropriate to critique communitarian writings.[48] These theorists claim to provide a sound alternative to Rawls's disembodied theorizing, but their own "situated selves" are amazingly unmarked by race/gender. However, I interpret Rawls's project as a grand attempt to construct a narrative of a modern, purified refounding through which democratic-liberal practices and beliefs are articulated, justified, and secured. Rawls mounts a heroic effort both to better redo the original founding and to take into account the ethical heterogeneity of our contemporary, deontological world. Therefore, I consider his work the most exemplary instance of liberal theorizing and a fair test of its political imagination. I also find his theorizing tragic in that, despite his deep commitment to justice and his admirable openness to others' criticism, the procedures he recommends to secure fairness ensure the failure of his attempt. His failures are instructive, for they also point to more promising routes to undoing race/gender melancholia.

In an interesting set of footnotes, Rawls says that "there is no social world without loss is rooted in the nature of values and the world. Much human tragedy reflects that. A just liberal society may have far more space than other social worlds but it can never be without loss...we may often want to say that the passing of certain ways of life is to be lamented. It is too optimistic to say that only unworthy ways of life lose out in a just constitutional regime."[49] As the next chapter will make clear, my own view of the social world is probably far more conflictual and tragic than his. However, I will argue that the space Rawls constructs to arrive at justice is too narrow and that the losses his vision requires often reflect the constraints of his approach rather than the innate nature of values or the world. Rawls states his purpose is to "get a clear and uncluttered view of what...principles of justice are most appropriate to specify the fair terms of cooperation when society is viewed as a system of cooperation between citizens regarded as free and equal persons, and as normal and fully cooperating members of society over a complete life."[50] However, the means he recommends to secure justice are self-defeating. They ensure that Rawls's approach will fail, even according to his own criteria. As Rawls states, his justice as fairness or "other liberal conceptions like it, would certainly be seriously defective should they lack the resources to articulate the political values essential to justify the legal and social institutions needed to secure the equality of women and minorities."[51] His approach does lack these resources.

According to Rawls, without fair regulating principles, political justice cannot exist. His story of how we arrive at such principles simultaneously generates the means to subsequently choose and evaluate basic policies. The device he proposes through which these principles are derived—the original position—is fatally flawed. Sheldon Wolin is half right when he says the:

> most crucial omission from the original position is any recognition that a political society inevitably carries a historical burden as part of its identity, that it has committed past injustices whose reminders still define many of its members. Rawls, by contrast, gives a picture of an expiated community that has settled its injustices on terms that merely need to be recalled, as in the antislavery amendments to the constitution.[52]

Wolin is correct that the nature of the original position renders those who assume it unable to recognize the historical burdens of their particular society. This blindness undermines any possibility of attaining justice; instead, as I will argue below and in the next chapter, effective practices of justice require subjects whose eyes are wide open to their own and others' positioning. However, he is wrong to claim that Rawls's community is already expiated. Instead, I think Rawls intends the original position itself to be a practice of expiation. Its necessity arises precisely from Rawls's recognition of our society's historical burdens. While this recognition cannot be retained once in it, the original position can be seen as a treatment for the flawed political consciousness and institutions of modern Americans. The severity of this treatment tells us a great deal about the stubbornness and pervasiveness of its targeted disease. If we pay attention to what our "artificial" representatives are supposed to block out, the conditions of injustice political liberalism confronts will be clearer. The heroic and impossible measures it asks of its subjects implicitly acknowledge the pervasive effects of a history they are not allowed to discuss. However, as I will elaborate below, the original position can also be interpreted as an instance of Cheng's fantasy of impossible perfection.[53] Perhaps, as Holland suggests, "fantasy is the only technique whereby the American liberal tradition can come to terms with itself."[54] However, since fantasy both partakes of and reproduces the social illness it is meant to heal, it rarely offers effective treatment. Instead, fantasy may inhibit accurately diagnosing social problems and inventing effective remedies.

As is well known, Rawls argues that for the principles regulating the basic structure of a state to be fair, they must be arrived at behind a "veil of ignorance." Once we are behind this veil, we are in the original position, and only from this position can fair principles be articulated. Rawls is unclear on how we are to understand the original position. Sometimes he refers to it as a "device of representation"[55] by which "the idea of the original position serves as a means of public reflection and self-clarification."[56] It enables us to bring all our considered convictions to bear on one another. Conforming to its requirements enables us to establish "greater coherence among all our judgments" and "deeper self-understanding."[57] At other points he claims an ethical status for it, saying it is to "model" the conviction that political propositions should neither be proposed nor accepted on the basis of social position.[58] We can think of the original position as "the point of view from which noumenal selves see the world."[59] The original position is a "procedural interpretation of Kant's conception of autonomy and the categorical imperative. The principles regulative of the kingdom of ends are those that would be chosen in this position, and the description of this situation enables us to explain the sense in which acting from these principles expresses our nature as free and equal rational persons."[60] It can also be understood as an epistemological standpoint, since it models "both freedom and equality and restrictions on reason in such a way that it becomes perfectly evident which agreement would be made by the parties as citizens' representatives."[61] Alternatively, it seems to fit within the rubric of formal logic; the original position is a hypothetical and ahistoric situation.[62] It is a mode of reasoning that we can enter "at any time simply

by reasoning for principles of justice in accordance with the enumerated restrictions on information."[63] By engaging in such reasoning
we "simulate being in the original position."[64] Taken up correctly,
from this viewpoint, "the same principles are always chosen."[65] The
original position also appears to have an empirical dimension. Rawls
believes it is a natural (innate) condition[66] and accessible to anyone
with a normal capacity for reasoning. It is a "natural guide to intuition"; a "viewpoint" anyone can take up at any time[67]; "a thought-
experiment for the purpose of public- and self-clarification."[68] On
the other hand, the parties inhabiting our device of representation
are merely "artificial creatures." "The deliberations of the parties,
and the motives we attribute to them" should not be mistaken "for
an account of the moral psychology, either of actual persons or of
citizens in a well-ordered society."[69] These parties exercise "rational
autonomy," which is a way to model the "idea of the rational (versus
the reasonable) in the original position."[70]

What are we to make of these convoluted and contradictory descrip-
tions? Rawls offers the idea of the original position as a device of representation to refute the claim by Sandel and others that he is making
assumptions about the nature of persons. In reply, Rawls asserts the
original position is a "role" a person can play without being committed to (or enacting) any metaphysical doctrine about the nature
of the self. However, he appears to be using "representation" in an
unusual way. Since the process, properly repeated, will always produce the same results, no more than one (empirical) "representative"
is necessary. Any and all deliberators will arrive at the same principles. The parties in the original position are not "representatives" of
a constituency, for this would mean knowing their commitments and
bargaining with others similarly informed. Rawls is quite clear that
"the original position is not to be thought of as a general assembly
which includes at one moment everyone who will live at some time.
It is not a gathering of all actual or possible persons. To conceive of
the original position in either of these ways is to stretch fantasy too
far; the conception would cease to be a natural guide to intuition."[71]
The original position is clearly not meant to be a guide in the sorts
of deliberation in which most ordinary representatives are engaged.
Such deliberation concerns specific political conflicts, not choices of
principles to regulate the basic structure. Conflict would not exist
without clearly situated differences among the parties. Deliberation
cannot occur without attention to the particulars of the issue, the
parties represented, and the effects of competing responses. All parties know that the outcomes will produce consequences some will

prefer more than others. It is also not clear how the original position can serve as a device to guide the political deliberations of ordinary people. As artificial persons, the parties in the original position are not "representative" of actual citizens, representative here in the sense of exemplars. If the parties in the original position do not share the moral psychology of actual persons or of citizens in a well-ordered society, their process cannot guide actual citizens' deliberations.

Rawls's characterization of the original position as a viewpoint is more coherent. What is being "represented" (imagined is a more accurate term) is a mental process, a mode of rational deliberation. Achieving such a position *is* a "fantasy." Like all fantasies, however, it tells us a great deal about what the conscious mind of the fantasizer cannot acknowledge or reconcile. What is being modeled is a process of splitting and denial. This splitting is required by the effects of the material it blocks out (race/gender domination and other forms of unfairness), but to maintain the position (and its plausibility) requires denying the social relations that necessitate it. The tragedy is that like all pathological defenses, Rawls's prescription undermines rather than safeguards the positive impulses it is meant to protect. Despite Rawls's deep commitments to justice and equality, his citizens will end up far from the possibility of instituting more just practices.

Rawls's narrative is a story shaped not only by denial but also increasingly by despair. It is a highly despairing fable about the absence of fairness in contemporary American culture. Indeed from his 1970 *Theory of Justice* to *Justice as Fairness*, published in 2001, Rawls's own tone grows increasingly melancholy. In a remarkable footnote in *Justice as Fairness*, Rawls says, "Germany between 1870 and 1945, is an example of a country where reasonably favorable conditions existed—economic, technological and no lack of resources, an educated citizenry and more—but the will for a democratic regime was altogether lacking. One might say the same of the United States today, if one decides our constitutional regime is largely democratic in form only."[72] Implicitly Rawls tells us that those with power to decide in the phenomenal world are unable to arrive at proper principles or practices of justice. The background institutions of any society, including the contemporary American one, are pervaded by inequalities arising from cumulative social, historical, and natural tendencies. Outside the original position, people are not equal. Some have undeserved advantages. These arise from contingent but persistent social arrangements. Among these contingent advantages or disadvantages are a person's class and race/gender positions. These contingent social positions shape people's thinking; the "particular features and circumstances of the all-encompassing background framework" distort our viewpoints.[73] The original position is necessary, because only if one fully erases one's contingent positioning is a neutral (disinterested) viewpoint possible. Otherwise, the proper principles could not be found; they would always be mistaken through the distorting lens of one's particularity. This is as stark a statement about the relationship between knowledge and power as any Michel Foucault is accused of making.

However, unlike Foucault, Rawls assumes that social positioning is only negative, a source of constraint rather than a site and effect of power that simultaneously enables and restricts the subjects it produces. His phenomenal selves are egoistic, and the gratification of their interests is necessarily at the expense of others. A zero sum situation of structured disadvantages exists in which dominant persons use their power to accumulate further advantage; "the conditions for a fair agreement on the principles of political justice between free and equal persons must eliminate the bargaining advantages that inevitably arise within the background institutions of any society from cumulative social, historical and natural tendencies."[74] Given these patterned relationships, the possibility of justice depends on controlling for their effects. "These contingent advantages and accidental influences from the past should not affect an agreement on the principles that are to regulate the institutions of the basic structure itself from the present into the future."[75] This requires creating a viewpoint that does not reflect the experience or position of any historical/contingent subject. The original position articulates a kind of historical agnosticism: it acknowledges many actual positions are possible, but no deliberator knows their original context or destination. Being abstracted from their context presumably frees them from their situated interests and causes them to think as free (e.g., undetermined beings).

Unless citizens remove ourselves from ordinary framework of thinking and practices, there is no ground from which a fair agreement on basic principles can be reached. Undisciplined by the abstraction of the original position, people will make choices based on their social positions. Existing advantages will mostly likely be sustained. Only by absenting themselves from constitution by dominant practices, only by not being themselves, can political actors enter the kingdom of ends. The biblical resonances of the word original are not misleading. Like all Edenic stories, implicit in Rawls's narrative is the background for which Paradise serves as a contrast. This background is not a kingdom of ends and is pervaded by unfairness. The original position is a prelapsarian moment, a mode of thinking unmarked by the "sins" of the inequalitarian ascriptivism intrinsic to American political subjects and practices. Rawls's narrative is also a fantasy of a refounding in which the deliberators, innocent of the sins of their fathers, will not repeat their unjust acts. Unlike the United States' actual founders, Rawls's deliberators will not write race/gender domination into their basic political structure.

RETELLING THE FOUNDING: THE SPLIT SUBJECT

Despite Rawls's disclaimers,[76] his theory does rely on a metaphysical view of the nature of the self. To "simulate being in the original position,"[77] Rawls's subject must engage in the psychic process of splitting. We (and it) are to believe that it can project its social determinants outward, beyond the veil and that the split off material no longer has any influence. No unconscious processes operate within its psychic world, and nothing remains inaccessible to consciousness or outside its control. Rawls's founding subjects are individualized but never consciously embodied. Parties to the original position must have no knowledge of their "race and ethnic group, sex and gender, and their various native endowments such as strength and intelligence."[78] They are not allowed to know "the social position of those they represent, or the particular comprehensive doctrine of the person each represents."[79] The parties do not know their class position or any special features of their psychology.[80] What remains are rational entities uncontaminated or tempted by social relations and unconscious processes. Once split off, heterogeneous determinants cannot affect otherwise rational persons,[81] and therefore, their reason can now provide the neutral ground our ordinary background practices cannot. We no longer act "as though we belonged to a lower order, as though we were a creature whose first principles are decided by natural contingencies."[82] Instead, we express "our nature as free and equal rational persons"[83] by choosing the proper (disinterested) principles of justice.

The plausibility of Rawls's theory depends upon believing that splitting works as posited and that therefore a radical disjunction between reason and the subject's social context and unconscious processes (including the political unconscious) is possible. A belief in noumenal minds depends upon their presumed capacity to distribute the phenomenal world elsewhere; no one claims the empirical world simply vanishes. Reason might be disembodied, but if permanently detached from the phenomenal world, rational persons die. The phenomenal world remains in the background; others contain it, live it, while rational deliberation proceeds, and even the deliberators return to it after taking off the veil. It also assumes that all psychic processes are knowable and controllable by reason. If reason cannot split off from and project outward the phenomenal world and control unconscious processes, the "enumerated restrictions on information"[84] would be ineffective. This is what I believe is the case. The denial of contingent determination does not remove its effects, increase the plausibility of disembodied, transparent rational deliberation, or produce justice. The phenomenal world, with all its heterogenous determinants and unconscious processes, disappear behind the veil of ignorance only from the point of view of those sharing this belief. The apparent disappearance of all marked and unconscious aspects of its subjects is an illusion. As Gilroy says, the "modern subject may be located in historically specific and unavoidably complex configurations of individualization and embodiment—black and white, male and female, lord and bondsman."[85] The assumption of a veil blinds those who operate behind it to their own determinants. Imagining it enables the subject to sustain a fantasy that it is the master of, not formed by forces not completely in its control, including its social history and unconscious. Inadvertently, it supports the idea that a "race neutral" position is possible, that in principle at least some of us can "rise above" enmeshment in the traces of an irrational past. Deliberators collude with others who agree to imagine themselves as similarly situated, as unmarked. Their proceedings are as uncolored as themselves. The fantasy of abstraction secures the belief that neutral political principles exist and that as the unmarked, subjects can attain objective knowledge of them. In their veiled ignorance, deliberators mistake defensively constructed ideas for generally applicable principles of justice. Thus, the fantasy of impossible perfection underwrites a belief in "pure" reason.

Rawls maintains otherwise. In the "present case," he states, "the conception of a person is a moral conception, one that begins from our everyday conception of persons as the basic units of thought, deliberation and responsibility."[86] This is a political conception and "given the aims of justice as fairness, a conception suitable for the basis of democratic citizenship."[87] This a rather odd conception of persons, one not necessarily congruent with "everyday" ideas. It does reflect an unthought (and for Rawls, unthinkable) consequence of social relations. Positions of social dominance enable their occupiers to believe that they (and hence their thought) are undetermined by social relations and unconscious processes. Contrary to Rawls's claims, reason does not enable subjects to operate as undetermined beings; rather, a position of relative privilege enables some to imagine such autonomy. A belief in noumenal minds reflects the asymmetric distribution of power, of determination and control. Social privilege is converted into uncontaminated thought. Reason here functions as rationalization; it constructs a story about the capacity of the subject that masks its need for and dependence on the unfreedom of others. For example, Rawls's deliberators know that a group of "least advantaged" may exist. However, to enter the original position of ignorance about their own condition, they must construct a compromise formation. Yes, constraints on freedom exist. However, it is true only of these determined others, not of all. Furthermore, such constraints do not compromise one aspect of a human capacity—reason. Thought can be free of all phenomenal determination. In taking up the correct viewpoint through reason, some persons can remove themselves from the phenomenal world. There can and does exist an unraced/ungendered space from which thought is articulated. Our claim to innocence can be sustained.

However, anxiety persists. Bonnie Honig characterizes Rawls's well-ordered citizen as unstable and anxious. Of Rawls's citizen, she says, "With his self-control always at stake, always in doubt, the responsible subject is anxious to distance himself from whatever pushes, pulls, attracts or impels him from inside or outside. He cannot silence his disruptive internal impulses as long as what he sees as their external manifestations persist."[88] Among these disruptive internal impulses, I believe, are race/gender fantasies, the stirring of the raced/gendered other within, rebellion against the disembodied situation of the noumenal self, and the thwarted aggression and pleasure seeking of a will to power exiled from the practice of politics. Even for those operating as units of thought, reason requires a supplement. This is evident in the strategies Rawls employs to persuade citizens to adopt equalitarian and rights-protective policies. He relies on two quite different principles. One is an appeal to social anxiety and self-interest—in a (implicitly unfair) world no one knows where they may end up, so it is in everyone's interest to generate universally fair principles. The other is a quasi-theological ethical injunction: if you are truly free, you will treat your fellows with the respect due yourself and regard them and yourself equally as ends, not means. This appeal to social anxiety, while masked by ethical discourse, reveals how the background bleeds into even into rational discourse.

Rawls provides further evidence that we can neither think our way out of the background framework nor do without it. His deliberators need to know a lot of general information. "There are no limits of general information,"[89] since the parties must arrive at conceptions of justice appropriate to their own system of social cooperation. They have quite a few "general facts about human society."[90] These include "political affairs and the principles of economic theory...the basis of social organization and the laws of human psychology."[91] They also have a list of acceptable concepts of justice to choose among.[92] It is not clear if among the general facts they would know are the differential effects of race/gender on the framework of the society for which they are deliberating. Rawls appears to assume that permissible information is objective and would not reflect the inequalities in the background framework. The knowledge about "economic theory," "the laws of human psychology," or the "basis of social organization" deliberators have access to is neutral in regards to ways of life, power relations, race/gender positions, and so on. This is quite implausible. For it to be useful in deriving conceptions of justice appropriate to historically situated social systems, such information cannot be utterly formal and abstract. Furthermore, socially relevant knowledge is saturated with the contexts in which it is produced.

Critique of Pure Reason: The Impossible Fantasy of Perfection

Despite his commitment to justice, Rawls reveals the helplessness of political liberalism to recognize or remedy impediments to its realization. He models a silence in the founding and a fantasy about the innocence and perfection of human reason and agency that are fatal to the possibility of justice. By permitting his agents to imagine a moment of purity, Rawls inadvertently (and, given his commitment to bettering the situation of the least well-off, unintentionally) participates in a deeply consoling fantasy of dominant groups. Their phenomenal privilege need not undermine their (and their society's) capacity to be fair. There is a viewpoint available outside of time and social networks, if only they will let their reason take them there. Then they can be their best selves—unmarked by race/gender relations and unmotivated by any will to power or unconscious fantasy. Fundamentally, the problem is in identifying or implementing the correct principles, not in systemic relations of power and their effects on everyone. This set of assumptions permits some to accuse those who attempt to insert questions of the race/gender bases of privilege of "reverse racism." Such attempts, for example, affirmative action or implementing policies to insure racial diversity, are then construed as violations of the ideal "race neutrality" (perfect abstraction) the enlightened embody.[93] Again, tragically, this is quite the opposite of what I think Rawls intends. His second major principle (the difference principle), that to the extent that it does not violate any individual's liberty, "social and economic inequalities...are to be to the greatest benefit of the least-advantaged members of society,"[94] is certainly congruent with affirmative action policies. The problem is that his description of the original position does not adequately account for the derivation of this principle, nor does he provide any persuasive means to convince subjects in our present circumstances to accept its application.[95] As Coles accurately points out in reference to the difference principle, "concern for the least well-off is empty if they are variously objects of disgust, marginalization, and everyday indifference."[96] Building support for applying the difference principle would require making use of resources, including imagination, empathy and inquiry into the operations of race/gender grids, including the political unconscious. Such mobilization would extend the realm of the political beyond the bounds of public reason and reasonableness.[97]

When deployed to legitimate the fantasy of a pure founding subject, Rawls's secure ground operates as a device of rationalization. To move politics onto the ground of abstract reasoning about general principles is to depoliticize it and obscure the workings of power. To maintain this mystification, we can either (re)create a (secular) theology or deny unfairness. I take this to be a parable of the intrinsic limits of liberalism. What happens in the original position parallels Rawls's text and the text reflects the practices to which he is committed. Too much credit is given to the emancipatory possibilities of reason (theology). Unrealistic (and unpolitical) representations of "neutral" and "well-ordered" political structure are generated. Too little attention is paid to systemic relations of power that produce many of those "accidental" distributions of advantage. In the narrative (as in Smith's account of the "transformative" strand) these appear extrinsic to the construction of basic regulatory principles and their representatives. Yet, such advantages generate unarticulated guilt about the misdeeds of contingent subjects. This in turn propels a flight to formal reason rather than a pragmatic consideration of how situated and imperfect citizens can act responsibly. The founders can once again present themselves as abstract, perfect individuals, unmarked by desire, will, unconscious processes, or social relations. Consequently, far too little value is given to developing or mobilizing potential resources in political struggles for justice—will, desire, the interactions of heterogeneous subjects outside the articulation or administration of law. In the next two chapters, I will discuss how some of these resources might be mobilized.

In his narrative, Rawls misconstrues phenomenal as well as noumenal selves. He splits the phenomenal world in two—into our situated knowledges without which no useful principles can be articulated and the situated subjects that cannot speak. He acknowledges that justice is of the worlds we find ourselves in, but the concrete subjects who live there cannot enact it. However, he mistakes the problem. What Rawls calls "contingencies" or "accidents of history" (and what I would call in our present context, race/gender domination) have, after all, systematically distributed great freedom to some subjects. The problem is not an intrinsic unfreedom of our bodies as opposed to our minds, but the "social facts" of the operation of bodies as sites of power. Justice is not undermined by the vulnerability of our phenomenal (or noumenal) existence to contingent determination per se, but by how determination is distributed. Our inquiry into the production of privilege and unfreedom is blocked by sustaining this split between noumenal and phenomenal selves. Without such inquiries, we are unlikely to reduce the injustices such power relations sustain. We cannot see how those "contingent advantages and accidental influences from the past" are socially constructed effects of power that differentially construct and empower us.

While Rawls portrays the original position as an ethical viewpoint, adopting such a view will reenact and perpetuate injustice. While it is meant to erase the effects of contingent advantages, instead it reinstalls them. Many of the effects of these contingent advantages play out unconsciously, and the veil of ignorance renders them even less accessible to their subjects. We know we have attained the original position when no disturbing reminders of phenomenal contingencies appear. Given actually existing background conditions, what could this mean in practice? Markers of difference must disappear. Here the fantasy of perfection is enacted. Race/gender blindness in a society whose social and historical background produces race/gender social positions as contingent but inescapable (and hardly "accidental") social facts requires erasing those marked as other while leaving the implicit norm undisturbed. Thought behind the veil, public discourse, or even standards of "reasonableness" cannot escape the social and unconscious processes of "normalization" in which the "norm," white/male, is invisible. The fantasy of race/gender blindness leaves other subjective positions as the disturbing markers of difference, subject to expulsion from the community of rational discourse. Raising problems of contingent determination marks oneself as part of the "lower order" that is unable to operate as a free being. Since the original position requires obviating race/gender, treating ourselves or others as privileged or disadvantaged on account of race/gender positions would violate our nature as free beings. We are to act as if the social facts were other than they are; if no accumulated inequalities existed, our constructed identities would not undermine the possibility of justice. Yet, we cannot talk about the facts, because to do so would suggest our citizens are more than units of thought, deliberation, and responsibility and that thought and rational deliberation might not be so pure or reliably self-correcting. Constituting race/gender fantasies remain unanalyzed and powerfully in play; therefore, race/gender melancholia lingers, untreated. By making justice contingent on splitting and denial and offering the hope of a space outside of the consequences of our histories and our heterogenous subjectivity, liberalism, as represented by Rawls, ill serves its own best commitments.

Politics for Fallen Angels: Subjectivity, Democratic Citizenship, and Undoing Race/Gender Melancholia

> *Democratic citizens are by definition empowered only to be dis-*
> *empowered. As a result, democratic citizenship requires rituals to*
> *manage the psychological tension that arises from being a nearly*
> *powerless sovereign.*[1]

In the last chapter, I argued that rather than offering resources for undoing race/gender melancholia, the political liberalism John Rawls conceives inadvertently exacerbates it. This consequence is partially due to the construction of subjectivity that his political liberalism posits and requires. Imagining that subjects can abstract themselves from all the networks of power and unconscious dynamics in which they find themselves is mistaken. As I argued in the last chapter, the veil of ignorance cannot perform such magic, because even if we could successfully carry out this thought experiment and remove all knowledge of our specific social locations, operating behind the veil will not provide individual subjects with transparent access to unconscious dynamics and content. Ignorance of unconscious processes cannot eliminate their effects. For the same reason, neither the rule of reasonableness in making demands on the public sphere nor the process of submitting such demands to public reason will sufficiently correct the political unconscious's effects. Instead, this approach will disable contemporary American citizens from making use of resources that can bring race/gender melancholia into conscious awareness and build support for policies to diminish its consequences. Remedies for race/gender melancholia and the race/gender domination it both reflects and prolongs must be multidimensional. Among the many remedies race/gender melancholia requires are different practices of subjectivity and citizenship. In this chapter, with the aid of Michel Foucault's late essays on "Care of the Self," I will develop and support these claims.

BEHIND THE VEIL: RACE/GENDER DOMINATION AND THE PARADOX OF DEMOCRACY

Public spaces are important sites of generating, enacting, and potentially altering race/gender melancholia. As currently practiced, however, American citizenship provides insufficient resources to confront the effects of the past in the present. In part this is because our practices of citizenship continue to elide a crucial paradox of democratic politics. This elision has been facilitated by race/gender domination. The paradox is that, although modern narratives of democracy institute popular sovereignty, equality, and consent as defining and constituting features, the successful practice of democracy requires citizens to engage in acts of sacrifice. Sacrifice is intrinsic to democratic citizenship because despite our founding narrative of democratic sovereignty and individual freedom, in actual political practice a disjuncture often exists between the individual will and the law. In modern democratic politics, to be legitimate, generally outcomes require only consent of the majority. On any one issue, this potentially can leave many citizens feeling discontent, disadvantaged, or disappointed. The stronger the democratic promise, the larger the gap between it and actual outcomes is likely to be. The more citizens expect autonomy and self-rule (understood as the coincidence of desire and outcome), the more frequently widespread disappointment and frustration will ensue. In a small polity, much less a large one, it is highly unlikely that even if perfectly democratic procedures or a Habermasian universal pragmatics could exist, that decisions will always be equally satisfactory to all citizens. The relative scarcity of social resources and the diversity of human desires and ideas of the good (subjective and collective) insure that any outcome will favor some and disappoint others. Citizens must therefore tolerate often not getting their way or exerting control. Furthermore, once a decision is arrived at, even if it is not the outcome we want, as long as we remain members of the polity, we must bear the burdens of its consequences. These consequences may include loss of valued resources or even our lives. Despite our disappointment (and perhaps envy or resentment of the winners), we must also maintain our loyalty to the polity and our investment in keeping its institutions and processes going.

In the United States, slavery, race/gender domination, and their lingering effects have enabled public discourse and practices to elide this paradox.[2] Danielle Allen argues that for much of our history, citizenship was structured through relationships of dominance and acquiescence, not equality. One effect of race/gender domination is that the sacrifices and disappointments endemic to self-rule are distributed unequally. Domination systematically skews the distribution of social goods in favor of the privileged. The acquiescence of the disadvantaged perpetuates the illusion that the system is fair and its principles are pure. The necessity of sacrifice within democratic rule is thus obscured by the systematic maldistribution of sacrifice and reward; rewards are unfairly distributed to those in privileged race/gender positions while subordinates suffer an unfair portion of sacrifice. Only when the disadvantaged begin to insist on a more equitable distribution of social goods (including political recognition and respect) and a redistribution of sacrifice is the democratic paradox more evident.

However, despite the formal incorporation of race/gender subordinates into the body politic, as I have argued in previous chapters, asymmetries of benefit and sacrifice remain. Americans have never effectively and publicly recognized the immeasurable, involuntary sacrifices enslavement and its consequences extract from African Americans.[3] Neither have white Americans acknowledged their enjoyment of the continuing psychic, political, and economic benefits and privileges such sacrifices produce. Performing public practices of mourning could counteract some consequences of these asymmetries. In the United States, however, there is an absence of mourning, of consciously coming to terms with one's investments in and constitution through intersubjective relationships of domination/acquiescence. If we do not mourn, we cannot imagine redoing these relationships, including redistributing sacrifices and benefits more equitably.

Furthermore, as De Tocqueville and Janara point out, the democratic promise of equality creates a corollary sense of entitlement among its citizenry.[4] Each citizen feels they ought to have what others do, that in principle any "X" could be theirs. Combined with the reigning mode of political subjectivity—individualism—and the social flux intrinsic to the absence of traditional status hierarchies, entitlement simultaneously produces anxiety and envy. While having equal access to social resources is assumed as one's democratic right, the lack of legitimated hierarchy means no stable place or outcome is guaranteed. Status insecurity, envy of those who have what one does not, and a gleeful but illicit desire for and pleasure in exclusivity result. (Why does X have what I do not? It could, therefore, should be mine. If I possess X I will be better and more secure in my status than Y, but having X only counts if Y cannot.) Thus, as Janara puts it, "the psychodynamics of envy, desire and materialism [are] native to democracy."[5] Race/gender domination secures some degree of guaranteed status for the privileged, but challenges to it intensify anxiety and render its management more problematic. Furthermore, contrary to the Rawls's claim, a belief in the fairness of the basic structure is unlikely to provide sufficient consolation for loss of an intensely desired object. It is a mistake to underestimate the independent power of emotions, desire, and unconscious fantasy in political life or to overestimate subjects' willingness or ability to be governed by reason alone.

Modern political theorists rarely acknowledge the democratic paradox.[6] Therefore, there is little discussion of the psychodynamics of democracy or how to manage its intrinsic frustrations.[7] Little attention is given to developing practices that will preserve the losers' investment in the game, teach winners to moderate the advantages of victory or contain envy, resentment, and greed. Instead, theorists utilize a variety of strategies to mask or finesse democracy's paradox. While Rawls, for example, recognizes the risks of cooperation, he incorrectly imagines that they can be eliminated permanently up front by excluding desire and pursuit of comprehensive goods while formulating the basic rules of social arrangements.[8] Conflict and disappointment disappear as ongoing problems requiring constant political work. Somehow reason, or reasonableness, will magically reconcile us to a rule of law that often thwarts our wishes. Others, such as Jurgen Habermas, locate the difficulties in attaining a universally satisfactory consensus within the current, imperfect procedures or processes governing public life, not the irreducible diversity or will to power or unconscious dynamics we encounter in human interaction.[9] They hold out the undeliverable promise that transparency of practices is possible or that the pragmatics of appropriate language games will free us from the messy consequences of our heterogenous subjectivities. Failure to incorporate psychodynamics within democratic principles and practices also results in positing problematic binaries such as (rational) law/ (irrational) culture or "ascriptive traditions." This is disabling in addressing race/gender dominance for, as the work of Rogers Smith exemplifies, we are then unable to see the effects of envy and other affects within apparently unproblematic democratic principles and institutions and thus cannot imagine effective countervailing practices. Instead, such authors construct

POLITICS FOR FALLEN ANGELS

another simplistic, dichotomous narrative of American politics featuring the good "egalitarian transformative" order versus the bad "white supremacist" one.[10] Defeat the villain and all will be well. Advocates of politics as spontaneous action such as Hannah Arendt, Jacques Ranciere, and Linda Zerilli appear to bypass the paradox by limiting the political to contingent, singular events. However, in these accounts what remains unexplained is how actors learn to govern themselves so that they restrict their actions to expanding the realm of freedom or justice, not intensifying domination.[11] Another tactic is attempting to banish diversity altogether by positing a unitary subjectivity that properly practiced will express a uniform desire. Deviations are explained through a variety of narratives, from sin to lack of reason, false consciousness, inadequate identification with one's true group, or perhaps foreign ethnicity or blood. Deviants must be corrected, contained, disenfranchised, expelled, or destroyed for the public good.

CHANGING THE SUBJECT

Thus, although since the passage of the 1960s civil rights legislation, the democratic paradox may be more evident, Americans are no more fit to manage it. A consequence of our untreated race/gender melancholia is that American citizens lack the practices of subjectivity and political action that would enable them develop and sustain more egalitarian democratic politics and to manage the potentially destructive emotions they evoke. The habits regenerating and supporting domination and acquiescence are deeply ingrained in the citizenry. They will not simply wither away; instead we require new practices of subjectivity and political action. The lingering race/gender disparities in distributions of social goods and esteem, the structuring of our current institutional politics by a desperate search for someone bad whom we may legitimately dominate—terrorists, gays who want to marry, foreigners who will take our jobs or resources, those who threaten the (Christian) values founding the state, and so on—are all evidence of our collective inability to forswear old subjective and political habits and reconsider our practices. Emerging from our melancholic state requires new habits of mind and feeling, different kinds of political practices and spaces, and a far more capacious view of politics itself. Later in this chapter, I will offer a few tentative suggestions for what these might entail. However, next I discuss some tools for beginning to think outside dominant American narratives of subjectivity and politics.

SOUL SERVICE: FOUCAULT'S LATE ESSAYS, SUBJECTIVITY AND "CARE OF THE SELF" AS ETHICAL AND POLITICAL PRACTICES

Clearing Space

As we have seen in previous chapters, part of what reproduces race/ gender domination are particular practices of subjectivity. The dominant narrative of subjectivity within American politics is individualism. While its origins are heterogenous, currently individualism is a disciplinary norm that sustains race/gender domination. This narrative is now intertwined with race/gender melancholia. One of the symptoms and effects of melancholia is denial of the effects of the ongoing legacy of past social relations, especially slavery, on the present constitution of subjects. As I argued at the end of chapter 4, individualistic self-representations are produced through denying subjects' race/gender positioning. Intrinsic to privileged race/gender positions is the authority to represent oneself as unmarked by social relations. Such individualism serves to ward off consciousness of or to deny the disturbing effects of race/gender on all subjects. It is an identity politics, a set of practices, that denies the particularity of the identity it fabricates and enacts. It generates a notion of freedom as undetermined action. Only disembodied, unsituated subjects can be free or fully exercise agency. This narrative generates its own vicious circle in that to imagine oneself as free, one must project the relations that effect subjectivity elsewhere. One also needs to project such material elsewhere to avoid location on the devalued, determined side of the perfection/denigration binary. The devalued state of those in subordinate race/gender relations intensifies the horror of imagining oneself as socially produced, like "those" people. It also intensifies investment in sustaining the fantasy of unmarked perfection. Horror may be defended against by unconscious hostility to the other, consciously expressed by an emotionally charged desire to exaggerate differences among groups.[12] Therefore, within race/gender melancholia, no escape is possible from the binaries it generates—including free/ determined and agent/object. Social and political practices, unless congruent with the will of an autonomous ego are constraints on agency and identity.

Among the ways to resist race/gender domination are reconfiguring practices of subjectivity. Such a project also entails rethinking the relations between freedom, moral responsibility, and disciplinary and governmental practices.[13] Shifts in the practices of race/gender domination render this project more urgent. Since the 1960s, cultural norms have altered such that overt expressions of race/gender denigration are discouraged. Furthermore, since the passage of the Civil Rights Act and the removal of tangible expressions of domination such as segregated facilities and explicitly race/gender-specific allocation of work, dominant groups are more likely to believe that such domination has ceased. However, as I argued in chapter 2, if one looks at patterns of the distribution of power, resources, and social status and norms, there are many reasons to believe this is not the case. Instead, the practices sustaining race/gender domination have altered. As Charles Lawrence argues, guilt regarding the violation of social norms of "fairness" or correct attitudes results in the repression of socially incorrect feelings or actions.[14] These feelings and beliefs remain unconscious and are often enacted in disguised or apparently race/gender neutral ways. For example, dominant subjects may express racial antagonism or denigration through avoidance, seeking out neighborhoods without subordinate group residents. The obvious asymmetries in income, resources, and the like, between dominant and subordinate groups may be rationalized by "scientific" findings on pathological cultures, deviant families, or innate biological differences. The desire to maintain control and distance may be enacted through the rubrics of fighting crime, restricting immigration, or protecting family values.

Once unconscious feelings and ideas become more prevalent sites and sources of race/gender domination, the practices they engender are less accessible to resistance and of course easier to deny. The pseudo-rationality of the overt material through which they are enacted disarms those seeking to resist relations of domination. Practices that are simultaneously irrational and normal violate expectations of rationalist individualism. Yet, these are what Wittgenstein calls the ungrounded ground of shared social worlds, the tacit understandings, beliefs, and meanings that enable the intelligibility of subjects and practices. Like language games, we learn by doing, by taking up the norms and disciplines around us so that we can construct subjectivities comprehensible to our self and others.

Contesting a tacit or unconscious meaning system is difficult. Sometimes the inevitable contradictions and gaps within any system provide leverage or sites for resistance. Often, however, what is required are ways to delimit the system, so that it appears as a social artifact rather than an eternal truth. However, only certain practices of subjectivity are likely to engender a critical skepticism toward normalizing processes. Given the power of normalization and the inaccessibility of

unconscious material, such practices will most likely require intersubjective interactions and practices through which we can acquire self-
critical disciplines and new habits. These disciplines enable a certain
degree of engaged detachment in which modes of subjective organization, including race/gender melancholia, might appear puzzling or
problematic. Rendering a mode problematic is an important aspect of
generating spaces for new ones to develop. Opening new spaces could
diminish race/gender melancholia's power. As its grip lessens, active
mourning could begin to displace melancholic paralysis.

How Is the Subject

Michel Foucault's work on "Care of the Self" is focused precisely on
the question of how to establish and enact disciplines that render the
given or "normal" problematic. These disciplines also enable us to
govern ourselves so that we pursue and engage in ethical practices
of freedom. My project here is to describe his results and to think
about how we might appropriate them to improve practices of contemporary American citizenship. I argue that Foucault explores techniques that could help us evaluate and reinvent the heterogeneous,
context-specific practices that constitute and alter subjectivities.
Adopting these practices will enable us to better manage the paradox
of democracy and resort less frequently to practices of domination
and subordination.

Only in his last works does Foucault fully open up this line of
inquiry. In these essays and lectures, he radically rethinks subjectivity and his previous ideas about power and political action. As he
says, as his work proceeds, "I have been obligated to change my mind
on several points."[15] Central to this rethinking is his elaboration of
practices he calls "technologies of the self." Technologies of the self,
while related to and potentially shaped by other modes of power, such
as biopower, are not its derivative effects. In exploring them, new
possibilities of exercising freedom and creativity emerge.[16] Among
these possibilities are new ways of practicing social theorizing that
enable us to bypass ones that generate unproductive stalemates. For
example, Foucault's genealogical approach enables us to avoid the
structure/subject dichotomy that, as I discussed in chapter 2, makes
it so difficult to conceptualize race/gendering. Instead of trying to
establish the degree or means by which structures determine subjects
(or subjects make structures), Foucault's method is more dynamic
and context specific. He constructs genealogies of the practices that
constitute subjectivities in particular times and places. Adopting his

orientation entails tracking the heterogeneous, context-specific practices in and through which distinctive modes of subjectivity and other social processes emerge, mutate, and act. Unlike a traditional approach, Foucault does not represent social reality as constituted through two levels—a macro level of social structures and a micro level of individual subjects. In this approach, structures are more or less rigid matter that constrains in varying degrees the behavior of actors, the individuals within a system. This view is similar to Freud's initial "topographical" model of the mind, in which layers that differ in their nature lie atop each other and must somehow be coordinated and their relations explained. Instead, Foucault's genealogical method reminds me of wave/particle theories in contemporary physics. His focus is not on what or where—what determines what, where does ultimate causation lie—but rather on how, as well as on dynamic transformations. Matter is simultaneously energy, forces, and grids of power. He shows how practices can congeal into and function like material, structural forms, for example into regulations or law or an apparently fixed subjective identity (e.g., white/female). Yet from another perspective, these apparently solid social facts (e.g., identity, norm, or law) dissolve into a contingent grid of power relations and other dynamic processes.

Among other reasons, this approach is helpful because it enables us to ask not who a subject is but how it is. The how question is particularly important in analyzing dynamic processes such as the political unconscious, which are simultaneously constituted by structure like institutions of law and the distribution of social resources and intangible phenomena such as fantasy and emotions that subjects experience as deeply personal and idiosyncratic. However, Foucault's approach is so outside a paradigm prevalent in Western philosophy and psychology that it is difficult to fully appreciate and make use of its radical departures and rich possibilities.[17] In my own struggles to understand it, I find myself constantly misunderstanding his ideas. It is tempting to fit them into more familiar theorizing and hence miss their import. Therefore, hoping to do justice to Foucault's innovations and to invite readers into his unusual universe, I will take readers through what some may find an unnecessarily long journey through his arguments.

Foundational assumptions of a paradigm prevalent in Western philosophy and psychology include that intrinsic to humans is a self that is the locus and cause of our identity. Further, it is assumed that each self possesses and is constituted by an essence or substance that is best understood in terms of interiority—that is, something that occupies us and *is* us deep inside. To the extent that we actualize this essence and it governs our actions, we are free. As I discussed in the last chapter, this approach offers the hope that once we strip away all contingent influences, we can exercise a facility (such as reason) that will enable us to escape or control for all those accidents that render our judgments and basic social arrangements unfair or suspect.

On the contrary, Foucault investigates what gave rise to the belief that we are what is deep within us and that we are obligated to speak this truth, for only by knowing it can we fully be ourselves. He agrees that modern subjects must produce the deep truth of themselves. Our social context compels each subject to both master and know itself through speaking its truth. To speak truth, it must practice particular truth games. A truth game is constituted through certain sets of rules that enable the production of truth. On the basis of its principles and rules of the game's procedures, the validity of a truth claim is adjudicated. What is produced as truth will vary according to the game being played. Each game creates expectations about what will be produced when it is played properly. However, Foucault asks, "Why truth? Why are we concerned with truth, and more so than with the care of the self? And why must the care of the self occur only through the concern for truth?"[18] Instead of assuming a deep truth exists, Foucault begins with the assumption that the subject "is not a substance. It is a form, and this form is not primarily or always identical to itself."[19] Unpacking this statement is neither simple nor easy. In making this claim, Foucault does not offer an alternative account of the self. Rather, as he rejects the idea that it is a substance amenable to more or less adequate accounts, he abandons the entire framework in which the issue is intelligible. He shifts discourse from investigations into the self's true nature to subjectivity. In doing so, he moves outside two positions dominant within existing discourses concerning the self. He is neither an essentialist nor a social constructionist. While his emphasis on socially situated practices might overlap with social constructionist ideas, Foucault pursues a radically different trajectory. He does not assume a coherent, stable inside is eventually constructed from social relations. Inside/outside is not a relevant binary in his discourse. Rather, for him, no one thing is being constructed; subjectivity is a dynamic process, more a complex network of often conflicting forces, demands, and resistance with multiple lines and forms of explanation. For him, no privileged sites of subjective formation can be assumed, and the subject is neither a dependent effect of determinant causes or social relations nor an undetermined autonomous actor. Therefore, as I argued about race/gender in chapter 2, his approach requires us to think about subjectivity as a verb, as what we do, not who we are.

To grasp Foucault's approach, we must follow him in refusing the binaries of thought/action and structure (objective)/experience (subjective). For him, practices are forms of activity inhabited by thought. Thought is broadly conceived as "every manner of speaking, doing, or behaving in which the individual appears as a knowing subject, as ethical or juridical subject, as subject conscious of himself and others...thought is understood as...action insofar as it implies the play of true and false, the acceptance or refusal of rules, the relation to oneself and others."[20] While bounded and historically specific, these practices are not invariant or deterministic structures. As subjects practice the practices that constitute them, both subjects and practices mutate. Autonomy, paradoxically from the substantive point of view, is an effect of particular practices or technologies of the self. Contrary to frequent claims, Foucault does not deny agency, but rather relocates its conditions of possibility. He refers to subjects, not persons, of processes of subjectification, not identity. Subject connotes the double sense of actor and acted upon, not as separate aspects of our being, but as mutually constituting and contemporaneous processes. These processes simultaneously enable and constrain, empower and subjectify. It is easy to misunderstand what Foucault means by subjectification. Modernist narratives of the autonomous self create a binary: subject/object. If we are not self-generating subjects, then we are mere objects, utterly determined by our circumstances. In constructing a different discourse, Foucault rejects this binary and instead tracks its genealogy. In tracking this genealogy, the practices required to generate such a subject become evident. As Foucault puts it:

> I have tried to get out from the philosophy of the subject, through a genealogy of the modern subject as a historical and cultural reality. One can proceed with this general project in two ways. In dealing with modern theoretical constructions, we are concerned with the subject in general. In this way, I have tried to analyze the theories of the subject as a speaking, living, working being in the seventeenth and eighteenth centuries. One can also deal with the more practical understanding found in those institutions where certain subjects became objects of knowledge and of domination, asylums, prisons, and so on.[21]

In pursuing this project, Foucault "wished to study those forms of understanding which the subject creates about himself."[22] He originally focused on three techniques or kinds of social practices:

production, signification or communication, and domination. Technologies of production "permit us to produce, transform, or manipulate things."[23] Technologies of sign systems "permit us to use signs, meaning, symbols, or signification," and technologies of power "determine the conduct of individuals and submit them to certain ends of domination."[24] Multiple technologies of power, each with their own distinctive practices and knowledges, exist. These techniques are procedures "suggested or prescribed to individuals in order to determine their identity, maintain it, or transform it in terms of a certain number of ends, through relations of self-mastery or self-knowledge."[25] Such techniques are historically specific and variable. Both practices of self-mastery and self-knowledge change. Technologies of self include those of government or governmentality. Through techniques of governmentality, relations of domination are often established and maintained. Yet, these techniques of self can also generate resistant practices. Governmentality for Foucault is a variegated set of policing-type practices exercised through both formal technical-rational networks and non-state surveillance activities. Technologies of government incorporate "rational forms, technical procedures, instrumentations through which to operate, and . . . strategic games that subject the power relations they are supposed to guarantee to instability and reversal."[26]

Biopower is an instance of governmentality. Foucault claims that like all practices, biopower emerges through contingent but historical processes. It is a new kind of governmentality that evolves over the eighteenth and nineteenth centuries in Europe. Biopower generates and is constituted by the production of new sorts of truth and by particular regulatory, disciplinary, and confessional practices. The concrete and precise character of its knowledge of and interest in human bodies are unusual. It is based in and effects a "real and effective 'incorporation' of power. It circulates through and roots itself in the concrete lives of individuals and populations through multiple and variegated means."[27] In United States, for example, race/gender is a prime locus of biopower. The modern fabrication of race/gender entails an "incorporation" of power made possible by newly emerging discourses. The nineteenth and twentieth "sciences of man"—psychology, anthropology, genetics, sociology, for example—generated and practiced innovative ways of sorting bodies into and assigning discrete characteristics to newly "scientific" race/gender positions.[28] The effect of biopower is such that, by the 1920s, "to become 'Caucasian' . . . was not simply to be 'white' . . . it was to become *conclusively, certifiably, scientifically* white. 'Caucasian' identity represents a whiteness discovered and apprehended by that regime of knowledge whose cultural authority is greatest."[29] Transmuting race/gender into a "natural fact" enabled further exercises of power, as these bodies of "objective knowledge" were then deployed to legitimate a wide variety of social policies and regulations regarding (among others) immigration, welfare, education, health care, employment, and public health.[30] New professions such as social worker, therapist, policy analyst, and so on arose to devise and implement these policies and regulations. Training within the new disciplinary fields legitimated the expert's exercise of power.

The purpose of disciplinary power is to ensure a cohesive public body. The heterogeneous elements of a population can be made more coherent through practices of "normalization." These practices are supported and exercised both by the state and by new bodies of knowledge, especially medicine and the human sciences. Under the humanistic rubric of the state's interest in and obligations to the creation and protection of the "well-being" of its inhabitants, global surveillance of its members is increasingly instituted. The state needs experts to amass the knowledge it requires and to execute the policies said to effect and maximize this well-being and protection. Instances of such knowledge and associated practices include medicine, education, public health, prisons and schools. Concepts of deviancy, illness, maladjustment, and so forth are products of the same discourses that create the normal. These concepts also name the dangers the normal must be protected against. They justify the need for new and better knowledge to control the problems and for the exercise of power. The knowledge is simultaneously individual and global. It entails the study of specific "traits" possessed by individuals that cause their deviations and the search for methods that can be applied to all such individuals to effect the desired disciplinary results in the populations as a whole. "Prevention" of disease or crime requires at least the potential extension of these knowledges and practices to everyone. The state's interest is in ensuring regularity of behavior, not only in punishing crimes after the fact. The more peaceful (e.g., controlled) the population, the more the state's power is legitimated and ensured. As the state becomes more powerful, it can dispense disciplinary legitimacy. It supports, regulates, and enforces the monopoly of certain professions over specific domains and practices. Failure of disciplinary practices becomes the basis for "experts" to ask for more resources and power to pursue and exercise their knowledge in the name of the public good. In the next chapter, by analyzing some contemporary American political practices, especially our drug and prison policies,

I will illustrate how useful Foucault's concept of governmentality can be. Foucault's approach enables us to see how these are related not only to their professed frames (public health and safety), but to race/gender domination and melancholia as well.

In addition to processes of normalization and discipline, confessional practices also contribute to fabricating the modern subject. Confessional practices emerge within certain discourses such as psychology. These forms of knowledge posit the existence of a particular form of being, the "individual." These discourses teach us any individual "self" is knowable. The individual has certain "natural," "universal," or "true" traits. As we engage in these disciplinary practices, we come to experience this self as true and foundational. However, such experience is not "true" in some ontological or essentialist sense. It is an effect of a subjectivity constituted in and through certain practices. In other practices, such notions and experiences might not exist. For Foucault, sexuality is one of the most important traits confessional practices fabricate. They teach us that if we observe properly, we will see our "deep insides" include something bodily but at least partially knowable by consciousness, a source of both pleasure and danger. These discourses name this dangerous force "sexuality." By transforming pleasure into "sexuality," these confessional discourse/practices generate further practices/knowledge of self-control and self-knowledge. Sexuality is controllable only by the person exercising surveillance upon her or himself.[31] This surveillance is said to lead to both "self-knowledge" and freedom from the effects of these forces. However, to attain such self-knowledge and self-control, the individual must consult an expert whose knowledge provides privileged access to this dangerous aspect of the person's "self." The force and expertise these discourses constitute now legitimates the expert's (and discourse's) exercise of disciplinary power. The subject's investment in the new modes of subjectivity so produced (e.g., the "hetero- or homosexual") fuel the reproduction of their correlative knowledge/power vectors.

CARE OF THE SELF: POWER AND PRACTICING FREEDOM

The practices of surveillance, confession, normalization, and biopower that distinguish technologies of governmentality threaten to crowd out other possible technologies of the self. Foucault wishes to resist this potential monopolization through juxtaposing resistant practices of subjectivity; he groups these as "care of the self."

Since race/gender is in part produced through governmentality, Foucault's elaboration of alternatives to it is important to explore. In pursuing his project, Foucault discovered a fourth type of technique: "Techniques that permit individuals to effect, by their own means, a certain number of operations on their own bodies, their own souls, their own thoughts, their own conduct, and this in a manner so as to transform themselves, modify themselves, and to attain a certain state of perfection, happiness, purity, supernatural power."[32] He calls these "technologies of the self." Foucault insists that while technologies of the self interact with those of domination, they are not themselves technologies of domination. On the contrary, technologies of the self can be practices of freedom, creativity, aesthetics, and ethics. Such freedom is not absolute or unaffected by its social context. Any self technology does imply "a set of truth obligations: discovering the truth, being enlightened by truth, telling the truth. All these are considered important either for the constitution of, or the transformation of, the self."[33] Furthermore, the available technologies of the self are "not something invented by the individual himself. They are models that he finds in his culture and are proposed, suggested, imposed upon him by his culture, his society, and his social group."[34]

Relations of power are intrinsic to technologies of self, as they are to other forms of subjective constitution. However, Foucault does not equate practices of power with those of domination.[35] Unlike some liberal theorists, Foucault does not define power only in terms of constraint or imposition, neither does he solely identify it as the opposite of freedom or autonomy. For him, unlike many social scientists, power is not best understood as A's ability to get B to do what B otherwise would not have done. On the contrary, for Foucault, power relations require freedom. In his view, power is relational. These relations exist only among practicing subjects. Power relations are "possible only insofar as the subjects are free."[36] It is because there is freedom that relations of power exist. Within a relation of power, subjects may not be equally situated, but each must have some degree of freedom. In power relations, subjects try to control or alter others' behaviors, and they resist others' efforts to control them. Such attempts would be unnecessary or impossible if others in one's social field were mere objects. In engaging in a practice, however, subjects encounter others who are likewise engaged. Since no practice is uniform, differences produce friction and resistance; subjects tend to insist on their own practices. Furthermore, since these relations exist in different forms and at different levels, any subject's situation will vary depending on the relations in which it is located. I might be quite advantaged in one relation and disadvantaged in another. Thus, resistance is intrinsic to power relations[37]; power relations are "strategic games that subject the power relations they are supposed to guarantee to instability and reversal."[38] Power relations are also mobile and mutating, so positions within them (and the positions available) can shift. In contrast, a state of domination exists when an "individual or social group succeeds in blocking a field of power relations, immobilizing them and preventing any reversibility of movement by economic, political, or military means."[39] In practices of domination, the strategic options available within a power relation never succeed in reversing the relations among its practitioners. The power relations are fixed and extremely asymmetrical. It is a game whose rules ensure that only one party can win.[40]

To articulate practices of care of the self, Foucault investigates texts by classical Greek and Roman writers.[41] In my view, what matters about this investigation is not whether it uncovers the truth or deep meaning of the texts. Foucault does not claim to excavate a pristine point where philosophy went astray or forgot something or to rediscover a principle that should have been our foundation all along. Contact with a philosopher does not revive the old, but can produce something new.[42] Rather, what is important is how Foucault imagines other practices of subjectivity via his encounter with the texts.[43] Foucault argues that in classical Greece and Rome, care of the self was conceived as a task that one must engage in throughout life. It is an activity, not only a form of contemplation. The subjectivity practiced was not defined "entirely in terms of knowledge," and philosophy was not defined "in terms of the development of the knowing subject, or of what qualifies the subject as such."[44] Furthermore, the purpose of these practices was not to renounce the self or to prepare for the soul's salvation in an afterlife. Instead, in practicing them, the subject constitutes itself as an ethical being whose relation to itself and others enables it to engage in a proper mode of life. Care of the self is not a preparation for living; it is a form of living.[45] It is a kind of work with its own methods and objectives. In the modern world there has been "an inversion in the two principles of antiquity, 'Take care of yourself' and 'Know yourself.' In Greco-Roman culture, knowledge of oneself appeared as the consequence of the care of the self. In the modern world, knowledge of oneself constitutes the fundamental principle."[46] Care of the self "was considered both a duty and a technique, a basic obligation and a set of carefully worked out procedures."[47] It is also a creative and aesthetic practice in which innovation and consideration of beauty and pleasure are central. The point of this technology was to attempt to "develop and transform oneself, and to attain a certain mode of being."[48]

Furthermore, in the classical world, knowing oneself did not necessarily mean discovering the deep truth lying within. In some practices, truth and the subject are not linked through "uncovering a truth in the subject or…making the soul the place where truth resides, through an essential kinship or an original law, the truth; nor is it a matter of making the soul the object of a true discourse."[49] Rather, knowing oneself required internalizing texts concerning how to care for oneself so that the substance of these teaching is literally incorporated and assimilated as one's own practice. Philosophy provides "soul service"; it is a therapeutic practice, dedicated to the care of the soul. It is less concerned with the question of under what conditions can the subject produce reliable truth and more about how subjects should live. Certain kinds of knowledge are necessary for living well, but such knowledge has multiple sources, many of which do not depend for their production or truth upon a purified foundational subject.

Care for the self is not a narcissistic or solitary practice. Relations with others are intrinsic to this mode of being, for care of oneself is understood as necessary for the proper exercise of citizenship and interpersonal relations. One is obligated to care for the self partially out of our duty to others. Extensive work on the self is required if one's practice of freedom is to take place within a way of being that is beautiful, honorable, and worthy of praise.[50] If one does not practice the correct power over oneself, one cannot rule others well or be a good friend, relative, parent, or spouse. A tyrant is one who is a slave to his desires and forces others to satisfy them. Furthermore, it is understood that carrying out this task requires an assortment of activities and resources, including relations with other persons, especially friends and teachers.[51] Indeed, Foucault argues that in ancient Greece and Rome, practicing care of the self enabled a rich variety of relations (and hence subjective practices), particularly ones between adult males, for which there is no modern equivalent.

PRACTICING CONSTRAINT

Foucault's emphasis on habits and practices and the ones he recommends suggest some techniques for containing the malignant psychodynamics of democratic citizenship. Through his ideas about care of the self, he intends both to induce skepticism regarding dominant narratives of subjectivity and power and to suggest alternatives.

As we have seen, in the disciplines of the care of self, subjectivity is constituted through an ongoing set of practices oriented toward enabling us to act such that we meet our obligations to our ethical commitments and to others. The orienting point is the ethical commitment, and one must learn and acquire as habits what must be done to approximate it. Taking on ethical commitments is itself a practice that must be learned and sustained. Care of the self entails developing habits that sustain such practices, including an engaged detachment and skeptical attachment toward all of them. Acquisition of habits is never permanent; hence these processes are more like disciplines requiring constant practice than a solid and stable self-formation. Practice cannot occur outside its appropriate contexts, and it requires the aid of mentors, exemplars, discipline specific knowledge, and interaction. Furthermore, in taking on a practice, we recognize that as heterogeneous subjects, our practice will never attain perfection. This awareness does not negate the worth of our ethical commitments or our efforts, but it can help contain the hubris of the fantasy of impossible perfection. We are servants of the practice; it does not exist to perfect us.

Foucault's investigations point us to the question, how would we, as contemporary American citizens, begin to constitute ourselves as ethical beings whose relations to ourselves and others enables us to engage in proper modes of life? One move would be to develop a chastened constraint and humility in regard to claims about our own subject positions. We would have to abandon the belief that any subject position outside constituting power grids is available. Imagining oneself outside power is an appealing fantasy, because one can then plead innocence in relation to patterns of injustice, or in Allen's terms, sacrifice and rewards. Whatever inequalities exist have nothing to with me. Recognizing one's locations within power grids, on the contrary, is necessary both to resist the processes of idealization and denigration intrinsic to race/gender melancholia and to open up shared spaces constructed through practices of empathy, respect, and recognition. As I will argue below, empathy as a mode of relating differently located subjects is an essential element in reducing the distrust stemming from our long-term habits of unequally distributing sacrifice and reward. Since Foucault believes that all power grids simultaneously enable and constrain and are composed of heterogeneous forces, abandoning belief in an unfabricated subject does not imply that any individual is simply a predetermined mouthpiece for a uniform identity. Foucault does not argue that our subject positions doom us to think or act in an inescapable, uniform way. There is no such thing, for example, as The White Male, nor does such a position always homogeneously determine the actions of subjects located there. Rather, his approach suggests that we have to take up our position(s) as a question open to investigation. We have to maintain a curiosity about how our subject positions constitute our various practices and recognize that their effects (and their intertwined dependence on others) are not always transparent or accessible to us. So, for example, in the recent Senate hearings regarding Justice Sotomayor's nomination to the Supreme Court, Foucault's approach would require that the white/male senators who criticized her for recognizing her social locations would also have to acknowledge their own. Rather than condemning Sotomayor for her partiality, the senators could have tried to take up the practices of a "wise Latina" and enlarge their understanding of their own subjective enactments and thus acquire a broader range of possible moves. In recognizing their own locations in power grids, the senators could have used their privilege to reduce it, inviting others as equals into a public space of inquiry. In turn, this exercise of respect toward denigrated others could have built trust through undertaking a common project. Within this opening, subjected citizens could more safely explore how their own positions institute both wisdom and constraint. Instead, in locating themselves as the already realized ideal and Sotomayor as the underdeveloped other, the senators reenacted the dynamics of idealization and denigration that express and reinforce race/gender melancholia. They idealized themselves as unmarked by any race/gender positions and denigrated her as the polluting and marked outsider. Old habits again undermined new possibilities for practicing citizenship.

A practice approach to subjectivity both supports and necessitates acquiring these habits of skepticism, constraint, and humility. As Foucault recommends, a practice approach to subjectivity pursues not who the subject is, but "how is it?" "How is it" requires a genealogy that unpacks at least three kinds of practices—the practices constituting subjects, those that facilitate continuing to practice those practices, and those that sustain their appearance of being. The prior practices constituting subjects, those that presently constitute them, those facilitating practicing their practices, and those that sustain their appearance of being are not necessarily the same. Furthermore, all subjective practices interact in wider fields. How and with what they interact is constantly open to change. Changes in patterns of interaction may affect the subjective constellation in unpredictable ways. Since subjective time is not linear, old practices may recur. Although each technology of the self interacts with every other, each also generates its distinctive correlative subject—the working being, and so on. Thus, the subject's constitution and its relationship to itself change depending on what it is practicing. For example, how I constitute myself in practicing motherhood differs from how I would in teaching. These various forms of subjectivity are themselves historically constituted. Since, for example, mothering practices are historically and socially variable, the practicing of mothering has not always constituted the same forms of subjectivity and activity.

The historical contingency of subjective constitution has important political consequences; it means that practices of subjectivity are not fixed or immutable. They can be changed, and hence new relations and practices of subjectivity (within and between subjects) are invented and practiced. When we turn our attention to historical practices, the focus shifts to the generation, enactment, and reformation of subjectivities through networks of narrative, action, embodiment, fantasy, and power. From a perspective of how, it appears that modern Western narratives about the unmarked, neutral subject reverse the relations between rationality, autonomy, authority, freedom, and power. The supposedly neutral positioning substance theorists argue subjects require to attain and exercise political legitimacy is an effect of their engaging in a set of practices, including constructing stories about their subjective formation. Intrinsic to this narrative is the belief that certain subjects possess an unmarked identity and that the freedom, authority, and autonomy of this self generate its actions. History (at least the good parts) is its biography. (The generation of evil or sin belongs elsewhere).

Despite these claims, practices within asymmetric relations of power enable this mode of subjectivity. Such subjects can sustain a certain appearance of being because they practice, invent, and reenact certain subjectivities and relations of power, not because they exercise an innate capacity for agency grounded in an undetermined identity. Agency is an effect of certain practices, not a manifestation of the deep self's freedom. Among others, the *appearance* of stability, autonomy, and identity is generated and sustained by practices of domination, denial of contingency and will, and projection of determination onto marked subjects. This practice of identity entails control over the normative regulation of subjectivity and the exclusion of aspects that would disrupt its own subjective representation. Its practice of assigning determining substances such as race/gender to marked others allows the autonomous subject to be "free." As in the Sotomayor hearings, practices such as race/gendering are projected outward or denied. Unlike unmarked subjects, the others this generates are embodied, historically situated, and race/gendered.[52] Therefore, to subscribe to an idealized subjective representation enabled by these practices—the unmarked self—is problematic, especially for subjects who are also committed to practices of justice or equality. It is not a simple matter of "tainted" origins, for there is no necessary relation between the practices that generate a subjective constellation and those required to sustain it. Assuming such a representation is unethical, because its practice moves us further from treating others as equals deserving of respect and rewards those assuming it with unearned honor. Perhaps engaging in practices of domination is not necessary to sustain such a subjective representation, although I cannot imagine this. Within our current social arrangements, the unmarked subject can only sustain its self-representation by practicing splitting and displacement. It is unlikely that, if presently denigrated subjects attained full access to practices of freedom, they would then willingly remain the exclusive possessors of that which others despise and experience as constraint. Since we have to fabricate ourselves through practices, how else will we account for our power networks?

Instead of narratives of the unmarked or essential self, I prefer thinking about subjectivity through metaphors of travel and diaspora. As Bonnie Honig illuminates, diasporian histories point to the constituting effects on modern subjectivities of exile, relocation, displacement.[53] Paul Gilroy suggests rethinking modernity via the history of the Black Atlantic, a "webbed network, between the local and the global."[54] Rejecting binaries of Africa/Europe or white/black, Gilroy substitutes incessant travel, the middle passage, and practices of movement, mediation, and domination for roots and rootedness. The web is woven via ships and the slave trade between Africa, the Caribbean, Europe, and the Americas. The African diaspora into the Western hemisphere is thus an initiating force within Euro-American histories and subjective constellations, and the practice of slavery is one of the constituting elements in all diasporian subjectivities. Various mutually constituting practices generate the subjects of this history: master/slave, normal/deviant, male/female, adult/child, and so on. Each dyadic formation and their interactions shapes patterns of freedom, of race/ gender, of sexuality, of citizenship and law, and the resulting norms continue to initiate and pervade contemporary Western and postcolonial practices of subjectivity.[55] This frame invites a more respectful inquiry into the constitution of all American subjects. In positing that we are all implicated in, constituted through, and moving within specific webs and networks of power, it models practices of equality, recognition, and respect that are necessary elements of a less melancholic citizenship. Recognizing that an ahistoric original position is unavailable could encourage more honest investigations of how various networks and positions differentially empower and constrain their practitioners and where and how we might practice differently.

POLITICS AND ETHICS: FROM SUBJECT TO OBJECT CENTERED PRACTICES

Foucault's approach to subjectivity requires and facilitates a parallel shift in the fields of politics, citizenship, and justice.[56] This shift requires its own disciplines of restraint and care, especially in regard to practices of citizenship and our obligations to public spaces and our fellow citizens. It entails reconceiving the problems and practices of politics, citizenship, and justice through an object-oriented rather than a subject-oriented focus. Political practices would no longer be oriented toward acquiring the resources I need to be me or the protection I need so I can practice my subjectivity elsewhere. In other words, inquiry and activity would center not around questions of identity (who are we and what do we require to be or remain us) but action (what could be done and what are its consequences). Arguments for and justification of actions require consideration of their qualities and effects as processes and accounts of their (always imperfectly known and unpredictable) outcomes. Criteria for evaluation might include aesthetic or hedonistic ones or whether actions potentially enlarge or constrain the range of available practices and practitioners, but ontological or teleological claims about fostering development of an individual or collective deep inside would be irrelevant.

Since it renders claims based on who I am irrelevant, shifting the practices of democratic politics in this way might generate new capacities for an engaged detachment among our citizens. Instead of self-interest, our attention could turn to finding or constructing widely shared mutual objects. Such projects help build trust, for they signal and enact a concern for inclusion and respect for collaboration as equals. Among these projects, constructing and maintaining public spaces that can contain disagreement, conflict, and attention to (and frequent recalibration of) the distribution of reward and sacrifice must receive special care. Collaboration helps us develop moves outside the habits of unequal sacrifice and honor that have often structured American citizenship. However, given the power of citizens' political unconscious and emotions, an important feature of developing collaborative projects must be attention to how to manage the play of such material. Rubrics of "discursive democracy," in which discourse seems uninflected with passion or unconscious fantasy are inadequate for these purposes. In turn, developing trust within public spaces could facilitate the work of mourning as we collectively consider our current practices—what we are doing—and what we could do otherwise. As numerous previous failures show, it is pointless to call for a dialogue on race/gender unless work to develop trust occurs first. Otherwise discourse that is honest and can result in changed practices is unlikely to occur. Unless changed practices occur, calls to talk are mostly likely to result in increased distrust and cynicism, especially among those disadvantaged by current social arrangements.[57]

Object-centered approaches are quite different from those based on narratives of the unmarked subject. The political correlative of deep subjectivity is the juridical subject. Just as the subject is the foundation of knowledge in Cartesian epistemology, in modern liberal political theory the juridical subject founds and grounds the state. As I discussed in chapter 4, juridical subjects exist prior to the state; their modes of subjectivization are not effects of governmentality or historically contingent technologies. They temporarily surrender some of their innate powers; the congealing of these powers in institutions of the subject's creation originates the state. Freedom exists as long as the law conforms to their inner being. Conformity to such law is simply obedience to their own reason or will. This genre of political theorizing is thus an identity theory writ large. Modern liberal political theories reflect and depend upon assumptions about their founding subject to account for the state's existence and legitimacy. These assumptions also provide the standards for normatively evaluating the state's laws and policies.

This political discourse logically gives rise to correlative practices: interest group and contemporary identity politics. The logic of the discourse requires its practitioners to define themselves as split subjects; they possess both a universal (or in Rawls's term, "best self") and a particular will or desire. Their desire takes the form of unitary "interests."[58] There is a sovereign abstract "I" that can identify and put forth claims based on these bounded interests; for example, as a mother I am interested in childcare; as a patient, I am interested in health care. A group is an aggregate of sovereign individuals who share an interest. However, the subject cannot be merely an aggregate of its interests, because then it would lack the neutral substance necessary to articulate abstract, indifferent, and thus binding principles. Hence, as we saw in John Rawls's account, it must also possess an undetermined essence, and its capacity for autonomy (or reasonableness) and the ability to choose freely among its desires without being determined by them is rooted in and enabled by this substance. Thus, the capacity for autonomy requires a deep, undetermined subjectivity. As a desiring subject, it possesses its "interests," but in its universal or best being, the subject is not possessed by them. No desire or historically contingent practice constitutes the true subjectivity of the chooser. Furthermore, not only are the subject's desires conceived as extrinsic to its true self, but the existence of these "interests" is treated as unproblematic social facts. Neither the conflict and relations of domination that may produce a felt interest nor the fluid and contradictory aspects of subjects and their practices are acknowledged. Subjects are rational individuals who know what is in their interest; these subjects and their interests are not heterogeneous, mutually determined, uncertain in effect or internally contradictory.

Similarly, contemporary identity politics also adopts a logic of a unitary deep inside. This deep inside is not abstract or universal in the sense of constituting every subject. Instead, it is homogeneous and concretely universal. That is, it is a uniform essence constituting a specific class of subjects. This essence grounds a unique subjectivity and generates its difference from all other subjects. Identity politics requires its practitioners to constitute their being through a singular and particular but definitive quality (e.g., sexuality, gender, or race). There is a universal and discoverable truth of this being. Individual subjects speak its truth, and this truth warrants the legitimacy of their claims. The truth also serves as the basis for normative evaluation and ethical practices. So, for example, one can be held accountable for not being "black enough," that is, deviating from the prescriptive practices constituting black subjectivity. In discovering this truth and conforming to it, subjects liberate themselves and institute the possibility of freedom.

In my view, subject-centered politics—whether of abstract or concrete identities—are deeply flawed, and, as can be all too readily seen in the contemporary world, extremely dangerous. Resisting domination or inventing more just political practices cannot remain contingent on identity—that is, on the subject finding its "Truth" and seeking to bring itself and the world into conformity with it. This applies equally to the liberal abstract "individual" in its Rawlsian or other versions and to subjects in subordinate or dominant positions who engage in group identity politics. The virtue of the subject also cannot depend on its Truth, and its virtue cannot be the basis for stipulating equality of treatment or respect. Subject-centered politics remain within the problematic genre of (auto-)biography; they rest on nostalgia for a singular "subject of history." They articulate a yearning for a purposive history in which time is the unfolding of this subject's biography. A desire for a guaranteed happy ending motivates them; however variably it may be specified, whether it is to bring freedom into the world, unfold its innate capacities, serve God's will, die a martyr, and so on, the subject's redemptive fate is preordained. However, I remain unconvinced such a subject or fate exists. Although advocates of various possibilities abound, no decisive argument has persuasively identified a single, unitary Truth of our being—reason, victimization, human capacities, religion, and so on—that can unproblematically ground claims to justice or engender ethical practices. I have not been dissuaded from reading these eschatological stories as expressing the fantasies and dreams of situated, complex subjectivities. They express understandable but unrealizable longings to be elsewhere and to possess more than our imperfect practices can promise.

As appealing as they may be, such longings too readily initiate practices of irresponsibility, violence, creation and annihilation of a denigrated "other," and terrorism. They launch us into investigations of the worth and character of the subject as measured by a preordained (and subject position-specific) standard and into a search for the commonalities of a subject position that is simultaneously a disciplining of its objects into conformity. Its subjects must be uniform, unworldly, and pure. As the bearer of the redemptive possibilities for humankind, they cannot simultaneously be generators of and invested in relations of domination or even strategic participants in power games. The resistant leakage of inter- and intrasubjective heterogeneity and imperfection provokes predictable responses— nihilism, terrorism, and totalitarianism. The nihilist develops a protective cynicism and detachment. In contrast to purity all is corrupt, and thus we are responsible for nothing. The terrorist or totalitarian refuses to accept the impossibility of purity and assigns the sources of imperfection to others. For the greater good, vast force is justified to eradicate the polluting ones. Death, even random murder, is justified in the name of the good or the holy.

Developing object-centered political strategies offers new political possibilities. Complex attachments to particular objects and practices replace subject-centered theories and practices. Diversity does not preclude a mutual attachment to particular objects. For example, in the next chapter I will discuss how adopting a frame of a mutual attachment to justice among very differently situated subjects could shift practices of affirmative action. Objects include modes of pleasure, ways of life, discrete political acts, new power relations, public spaces of all sorts, particular kinds of social relationships, and ethical commitments as well as material resources. Instead of depending on a unitary or redemptive subject as the agent of change, we can develop practices of politics based on a mutual desire for particular objects or outcomes—for example, reducing or resisting domination in a specific social field. Attachment by highly diverse constellations of subjectivities to a particular object provides a powerful motivation for political activity. Subjects' bases of attachment to a common object need not be uniform. However, an attachment to a particular object renders coalitions both possible and necessary. These attachments will unfold and gather force in ways we cannot predict, generating, perhaps, new desires and relations of solidarity and opposition.[59]

Attachment to an object and the attempt to persuade others to pursue it requires different practices than interest-based politics. In object-centered politics, the subject must take responsibility for the object and its attachment to it as aspects and practices of its own subjectivity. Since subjectivity is not a stable substance, attaining the object cannot simply satisfy an already formed individual but may instead radically transform its subjectivity. In object-centered politics, the subject cannot claim a sovereign I or to act on behalf of an authority outside its own desire. Therefore, it cannot position itself as the servant of a pure good or the will of another, or as the representative of abstract reason or a sacred text, or as freedom's agent, or as any other force extrinsic to its own subjectivity. It has no trump available and must seek to persuade others on some other basis. Effective persuasion requires knowledge about one's audience and stimulates a desire to understand others' complex subjectivities. Since the most effective appeals often make use of a wide variety of practices including fantasy, emotion, or desires for beauty or pleasure, practicing persuasion also encourages development of and knowledge about a wide variety of subjective modes. In turn, employment of such modes deepens the appeal of public spaces and expands others' attraction to them. Furthermore, object-centered politics requires practices of humility, because practitioners of object-centered politics cannot claim a privileged or unproblematic relationship to their attachment. Engaged in practices of care of the self, subjects realize they need others to foster disciplined inquiry into the constitution of a felt need or desire. Perhaps our attachment to an object expresses enmeshment in a destructive way of life or its pursuit would inadvertently undermine other, more important attachments. Thus, attachments to objects and their pursuit become invitations to conversation, imagination, and even play, not fixed ends or a zero-sum game. Unlike the liberal interest seeking individual, practitioners of object-centered politics do not treat the public sphere as a space we briefly enter to obtain our good and then exit so we can enjoy it privately. Instead of retreating to walled-off private worlds, such politics encourages multiplying public spaces and tending carefully to them. However, unlike totalitarian regimes, object-centered politics does not seek to institute a monopoly by any one space or practice. As heterogeneous subjects we must recognize the multiplicity of modes of subjectivity; practicing object-related politics is only one among many possibilities, and it cannot be privileged as the most excellent.[60]

In recognizing the heterogeneity of our own and others' subjectivity, engaging in the practices of care of the self induces the detachment Rawls seeks from having us operate behind the veil of ignorance. However, unlike Rawls's procedure, it does so through a full recognition of the impossibility of any subject removing itself from the embodied, context specific practices that constitute it. Instead, recognizing one's context dependence stimulates a detachment and skepticism toward one's own attachments because the subject recognizes none can exist in isolation from the others, nor from the multiple fields in and through which our subjectivity is constituted. As a practice of a heterogeneous subject, any attachment will bear the traces of its multiple desires and positioning. So for example, I may have to query myself about how my race/gender positioning may be playing out in an attachment to a particular view of equality. Detachment arises from looking at one attachment from another's perspective and from engaging in disciplined discourse and other practices with a multiplicity of subjects, especially those less enamored of our particular desires.

Contrary to the claims of those attached to neutral, universal principles, acknowledging that there is no place outside power relations and historical practices need not lead to nihilism or indifferent amorality. Since there is no guaranteed good, redemptive end or neutral outside available, we have to make the best of, resist, or reinvent the historical practices constituting us.[61] Acknowledging our social constitution entails recognizing that subjects cannot escape the unending project of mutually constituting ourselves. As long as it is inescapable, we might as well maximize its possibilities. While such politics is not utopian, it is concerned with generating new practices within the worlds constituting subjects in present time. Its goal is not to reform the given, but to unmask its contingency, thereby opening up spaces to imagine new power games or to play existing ones differently. Freedom exists not in a return to or reconciliation with our pure, undetermined essence, but in the capacity to participate in power relations and their accessibility to us. In its focus on action and responsibility, this approach overlaps with Hannah Arendt's emphasis on action, but it rejects her contempt for "the social."[62] Since our desires and heterogeneous practices are us, we cannot escape them. Deploying our multiplicity is a requirement for, not an impediment to, acting justly and freely. We cannot articulate any useful principles or practices of justice or freedom without or outside the practices heterogeneous networks generate. Only intense engagement, not a Rawlsian veil of ignorance or a disembodied Arendtian *arete*, can engender reflection upon or resistance to their effects.

How do we foster such politics? Technologies of the self, particularly in the form of care for the self, are an important element. The care of the self can engender an attachment to practicing subjectivity such that ways of life are multiplied and endlessly reinvented. Innovation and creativity requires much more than tolerance or a commitment to diversity or inclusivity; for such practices can actually serve to simply validate the ways of life in which the subject is already engaged. For example, following Habermas, we could advocate protecting the efficacy of rational discourse and the autonomy of public space and ensuring a broader range of participants within them.[63] However, this approach leaves undisturbed important assumptions, including privileging reason and speech, rather than a multiplicity of practices including aesthetic and affective ones, as the means of arriving at public goods. Adherence to mere tolerance can permit subjects a passive attitude toward other ways of life; we can treat them as irrelevantly exotic though valid for others. Instead, no longer able to assume even a purely subjective truth lies accessible within, care of the self requires perpetual tutoring by and engagement with others. We recognize that others might attain a kind of knowledge of us, engage in a generative self-technology or be attached to a good to which we, immersed in our own practices are blind. Thus, we must actively seek them out and invite, imaginatively take up and take pleasure in attending alternatives, and repeatedly consider our how our own modes appear from foreign viewpoints.[64] Such experimental practices are self-reinforcing, for the more possibilities we actively engage, the more we unsettle the illusion of identity and recognize the consequences of routinely privileging a particular range of commitments.

Thus, contrary to many critics of Foucauldian approaches, their necessary ethical correlative is not an anything-goes relativism or self-indulgent narcissism.[65] While within such practices subjects lack recourse to any neutral trump to resolve conflict or a transcendental justification for our actions or chosen ways of life, it does not follow that we are no longer committed to them or obligated to their ethical stipulations. Subjects remain responsible for their commitments' consequences, intended or not, and to the spaces, networks, and relationships that are their conditions of possibility. Innocence is ruled out. Firmly located in our contexts, subjects recognize opting out of all contexts is impossible. Since it is unavoidable, whether we act, desire, and will is not a choice, but there may be a range of possibilities for how we do so. Part of what each subject realizes in interacting with others is how we are differently affected by determining social relations. One form in which power is exercised is the attribution of subjective practices. Depending on their positioning, some subjects can project onto others the denigrated practices of their own subjectivity; others suffer the violence of being targets of such projections. We discover that most subjects occupy several places at once—we resist, impose, enjoy, and suffer from different kinds of power. While such unevenness is unlikely to disappear, a commitment to multiplying ways of life can also engender investment in playing games of power that minimize domination. Uniformity, grandiosity, and denigration become suspect; they could be symptoms of domination, of a frozen power game that one is obligated to resist whatever one's position might be within it.

Fostering a suspicion of homogeneity or idealization and denigration and an appreciation of conflict does require certain kinds of subjective knowledge, disciplinary practices, and capacity for engaged detachment. However, rational thought is not a sufficient or unproblematic way to attain such knowledge and detachment. We can use our reason to rationalize, to obscure passions motivating a seemingly rational choice. The capacity for detachment rests on the subject's recognition of its own historical contingency, not a presumption of being nowhere or behind a veil of ignorance. Paradoxically, the more we acknowledge the contingency of our desires, the less we are determined by any one of them. Immersion, not abstraction, allows us to be more objective. Juxtaposing one desire against another, subjects realize their heterogeneity and multiple determinants. In acknowledging contingency, we also recognize that our desires and practices could be otherwise. If they could be otherwise, other practices are equally possible. Recognizing our will, we must take responsibility for such choices while acknowledging that other moves are plausible. While not vitiating our loyalty, our commitments will appear as choices whose continuance depends on our willingness to keep choosing them and their consequences and on our location within networks that generate their possibility and render them intelligible.

This engaged detachment is necessary for ethical behavior, including reworking our frozen melancholic state with its compulsive repetition of splitting, denial, denigration, and fantasies of perfection. Foucault defines ethics as the "considered form that freedom takes when it is informed by reflection."[66] Reflection, however, is a practice, not an innate capacity. Like any practice, it requires the appropriate technologies and power relations. Also like any practice, it must be endlessly renewed and taken up. The capacity for reflection depends upon the continual confrontation among subjects. Instead of a search for consensus, such interaction intentionally seeks disjunctions. Agreement will not necessary result from such interaction, nor is it the governing purpose. When genuine understanding is reached, unresolvable conflict will result as frequently as empathy, reflective equilibrium, or an ideal speech community.[67] Reflection and communication cannot dissolve the diversity of subjective practices and meaning systems. Hence power games are intrinsic to freedom. Object-centered politics cannot promise transparent communication or Habermas' universal pragmatics. However, subjects attempting to practice them continually struggle with how "to acquire the rules of law, the management techniques, and also the morality, the ethos, the practice of the self, that will allow us to play these games of power with as little domination as possible."[68]

Practitioners of richer technologies of the self cannot serve as ground for or guarantee emancipatory action or the end of history, or the final actualization of reason, freedom, or the good. Such subjectivities are not simply replacements for unitary ones and their teleological narratives. The worlds in which subjectivity is practiced are not narcissistic reflections of our practices, nor can they unilaterally or predictably determine them. Subjectivity is simply one aspect of the context in which we must act—the environmental surround enables, limits, and shapes us as much as we transform it. Past practices leave land mines, and we never know when our actions will set them off. The sheer contingency pervading human worlds ensures conditions of uncertainty and gaps between intentions and outcomes will persist. Disciplined practice of care of the self cannot promise an idealized perfection. Reflexivity cannot perfectly control other practices of subjectivity such as fantasy and is itself pervaded by them. Subjects may act on hate as readily as on empathy. Even concern for the other is not pure; it is animated in part by narcissistic fantasies, including those of one's own reparative powers and will to power, that inevitably encroach on that we wish to respect and preserve.[69] Recognition of how much we cannot control should intensify our attachment to what is in our range—better practices of justice and more fit modes of ruling. Hope for these rests in what democratic citizens might learn to desire or resist desiring, the openness of power games and the practices sustaining them, and our mutual care for multiple public spaces. Contrary to Rousseau, what freedom we might enjoy does not depend on willing the general, but on taking responsibility for very particular context-specific locations, including relations of domination/acquiescence, and ensuring the presence of other empowered subjects. We have to accept that practices of freedom and democratic citizenship require and reflect the willing by unstable subjects in concert with others, equally tenuously situated, of imperfect and uncertain alternatives and that empowerment is not simply the opposite of constraint. This acceptance requires the availability of practices, public spaces, and subjective technologies Foucault anticipates but we must endlessly reinvent.

However, if we as democratic citizens take up his challenge to play games of power with as little domination as possible, one of our shared objects must be undoing race/gender melancholia. As I have argued, this melancholia blocks us from recognizing and remedying practices that sustain race/gender domination. Unfreezing melancholia's paralysis requires accepting our embeddedness within the webs of the "Black Atlantic" and forsaking claims to and fantasies of colorless/genderless positioning. Mourning is about redoing our relationships with the past and with our lost objects. It requires an honest accounting of our losses and finding ways to live with them. A making good—to the extent we can—of past and present harms and their costs to the objects and ourselves is an intrinsic part of this process. Abandoning narratives of innocence and exceptionalism, American citizens can begin to look anew at our practices and see what we might do differently. As heterogeneous and imperfect subjects, we cannot expect to generate perfect policies or to restore the body polity to some imagined purity. Since race/gender domination is an effect of and is sustained by many networks of power and practices, its reduction will require equally various interventions. None will be perfect or total; some will have unintended or unfortunate consequences. Since race/gender domination is the living legacy of over four hundred years of heterogeneous practices, no quick or simple fix is likely. Some interventions may simply reduce the amount of harm or sacrifice current practices unfairly distribute to the disadvantaged, but this itself would not be an inconsequential achievement. Some, however, can extend the number of moves and subjects to whom the widest variety of games is accessible, thereby enlarging spheres of freedom. In the next chapter, I turn to some promising lines of action.

CHAPTER 6

In-Conclusion:
Remedies and Constraints

For such a guidance, we have no indubitable and universally agreed codes and rules. Choices are indeed choices, and that means that each is to some sense arbitrary and that uncertainty as to its propriety is likely to linger long after the choices are made. We understand now that uncertainty is not a temporary nuisance, which can be chased away through learning the rules, or surrendering to expert advice, or just doing what others do—but a permanent condition of life; we may say more—it is the very soil in which the moral self takes root and grows. Moral life is a life of continuous uncertainty. To be a moral person takes a lot of strength and resilience to withstand the pressures and the temptations to withdraw from joint responsibilities.[1]

Throughout this book, I have reiterated several claims: that race/gender domination persists, that one of the reasons for its persistence is that American citizens remain in a state of race/gender melancholia stemming from the lack of proper acknowledgment and mourning of the losses slavery and its consequences inflict, and that dominant practices of citizenship are inadequate to diagnosis or address our melancholia. Through examining a wide range of phenomena including empirical data regarding the distribution of social goods such as occupations, wealth, income, property, and power; interpretations of films illuminating the interplay of fantasy and social relations in the fabrication of race/gender; and analysis of theories and practices of citizenship, I have provided the reader with reasons to take such claims seriously. To better diagnose and treat race/gender melancholia, I have suggested adopting the practices that Foucault calls "care of the self." These practices entail transforming both our understanding of and our ways of doing subjectivity, ethics, power, and politics. I can imagine an understandably impatient reader protesting that these suggestions are so abstract and broad as to be utterly useless in daily life. Later in this chapter, I will offer a few more concrete examples of how such practices might be enacted. In my internal dialogue, I also hear other readers protest that a few movies, however fancy the interpretation, and an analysis of the rather abstruse writings of a Harvard professor and a French philosopher hardly constitute compelling evidence for such serious claims. To the second set of objectors, I can offer no indisputable rebuttal. I do not think one is possible, because as I argue in chapter 5, truth claims are context dependent, both for their sense and for the means of adjudicating them. All I can do is invite readers into my narrative and hope it is compelling enough to at least trouble their own.

However, in my support, I would also encourage the reader to carefully watch Spike Lee's recent 2006 documentary, *When the Levees Broke: A Requiem in Four Acts*, about Hurricane Katrina and its aftermath.[2] In it, themes of slavery and the costs of denigration spontaneously and frequently arise as the people he interviews recount their experiences and analyze why the flooding occurred and the governmental response (or appalling lack thereof) to it. People draw parallels between how post-flood family members were randomly placed across the country and the breakup of families during slavery. Others insist that because New Orleans is a poor, mostly black city, the Federal Government felt no urgency about coming to its aid. Even well-off white residents recognize that their location within a denigrated social location (poor/black city) worked to their disadvantage, as they confront governmental behavior that conveys persistent indifference and contempt. They often conclude that, evidently, their city and its residents are simply expendable.

Although Lee mostly comments on it indirectly by showing how devastated the city remains a year later, what is also disheartening is the apparent absence of any incorporation of the meanings of these events or urgency about their remedy into the mainstream of American politics. At the time of the hurricane, there was some talk of "how could this happen" in America—as if the poverty, neglect, and absence of public services that existed long before the hurricane were a shocking revelation or unusual. That the U.S. government might build inadequate levees, take its time in coming to the aid of a stranded group of mostly poor, black Americans once these inevitably broke, and then do so ineptly could only surprise someone who thought our first 400 years of race/gender history is an aberration. Nonetheless, Katrina did provoke widespread calls to finally undertake a serious national dialogue about race. However, this dialogue failed to materialize. Instead, old patterns of neglect and isolation remain, mostly undisturbed. Post-hurricane, the predictable response has been to find a scapegoat, some deviant official or agency to blame. This approach reiterates the familiar psychological defense of splitting to preserve the myth of perfection. Rather than seeing the flooding and its aftermath as another instance of the effects of the shadow at the heart of American politics, long-standing patterns of domination and neglect and their consequences are transformed into an aberration caused by a few uniquely inept officials or agencies. New Orleans's fate also exemplifies the disadvantages of its positioning as an exotic other to the mainstream norm. The socially shared fantasies of New Orleans as a hybrid creole-mulatto "big easy" outside the regulative norms of race/gender, sexuality, and pleasure, enabled a masking of how much its residents shared the ordinary burdens or privileges of others in their race/gender positions. Furthermore, such other-ing positioned New Orleans as not really "us," and hence not worthy of the respect and care "our" citizens deserve. As several people in Lee's documentary comment, the media and many federal officials termed survivors of Katrina "refugees," as if they were stateless foreigners, not American citizens. In this regard, the plight of New Orleans and its residents, pre- and post-Katrina, serves as a cautionary tale for those who think any mere celebration of "difference" unaccompanied by substantive redistribution of social goods and privilege might reduce race/gender domination.

So, to reiterate, what are these losses that we have yet to mourn and what can be done to mourn and alleviate them? Mourning would require overcoming the melancholic split between the all-good object—America's history and its "real" practices or "true" nature—and its incidental, extrinsic "bad" mistakes. Americans would see slavery and its ongoing effects as intrinsic to the great American experiment—essential to our accumulation of wealth and economic development, to our practices of citizenship, and to the fabrication of our subjectivities. Doing so entails unfreezing our disavowal of the presence of the past, with its infliction of social death on millions of people and the distribution of unfair privilege for others, and reworking our understandings of the context in which we take up citizenship and elements of our subjectivities. The effects of this past pervade our present, shaping the current distribution of social goods, including honor and respect. The process of mourning also requires all subjects to face our losses; idealized perfection is an unattainable, toxic fantasy, and the denigration it necessitates inflicts deep harm on us all.

Giving up privilege entails many psychological and perhaps material losses, and it is not easy. It requires ongoing management of resentment toward others whom we can no longer denigrate or exclude. Privileged subjects must reclaim qualities that we have projected onto denigrated others, including our own fabrication through race/gender grids. Mourning requires us to recognize and struggle against an often unconscious sense of entitlement and to consider the extent to which our benefits have harmed others. We have to constantly take into account that our privileges might be undeserved or a consequence of contingent positioning rather than innate individual virtue. Mourning requires subordinate subjects to ruthlessly investigate their own investments in patterns that sustain domination and their own wishes for an unmarked perfection or innocence. It requires an honest accounting of the costs of internalizing denigration and acting it out on one's self and others. Claiming a victim position or demanding perfection as a condition for doing anything reiterates old patterns. However, only if the privileged take responsibility for their privileges and their consequences can space open up for the denigrated to publicly acknowledge how they too have enabled old patterns to continue and to devise better ways of resisting complicity. Only under such conditions can the subordinated trust that honest introspection and exertion of appropriate efficacy will not fuel the privileged's further denigration, abdication of responsibility, and oppression.

I want to be clear that by mourning I do not mean those ritual, fleeting expressions of white guilt or its mirror opposite, what we used to call "guilt tripping" in the Civil Rights Movement. Expressions of white guilt mostly serve to reestablish white people's moral comfort. The implicit message is "I am good enough to see how awful you think I am," and the reiteration of this reasserts white dominance (i.e., "it's all about me"). Conversely, guilt tripping, including passionate denunciations of white devils or the utter evil of "the white man" and any deeds he could do only serve to momentarily puff up the sense of importance of the speaker and perhaps the audience's solidarity. Leaving splitting firmly in place, such rhetoric simply substitutes one occupant of all good or all bad for another. None of this has anything to do with what Freud calls the hard work of mourning—of looking at every aspect of our relationship with an object and carefully reworking it, taking responsibility for our wishes and investments in avoiding recognition of what we have denied, struggling to resist fantasy's temptations, and thinking about and instituting what is actually possible in a less than ideal here and now.

Instead, overcoming melancholia should produce an acute felt need for justice. No longer able to externalize the harm intrinsic to the good, assign blame solely to denigrated others, or agency exclusive to the privileged, the only way left to live tolerably with a less fantasy-ridden relationship with our collective object of the American polity and its subject/citizens is to transform its old, frozen patterns. While public discourse about race/gender dominance is important, mourning also requires other ongoing actions, such as the redistribution of social goods and establishing new patterns of respect and honor, to secure a transformed relationship with and within our collective object. Recognizing the multiple ways in which power is exercised, and trusting that the privileged will assume their just portion of the burden, the subordinated can realistically take on their own share of the project of transformation.

Mourning requires a collectively produced and acknowledged revision of the publicly favored narrative of our country's founding and character. While academic scholarship since the 1960s has produced much evidence that undermines the plausibility of this narrative, its popular appeal remains strong.[3] This narrative is often summed up as American exceptionalism. The main theme of this story is that the United States is unique among all nations. Unlike all other foundings, ours is innocent. With the birth of the United States something new emerges—a country that only incarnates the good and that possesses a limitless capacity to reinvent itself as it moves on through time unmarked and unconstrained by any traces of its previous actions. Uniquely constituted in and through freedom, we retain a special burden of spreading our essence (or protecting it) throughout the world. Since we are unalloyed good, our acts can generate only further goodness. Our special place among nations is also supposed to guarantee our safety and ensure protection against experiencing the tragedies others endure. After all, to the good, only good can occur. (Part of the widespread shock over the events of 9/11 is that they violated these narrative conventions.)

Recognizing that our founding both required and legitimated enslavement, race/gender domination, and persistent patterns of privilege and subordination disrupts this narrative. We need to mourn the loss of the fantasy that any subject or country could be all good and reject the pattern of splitting heterogeneous entities into homogenous, unalloyed units of bad or good (or the axis of evil and the liberators of humankind). This requires that we be able to hold onto a much more complex view of our object and of our and others' relationships with it—neither the object nor our selves are all good or all bad, or purely victims or villains. The United States is neither the "great Satan" nor God's chosen earthly agent. This more constrained view encourages recognition that even when others commit crimes against us they retain their subjectivity. Thus, as subjects ourselves, we ought to inquire into others' narratives and how they make sense of such actions. It is not necessary to agree with another's narrative to learn from it and productively take it into account as we shape our own responses.

What has it cost to sustain the fantasy of idealized perfection and denigrated others? Our longstanding patterns of denigration and demonization produce self-destructive acts. These include tremendous damage to our own citizens, failure to meet the obligations our own publicly endorsed ethical commitments impose, persisting patterns of undeserved privilege and disadvantage, and habits of subjectivity and citizenship that leave us ill equipped to remedy the damage. (Not to mention the recent, escalating pattern of foreign policy misadventures that left our citizens and the new president with a country increasing isolated, in debt, and the object of intensifying and widespread hatred.) Mourning entails the acceptance that none of this can be erased or undone. Unlike Rawls's fantasy of a prelapsarian original position, mourning cannot promise a return to an unmarked innocence or the finding of an unambiguously right path that existed all along as we were lost on a detour. As in post-Katrina New Orleans, the muck is everywhere. There is no pure "Africa" into which blacks can escape their Americanness or a colorblind utopia in which whites can practice our subjectivities outside the social grids of race/gender that fabricate us. In mourning, we recognize that all American citizens have so far "failed to find ways of slipping loose of habits of domination and acquiescence."[4]

Finding alternative habits and the practices of subjectivity and power that could sustain them will not be quick or easy. I do not expect the effects of race/gender melancholia to be adequately dissolved anytime soon. The pervasiveness and complexity of race/gender domination render it impossible to devise a simple four-point plan (or one of those dramatic "wars" Americans seem fond of declaring) to diminish it. Instead, we face the prospect of engaging in ongoing struggles on many fronts, equipped only with uncertain means and facing unpredictable outcomes. Thus, the policy suggestions in this chapter will seem puny in relation to the problems I have addressed throughout the book. At best, they might bring about modest (but useful) effects and inspire others to devise more creative practices.

The moves I recommend are meant to (1) ameliorate some of race/ gender domination's endemic gross injustices; (2) contribute to the necessary process of making the unconscious conscious. This itself is not curative, but rather offers a possibility of clearing space for practicing different relations of power and modes of subjectivity; (3) provide "trust building" practices that could provide concrete benefits so that "conversations" about race/gender are not empty exercises (or worse) means to avoid confronting the necessary shifts in power and narratives (subjective and cultural).

RULES OF LAW

What might some of these new habits and practices of subjectivity and power look like? Foucault's suggestion, that we need to focus on devising and acquiring "the rules of law, the management techniques, and also the morality, the ethos, the practice of the self that will allow us to play these games of power with as little domination as possible,"[5] provides useful orientation. Let's turn first to the rules of law. Here I will suggest several changes—a reinvigorated affirmative action program, legalizing drugs, and instituting the practice in government and economic organizations of a race/gender impact statement. The successful implementation of these changes will require attention to how in each context the political unconscious might be playing out and how to manage the effects of its processes. These suggestions hardly exhaust the range of what could and should be done, and for more extensive treatment I would refer the reader to the excellent policies and practices regarding health care, education, the justice system, policing, neighborhood development, democratic participation, support for rural communities, employment, environmental justice, and the digital divide recommended in *The Covenant with Black America*.[6]

Affirmative Justice as Redistributive and Ethical Interventions

My suggestions regarding affirmative action extend Katznelson's clear and well thought-out defense of and criteria for "narrowly tailored" practices of affirmative action.[7] Such practices "must be conditional on the character and strength of the ties that connect specific past harms to present remedies."[8] Once the imbalances are corrected, the policies will be eliminated.[9] As we saw in chapter 2, the New Deal and Fair Deal programs such as veteran's benefits, social security, and labor law constituted "a massive transfer of privileges to white

Americans."[10] One purpose of a targeted affirmative action policy is to correct the consequences of this unfair system of advantages. The consequences include imbalances in home ownership, access to education, actual or anticipated social security pensions, income and net worth, and preparation for well-paid employment.

A second purpose, and one that Katznelson does not discuss, is to open up meaningful discourse that can help undo race/gender melancholia. Furthermore, I think that without attention to this dimension, such programs cannot succeed. How these programs are articulated and justified is critical; it requires directly confronting our melancholic history and taking responsibility for it.[11] It is not sufficient to propose reinvigorating affirmative action without consideration of the psychodynamics of race/gender melancholia. Nor, as I argued in chapter 4, is it sufficient to hope, as Rawls does, that an abstract "difference principle" as one of the two principles of justice regulating the basic political structure could provide adequate support for instituting redistributive measures.[12] Effectively advocating distributions of social goods that favor the least advantaged requires us to locate such recommendations within rich, historically specific narratives of privilege and subordination. Otherwise, it is all too easy for some privileged subjects to dismiss such proposals as yet another handout to "those" perennially unworthy others and to deny the advantages prior systems have bestowed upon them. Therefore, an intrinsic aspect of all affirmative action programs must be robust practices of education and guided interpersonal interactions that create safe spaces within which all subjects affected by a specific program articulate their understanding of their own positioning and felt entitlement or disadvantage and have to actively confront those of others.'[13] Given the fact, as the recent controversy regarding the arrest of Professor Henry Louis Gates vividly reminds us, that differential positioning along race/gender lines often entails operating within different narratives that shape our interpretation of events and practices, such programs must take these varying frames and their potential effects into account.[14] These practices will necessarily be both educational, informing all affected subjects of the ongoing effects of past exclusionary governmental policies and confrontational, as interaction is likely to simulate powerful emotional investments and attachments.[15]

As remedies for past and present wrongdoing, affirmative action policies should not be understood as "preferential treatment." Instead, because targeted affirmative action policies affirm our collective attachment to justice, they are practices of affirmative justice. These policies address the demonstrable effects of prior and often continuous unfair treatment; they are meant to correct the violation of a basic premise of American law, equal treatment for all. Instituting them is a part of the collective mourning process in which we recognize the existence of patterns of exclusion and privilege and signal our collective desire to resist further investment in the unfair current effects of past and present injustice. If our ethical commitments are to be more than empty moral posturing, such correction is an object to which all subjects, however positioned, ought to be attached. Doing the right thing is often not easy, and without psychodynamically informed interventions, affirmative action programs may exacerbate aspects of race/gender melancholia such as the denigration of subordinated subjects by privileged ones. Therefore, it is necessary to maintain interactive programs that provide spaces for articulating feelings of resentment and disappointment and means of recognizing the sacrifice it often entails.

Targeted affirmative action programs would parallel those the federal government created through the G.I. Bill: "subsidized mortgages; generous grants for education and training; small business loans; and active job searching and placement."[16] Eligibility could be determined by evaluating present income and net worth, status of education and employment, and race/gender social positioning. Individual programs ought to be open to anyone who can demonstrate a direct connection between legalized exclusion and current condition. To administer such programs, community centers could be established, especially in the poorest and most isolated parts of our cities. To be successful, such programs would have to include an active and ongoing counseling component, including the equivalent of caseworkers for applicants, peer support groups, and follow up in employment and educational settings. Neighborhood support for home ownership, including community banks of tools, shared expertise, and low-cost maintenance crews is also important. Such practices are meant to counteract the long-term consequences of internalizing denigration and the powerful effect it has on a subject's sense of their efficacy and capacities. As Katznelson says, exclusionary programs "did far more than cost people money or opportunity. They also projected humiliation, while stunting human imagination and possibility."[17] To be effective, we must craft affirmative action policies that take these dynamics into account. However, despite the discomfort those in privileged race/gender positions may experience, the success of affirmative action policies requires that we attend to how exclusionary programs shaped those doing or benefiting from the projecting and stunting, as well as the humiliated. Unless we create affirmative action programs that take a fuller range of the ongoing consequences of the past into account, they are unlikely to succeed.

Drug Policies: Resisting Destructive Governmentality

(X) "marketed and sold their lethal product with zeal, with deception, with a single-minded focus on their financial success and without regard for the human tragedy or social costs that success exacted."[18]

While justified within the rubric of public health, our current drug policies are a primary site for enacting and sustaining race/gender domination. Race/gender melancholia inhibits us from adequately analyzing this malignant exercise of governmentality. Instead, many citizens embrace practices of surveillance and control (e.g., drug testing as a condition for employment) that expand biopower's reach. Despite no evidence that such tactics work, vast sums of money and quasimilitary ventures into other countries are deployed in an apparently endless "war" on drugs. In the four decades since declaring this war, we have spent more than 1 trillion dollars and arrested more than 37 million nonviolent offenders. Arrests for drug violations this year are expected to exceed the 1,841,182 arrests in 2007. This represented 13 percent of all arrests. In 2007, more people were arrested on drug charges than on any other violation. Last year approximately 25 percent of those in prison were sentenced for drug charges. Although there are five times as many white drug users, blacks are far more likely to be imprisoned for drug violations.[19] Enlarging the space for better practices of citizenship and fostering technologies of care of the self rather than the disciplines of governmentality require radical revision of these policies.

My second policy recommendation, therefore, is to legalize all prohibited drugs and to stringently restrict the sale of them to adults. Legalizing prohibited drugs does not preclude the development of other, nonjuridical approaches to discouraging their use. Moving away from juridical techniques can encourage subjects to engage in different practices and disciplines. Communities and non-state organizations remain free to devise innovative programs to deter behaviors they find self- or socially destructive and to foster and support ones that they believe will enable citizens to better meet our obligations to ourselves and others. Furthermore, any practice that fosters a sense of responsibility will stipulate that under no conditions should drug use be exculpatory. Drug users would remain responsible for committing crimes that harm others; for example, if reckless driving kills some-one, the crime is that death, not the physiological condition of the driver. If a user takes a drug and then violently assaults someone; they should be accountable for that assault.

However, our current practices of criminalizing drugs and impos-ing incarceration for their sale (except to minors) or use are futile and destructive. I offer several reasons for this claim. The first is that our current approach, the so-called war on drugs, is expensive and ineffective. The best available estimate is that this war costs taxpay-ers "upward of 40 billion annually in recent years."[20] Despite this expenditure, today drugs are cheaper, stronger, and more available than they were in 2000. This enormous sum could be better used for programs that contribute to reducing race/gender gaps. For example, more money should go to programs like Head Start, the 2008 budget for which, according to the Office of Head Start, U.S. Department of Health and Human Services, is approximately $6.8 billion. States could reverse their disproportionate spending on incarceration rela-tive to education. Currently they spend 1 in 15 tax dollars on "cor-rections." Between 1987 and 2007, state spending on this category increased 127 percent, while that on education has risen by only 21 percent.[21]

Even from a public health point of view, our current policies make no sense. The basis for sorting drugs into categories of legal and ille-gal is irrational. Nicotine is one of the most addictive substances, yet it is legal. Some people use illegal drugs occasionally without ever sliding into addiction; others are rapidly addicted to alcohol. Sheerly on a physiological basis (nicotine is associated with many forms of cancer and lung disease; alcohol with some forms of cancer and liver and other organ damage) both alcohol and nicotine are far more damaging to the body than opiates. According to a recent article in the *Archives of Internal Medicine,* smoking "is the leading cause of preventable death in the United States and worldwide. In the 20th century, smoking caused 100 million deaths. If present patterns per-sist, about 1 billion people will die from smoking-related diseases in this century."[22] The "X" I put before the quote at the beginning of this chapter refers to tobacco, which is by far the most dangerous drug Americans consume. According to a recent report, the top three causes of death in the United States in 2000 were tobacco (435,000 deaths; 18.1 percent of total U.S. deaths), poor diet and physical inactivity (400,000 deaths; 16.6 percent), and alcohol consumption (85,000 deaths; 3.5 percent). More people die due to lack of health insurance (approximately 18,000 per year) than from consuming illicit drugs. Illicit use of drugs caused 17,000 deaths. Of these, marijuana caused none.[23]

Certainly, it is no argument to say that because we allow some harmful substances, we ought to permit more. My quarrel is not with the (putative) goal of reducing harm, but with the means. Contrary to the common sense intuition that criminalizing drugs deters their use, the experience of countries that have adopted decriminalization policies, such as Holland, suggests that this is not so. According to Peter Cohen, former director of the Center for Drug Research at the University of Amsterdam, who has studied these issues for twenty-five years, there is no correlation between drug policy and prevalence of use. His research demonstrates that " 'drug policy is irrelevant'... It's quite logical, he says, to theorize that outlawing drugs would have an impact, but experience shows otherwise, both in America and in some European countries with stricter laws than the Netherlands but no less drug use."[24] Despite its decriminalization policies, use of all drugs is lower in Holland than the United States. One reason, some evidence suggests, is that decriminalization removes the appeal of transgression from drug use. Especially among young adults, subtracting this thrill may reduce interest in drug consumption.

In addition to their ineffectiveness and irrationality, as currently administered, our drug policies exacerbate existing race/gender inequities. According to a recent study, "African-Americans constitute 13 percent of all monthly drug users, but they represent 35 percent of arrests for drug possession, 55 percent of convictions, and 74 percent of prison sentences."[25] Criminalization further unravels the social fabric of already vulnerable populations. Increasingly high incarceration rates wreck havoc on existing families and undermine the possibility of future family formation. For example, black children born in 1978 had a one in seven chance of having a father sent to prison by their 14th birthday; for black children born in 1990, the risk increased to one in four. Since incarceration rates for black women are rapidly rising (many for drug or drug-related offenses), these children are increasingly at risk for losing their mothers as well. While for white children the risk of parental imprisonment increased 60 percent from 1978 to 1990, it remained relatively small at 1 in 25 in 1990.[26] Prior convictions, especially of felonies, often condemns subjects to a lifetime of poverty and economic insecurity. If we were truly concerned about the welfare of black children, rather than demonizing single black mothers, we would alter these destructive policies.[27]

Furthermore, there is ample evidence that rather than enhancing public safety, the enormous profits resulting from our selective prohibition of drugs contribute to increasing rates of violence and corruption of officials here and in other producing countries such as Mexico, Colombia, and Afghanistan. As Cohen says, "prohibition does not reduce drug use, but it does have other impacts. It takes up an enormous amount of police time and generates large possibilities for criminal income."[28] In a particularly ironic twist, one consequence of the vast profits produced by selling illegal drugs is the emergence of a new form of violence, narco-terrorism. For example, in 2008, the Taliban in Afghanistan reaped an approximately $400 million profit from opium sales, which they then channeled into such enterprises as purchasing and devising weapons to kill American soldiers. In America, especially in poor inner cities, turf wars over distribution contribute to the high rates of homicide and assault among young blacks. Drug profits bankroll the extravagant life styles of a small group of dealers, and the "bling" they accumulate glamorizes their trade and its appeal to those whose other current economic options are quite limited. Addicts turn to crime to support their habits and terrorize their neighbors. Users die due to drug adulteration and unpredictable dosage; shared needles spread HIV. The irrationality and inequities of our current policies suggest that they require serious overhaul.

If these current policies are so ineffective and discriminatory, why do they continue? Other than the employment of police, program administrators, "experts," and prison guards, who benefits? I think our current drug policies are best understood within the frames of Foucault's work on governmentality and biopower, as well as race/gender melancholia. As I discussed in the previous chapter, through regulatory means, governmental and biopower technologies prohibit certain behavior while simultaneously inciting others ("don't smoke marijuana; have a beer"). They create a threat (the drug menace) while simultaneously producing and legitimating the means of eliminating it (a war on drugs). Often these technologies entail the exercise of power under the rubric of an apparently neutral concern for "public health" or safety. Vast systems of expertise, social control, enforcement, and organization of the populace into normal/deviant, sick/well, and criminal/innocent evolve and are further elaborated and justified through the very practices that generated them. Once established and normalized, such governmental technologies exert enormous inertial force. They generate their own truth, power, legitimacy, professions, and practices. Occupying and controlling positions of normalization and truth, practitioners of these disciplines can construct opposing practices as dangerous, irresponsible threats to public security and well-being. Desiring protection from the threat now created, subjects demand its eradication and support those who promise to do so.

Resistance to normalized practices requires questioning what on their own terms seems irrefutable truth, not disciplinary power. In the case of our drug policies, resisting the dominant discourse is especially difficult since its technologies make use of other longstanding aspects of American culture, including our ambivalence toward pleasure and race/gender melancholia. Americans have long had an ambivalent relationship with the pursuit of pleasure. While technologies of "care of the self" might suggest alternative possibilities, Americans often equate pleasure with consumption, especially of material goods. Throughout American history, attachment to massive consumption of various goods alternates, or coincides with, campaigns for abstinence or purity. We prohibit alcohol and then legalize it again; use sexuality to sell everything from cars to mouthwash and then promote abstinence as a primary means of birth control or hesitate to encourage condom use to slow the spread of HIV. One of the ways this ambivalence has been managed is by splitting—drugs are divided into categories of "bad" and socially sanctioned. It is obvious but readily ignored that no drug is intrinsically criminal; it is social policies that make them so. What counts as criminal behavior is socially constructed. For example, in the nineteenth century, opiates were legal while aspirin required a physician's prescription. Our social practices split drug users into "addicts" or "consumers" and "patients." Appreciation of wine is a mark of sophistication, consumption of crack a symptom of moral failure or evil. Despite the risks of obesity or diabetes, like the numbed characters in *Monster's Ball*, many of us turn to food for comfort or stimulation. Those with access to medical care can sanitize their drug-aided pursuit of pleasure through a soothing medical diagnosis (e.g., "erectile dysfunction" for which Viagra or other medications are prescribed). When this ambivalence circulates through and is structured and made use of by race/gender grids, it enables the reinforcement of preexisting race/gender domination. Our drug policies become the means and rationale for putting a disproportionate number of black people into prison. Once again blacks are constructed as the incarnation of appetite and as predatory, dangerous, and out of control. The safety of the community requires their removal from it. Since they are the criminals, our consumption of socially sanctioned drugs is innocent, normal. These preexisting fantasies enable us to rationalize what would otherwise appear as the irrational, misguided use of resources and power that our drug policies actually represent. Race/gender melancholia disables citizens from adopting a skeptical attitude toward the lulling promises of "public health," and it undermines our resistance to this particularly destructive intersection of governmentality and race/gender domination.

It would be far better to redirect the money and other social resources to programs that might reduce the patterned disadvantages in America. Shifting money and power from selective drug prohibition would augment targeted affirmative action programs. For example, money currently spent on the drug war could be redirected to creating community banks that offered microloans to start useful enterprises. These enterprises could include ones that support the legally employed and community development and that address real threats to public health such as the unavailability of fresh food and medical care and exposure to environmental toxins. Developing practices such as urban farming and the "edible" classroom would not only make better food more accessible, but they can also support and encourage different technologies of the self and relationships among citizens (or potential citizens).[29]

Legalizing drugs would also undercut the financing of the urban thug, a destructive kind of subjectivity much lamented by some commentators.[30] Since we do not seem to apply the term when such behavior is exercised on a grand scale, such as the in Enron debacle (see the documentary, *The Smartest Guys in the Room*, for multiple examples of economic thuggery running wild) or campaigns of "shock and awe" that inflict far more death and destruction than generations of urban thugs could, I am suspicious of the discourse that produces only black men as "thugs." It would be foolish to deny, however, that among some subjects in poor black communities, this lifestyle is glamorized. I doubt that, without the financial incentives its drug component provides thuggery would retain much of its allure. The thriving drug trade does suggest, however, that there is a lot of misdirected entrepreneurial energy among those involved in it. When its current market is cut off, programs can be developed to redirect it. Of course, profits for the few would not be as great, but these would no longer be available.

Publicly Recognizing Patterns of Sacrifice and Reward

In my discussion of targeted affirmative action and drug policy, I have already exemplified my third recommendation for rules of law— developing and implementing an ongoing practice of incorporating a race/gender impact statement in all policy formation. Developing such a practice is important for several reasons. Doing so moves us toward better practices of citizenship because it encourages heightened awareness of a fact race/gender domination obscures—that distributions of sacrifice and reward are intrinsic to democratic politics. As I argued in the previous chapter, a paradox of democracy is that despite its promise of popular sovereignty, public policies inevitably result in losses for some and wins for others. As Allen says, these losses "do not disappear but are retained in the fabric of society."[31] If we are to build trust and communication among citizens, encouraging such mindfulness is necessary. It signals that the polity's effects on all citizens matter and that citizens and the leaders they install are accountable for the ensuing patterns of distribution. Furthermore, a continuous public accounting of the race/gender distribution of public goods is a necessary complement to a targeted affirmative action program. Its absence permits the false marking of subordinate groups as the only recipient of governmental "handouts" and feeds dominant groups' race/gender resentment. Without such accounting, many of the ongoing shifts of public resources to the already advantaged remain hidden.

This practice might also increase skepticism concerning claims that law or policy making is "colorblind." As I hope is now apparent, how race/gender domination shapes and is supported by many policies and practices is not always obvious or transparent. Often on the surface policies and practices appear neutral or colorblind. However, as I have argued, the pervasiveness of race/gender suggests that neutrality or colorblindness is likely to be the exception rather than the norm. We have to look carefully for its effects. Our decisions regarding the distribution of many public goods can exacerbate or diminish race/gender disparities. For example, as we saw in New Orleans during Katrina, decisions to favor funding highways over public transportation can disparately burden the poor. Since black people are over-represented among the poor, this will impact race/gender relations. The inability of many New Orleans' residents to escape the city, even under the threat of potential death, was an actual consequence of long-standing policy choices. It is also a dramatic allegory for the everyday burdens of many, as the absence of public transportation isolates people in often racially segregated inner cities and renders less available such goods as employment opportunities or even fresh, affordable food.

While some of our policies disproportionately burden those in subordinate race/gender positions, others distribute inequitable advantages. Agricultural subsidies are a good example. Reporters at *The Washington Post* recently conducted a nine-month study of these programs. They found that what "began in the 1930's as a limited safety net for working farmers has swollen into a far-flung infrastructure of entitlements that has cost $172 billion over the past decade. In 2005 alone, when pretax farm profits were at a near-record $72 billion, the federal government handed out more than $25 billion in aid, almost 50 percent more than the amount it pays to families receiving welfare."[32] Very few of the recipients of such aid are in disadvantaged race/gender positions. Currently the Black Farmer & Agriculturalists Association reports that less than 1 percent of all U.S. farmers (about 18,000) are black. Even policies meant to lower race/gender disparities can be poorly devised. For example, four years ago the tax code was amended to include a $1000 child tax credit. However, because currently families that earn less than $11,000 are excluded from the program, about half of all black children are members of families too poor to qualify for the full benefit. Approximately 28 percent of black families (and 9 percent of white ones) receive no credit; 21 percent (and 9 percent of white ones) receive partial credit.[33] Examples of the disparate distribution of burdens and privileges could (and should) be found in many current federal, state, and local policies. While perfect fairness is impossible, more open and honest public accounting is not. In turn, such accounting could provide a commonly shared basis for ongoing conversations about what citizens might do differently.

Race/gender impact statements are only one of the techniques we might invent to encourage mindfulness as a counter to race/gender melancholia's characteristic denial and blindness. Another technique is to institute public rituals of mourning, recognition, and honor. One such public ritual might be instituting an annual day of commemoration, similar to Memorial Day. On Memorial Day we honor all those who sacrificed so others could enjoy the freedoms of an ongoing life. Enslaved persons suffered social death and involuntarily lost these freedoms while others benefited from their labor and their losses. Yet despite their enormous contributions to the American polity, no Tomb of the Unknown Slave honors all those lost during the middle passage. We do not enumerate the sacrifices of enslaved persons as we narrate accounts of the noble deeds that shaped our polity. No president before President Obama publicly honored in his inaugural address the labor of the enslaved persons who, among many other contributions, helped build our nation's capital. Regularly making such deeds visible and offering public recognition and gratitude are important practices to cultivate. Such practices are necessary ingredients in the remaking of citizenship and undoing race/gender melancholia.

FABRICATING CITIZENS

As Myrdal points out, many Americans have found ways of living with the contradictions between our professed ideals and actual practices, including those of race/gender domination.[34] Therefore, we need better ways to fabricate citizens. This may seem a contradiction in terms, but as Cruikshank argues, it is not.[35] As contradictory as it may seem, technologies of governmentality are intrinsic and necessary to the production of democratic citizens.[36] The more democratic a state is, the more pervasive such technologies must be. This necessity arises from another paradox of democratic citizenship. Since democratic theories stipulate that the people, not the state, are sovereign, a "means of democratic government, one that did not violate the will of the people, had to be invented."[37] Understood as rule of the people and thus requiring their consent, democratic governance "cannot force its interests but must enlist the willing participation of individuals in the pursuit of its objects."[38] Segregation, for example, relied upon enforcement by ordinary white citizens who "imposed sanctions on blacks whom they perceived as violating boundaries."[39]

This invented means is the "self-governing" subject. Such self-governing citizens are not born; they have to be made. In democracies, the question is not if citizens will be made, it is how. The currently popular discussions by Putnam and others regarding "civic culture" and its role in the success of democracies gesture toward this fact.[40] However, this discourse's chosen terminology (culture, volunteerism, etc.) masks the ongoing technologies of power (including inclusion/exclusion, normalization/deviancy) intrinsic to the fabrication of democratic subjects. Subjects have to learn how to constitute their subjectivity so they can be the self-governors their democracy requires, and among the practices of a democracy are the productive forms of power that fabricate the citizens it needs. Rather than think of ourselves as either powerless or individualistically autonomous articulations of an unsituated free will or reason, as citizens we instead need to examine *"the extent to which we are already self-governing."*[41] Our current self-governance, for example, regenerates race/gender domination. The construction and perpetuation of race/gender mediated social meanings and practices require the conscious and unconscious collaborative efforts of many citizens, engaged in a wide variety of activities. If we want new kinds of practices of citizenship, "we must reinvent the means by which democratic citizens are known and produced."[42] Inventing new social meanings and practices without such mediation will require similarly collaborative efforts within every aspect of American life, from economic and political networks to daily subjective habits of thinking, feeling, and acting.

As I have argued, such reinvention requires confronting the limits of abstract individualism and political liberalism. Their narratives lack the resources either to account for how current citizens are fabricated or to imagine better practices.[43] Instead of imagining our citizens as disembodied, dispassionate, rational, self-interest maximizing, ahistorical, unmarked "individuals," we need to develop techniques to "look for insidious habits of thought, selective patterns of social intercourse, biased processes of social cognition"[44] and psychodynamic activities such as fantasizing, splitting and projection. Such techniques would enable us to recognize our complicity in sustaining race/gender domination, to examine how we conduct our lives, and to imagine better possibilities. I have tried to show that Foucault's care of the self offers many techniques suitable for developing subjects' capacities to discover and dismantle insidious practices. He recommends developing a multifaceted practice including critical subjective examination, constant struggle, multiple modes of social interaction, establishing ethical commitments and nurturing a sense of obligation to enact them, and seeking "soul services" to treat our inevitable dysfunctions.[45]

Practicing care of the self incorporates and requires the support of educational and other institutions and modes of social interaction far different from our current ones. For example, rather than "teaching to the test," educational institutions committed to fostering better citizens would insist on building subjects' capacity to ask questions, sustain a strong skepticism about all truth claims, care for common spaces, engage in social collaboration, develop a wide variety of techniques (including aesthetic appreciation and judgment and kinesthetic, ethical, emotional and social "intelligences") and maintain an engaged detachment toward our passions and those of others. While teaching to standardized tests may improve students' technical skills (for example, writing sentences with a noun and a verb), it seems to disable capacities for critical thinking, analysis, creativity, empathy, and curiosity better citizenship practices require. It also models and reinforces a mistaken tenet of individualism—that the success of any subject simply reflects their own efforts and worth. Learning is a competition, between the individual and the test; the best will win and the win signifies that they are the best. What matters are the individual score and the aggregate of individual scores, so that what can be rewarded is what can be easily measured. The "objectivity" of the measure is assumed and neither its meaning, value, or genealogy are to be subjects of inquiry. Training students through such technologies is unlikely to generate citizens who can tolerate complexity and ambiguity or exercise concern for other subjects and our public spaces. Instead, students are trained to maximize "individual" performance and reward and to rely on others to set safe boundaries and delimit in advance what they must do and know. This is quite different than the demands of technologies of care of the self, which require that subjects seek critical mentors and initiate uncomfortable conversations with unfamiliar others. Such technologies require giving up the comforting question, "is this going to be on the test?" or its equivalent. Instead, they encourage looking for what is not being said or asked. Attaining proficiency in such disciplines also requires desiring the unfamiliar. Among other moves, we would feel compelled to make frequent exits from our iPod/Blackberry/cell phone bubbles and from our comfortable isolation in gated communities and their equivalents.

The refabrication of citizenship also entails generating and sustaining a chastened sense among all Americans about the possibilities and limits of politics. Like Officer Ryan in *Crash*, we have to recognize that long-standing practices of domination enabled unrealistic expectations about politics and power. Politics is about management of conflict, not its permanent abolition through overwhelming exercises of unilateral force. Ultimate, unambiguous victory over X, whatever X is, is unlikely. A chastened politics requires that leaders abstain from promising the kinds of certainty, security, permanent resolution, unity, or tranquility that political practices can never deliver, and that citizens learn not to demand what we cannot have—for example, gains without losses or victories without costs. Rather than encouraging a search for the final, triumphant move, better citizenship practices substitute a shared object of caring for the spaces in which constructive conflict is possible. While we will continue to disagree about what to do, absent appropriate management techniques and the spaces they sustain, playing the game of politics as free subjects is impossible. As Foucault argues, our freedom consists in the variety and number of moves we can make, not in the absence of resistance to our will. To preserve or expand our freedom, space must remain open for further conflict and the possibilities of different future outcomes.

Citizens' abstinence regarding the introduction of their attachment to certain objects into public spaces will protect nonpublic ones, perhaps even encourage their flourishing. Furthermore, while some bases for asserting claims are ruled out, a vastly enlarged range remains possible. In public discourse, appeals to "reasonableness" should be only one among a multiplicity of permissible forms of claim making, including passionate and aesthetic ones, and citizens could propose innovative objects of shared attachment based on such claims. Coles, for example, envisions "experimental transfigurations of sensibility that might feed into institutional transformations affecting families, punishment, welfare, public spaces, technologies, land use, and relationship with the other-than-human beings."[46]

While many note that the American polity sorely lacks an ongoing dialogue on race/gender,[47] I have argued throughout this book that its absence is not accidental, neutral, or harmless, and its effects are toxic. Our failures to sustain such a dialogue reflect, among other forces, the power of the political unconscious and race/gender melancholia. Past failures, however, do not justify abandoning the effort. Creating spaces in which such dialogue can occur is an important aspect of undoing our frozen race/gender melancholia and generating new narratives about the losses slavery and its consequences continue to inflict. Engaging in such efforts can contribute to reinventing public spaces and refabricating citizenship. Dialogue requires the engagement, actions, and care of citizens located differently across race/gender grids. It is certainly the case, as Shelby argues, that to overcome internalized denigration and the self-contempt it generates, black people "must participate, in a meaningful way, in freeing themselves."[48] It would be a significant advance if blacks united in the kind of solidarity against domination and resistance to its practices he recommends. However, this cannot constitute an adequate strategy for addressing race/gender domination or undoing race/gender melancholia. Any lessening of these also requires that white subjects take responsibility for our contributions to and benefits from them and for the harms our positioning inflicts on ourselves and others. Domination cannot exist without those who, inadvertently or not, practice it. Without discussion of entitlement and privilege and their effects on all subjects, we cannot meaningfully talk about domination. Talk is not meaningful if it remains unconnected to actions that shift currently existing patterns of advantage and burden. Unless better practices of race/gender become an object of shared attachment, race/gender domination will remain the "black man's" burden, responsibility, and problem. Attempts to sustain discourse about domination will stay vulnerable to construction (and dismissal) as special pleading by undeserving others. Instead, we need discourses that insist the elimination of undeserved privilege is central to practices of justice and that create excitement about the new democratic practices for which abolishing entitlement could create spaces.[49] While giving up the benefits of privilege is never easy, desire for one object (justice or expanded democracy) can be mustered against another (entitlement). Doing so requires the support of public practices in which such behavior is modelled, honored, and incurs the respect of others.

The pervasiveness of race/gender domination means that its manifestations surround and are us. Although recognizing this is depressing, it need not be overwhelming or paralyzing, for it also means that opportunities for resisting or diminishing domination are equally pervasive. Care of the self entails the recognition that no aspect of our practices, from fantasy to work, consumption, and manifold forms of social interaction, should be exempt from ongoing moral scrutiny. Practices constitute subjectivity and are forms of action and exercises of power. All actions have consequences and support, enlarge, or foreclose ways of life. Disciplines of care of the self suggest critical attention to and informed practices of such matters as where we choose to live. If we are located in denigrated subject positions, how do we resist their effects and create maximum space to move differently? How do we encourage and support others to also resist and move differently? If we benefit from privileged subject positioning, how do we make use of it? Who do we mentor? How do we resist, or turn to better purposes, the powers of entitlement? Do we notice who our current practices include or exclude and seek to alter exclusionary ones that perpetuate race/gender disparities? What kinds of historical narratives and subjective practices do our children's schools support? What kinds of race/gender representation are presented in the media we consume, and what do we do with or about these images? What kinds of social interaction do we seek out and why? What are our race/gender fantasies, and how might we be acting them out? How do we manage passions, such as hate, fear, entitlement, and envy? What do we take for granted and why? What other points of view and modes of life do we regularly take up or engage? Who do we turn to reinforce or challenge the habits of mind and practices constituting our subjectivities? What do our actions and choices reveal about which citizens we consider worthy and due respect or honor? What do we demand of those who occupy governmental positions of power or who control the distribution of socially valued resources? In what ways are we already empowered, and how do we make use of our powers?

Even if practices of care of the self became ordinary aspects of the fabrication of democratic citizens, conflict, disagreement, and games that produce winners and losers will not disappear. Nor will the political unconscious, envy, resentment, or desire. I am hoping, however, that we can better make use of and manage these facets of democratic politics and subjectivities. The effects of persisting in familiar habits of race/gender melancholia, such as splitting and projecting all flaws onto denigrated others and sustaining fantasies of idealized perfection and omnipotence, grow ever more toxic. As recent events suggest, imagining the United States as a fantasyland exempt from the ordinary tragedies and limits constrained and embodied subjects incur, results in increasingly dangerous consequences for ourselves and others. Unless we forswear our practices of denial, unfreeze our race/gender melancholia, and bring the sun of consistent attention to bear upon the shadows at America's heart, our self-inflicted losses can only mount. To a subject attached to such objects as justice, this prospect is chilling and unbearably sad.

NOTES

INTRODUCTION

1. Barack Obama, "A More Perfect Union," reprinted in *Change We Can Believe In* (New York: Three Rivers Press, 2008), 226. This speech itself was necessitated by the recurrence of the past in the present, in particular, the foregrounding of the stereotype of the "angry black man." Jeremiah Wright, Obama's pastor, came to bear this representation. Neither Michelle Obama, who some commentators and politicians tried to construct as a bitchy "Sapphire," nor Barack Obama could escape our dominant race/gender grammar. Numerous authors have discussed the social construction of black women through tropes of Sapphire and the "bitch." They include Regina Austin, "Sapphire Bound!," in Adrien Katherine Wing, ed., *Critical Race Feminism: A Reader* (New York: New York University Press, 1997): 289–296; and Patricia Hill Collins, *Black Sexual Politics: African Americans, Gender, and the New Racism* (New York: Routledge, 2004). I discuss other constructions of black women such as Mammy and Jezebel in chapter one.
2. Ibid., 222.
3. Ibid.
4. Ibid., 228.
5. Ibid., 225.
6. Ibid., 215.
7. Barack Obama, *Dreams from My Father: A Story of Race and Inheritance* (New York: Three Rivers Press, 2004).
8. Ibid., 76.
9. Ibid., 115.
10. Ibid., 135.
11. Barack, Obama, *The Audacity of Hope: Thoughts on Reclaiming the American Dream* (New York: Vintage, 2008), 275.
12. Ibid., 288.
13. Toni Morrison, *Playing in the Dark: Whiteness and the Literary Imagination* (New York: Vintage, 1992), 48.
14. After the civil war, the "one drop rule," gradually emerged as the dominant basis for racial classification in the United States. According to this scheme, one drop of "black" blood rendered a person black. See James F. Davis, *Who Is Black?: One Nation's*

Definition (University Park: Pennsylvania State University Press, 1991). The ways race/gender played out in the election, also illuminate how little the dominant race/gender grammar has changed since the publication of one of contemporary black feminism's initiating texts, Gloria T. Hull, Patricia Bell Scott, and Barbara Smith, *All the Women Are White, All the Blacks Are Men, But Some of Us Are Brave* (New York: Feminist Press, 1982). On this point, see Jane Junn, "Making Room for Women of Color: Race and Gender Categories in the 2008 U.S. Presidential Election," *Politics and Gender* 5, 1 (March 2009): 105–110.

15. Kate Zernike and Megan Thee-Brenan, "Poll Finds Tea Party Backers Wealthier and More Educated," *New York Times*, April 14, 2010, A 1. See also, Charles M. Blow, "A Mighty Pale Tea," *New York Times*, April 17, 2010, A 15; and Kate Julian, "What's the Big Idea?," *Washington Post*, January 10, 2010, B 5. She reports that "according to a recent study by researchers from Stanford and the University of California at Irvine, negative views of the president do appear to be correlated with racial bias."

16. On liminality, see Victor Turner, *The Ritual Process* (London: Routledge and Kegan Paul, 1969).

CHAPTER I

1. Toni Morrison, *Playing in the Dark: Whiteness and the Literary Imagination* (New York: Vintage, 1992), 48.

2. See for example, Jennifer Hochschild, *Facing Up to the American Dream: Race, Class and the Soul of the Nation* (Princeton, NJ: Princeton University Press, 1995) and Rogers M. Smith, *Civic Ideals: Conflicting Visions of Citizenship in U.S. History* (New Haven, CT: Yale University Press, 1997).

3. David Brion Davis, *Inhuman Bondage: The Rise and Fall of Slavery in the New World* (New York: Oxford University Press, 2006), 6.

4. Paul Gilroy, *The Black Atlantic: Modernity and Double Consciousness* (Cambridge, MA: Harvard University Press, 1993), 4.

5. Davis, *Inhuman Bondage*, 102.

6. Ibid.

7. Sigmund Freud (1917), "Mourning and Melancholia." In *Sigmund Freud: Collected Papers v.4*, ed. James Strachey (New York: Basic Books, 1959), 159.

8. Morrison, *Playing in the Dark*, 48.

9. On the importance of narrative and imagination in the constitution of states, see Benedict Anderson, *Imagined Communities: Reflections on the Origin and Spread of Nationalism* (New York: Verso, 1991); Catherine A. Holland, *The Body Politic: Foundings, Citizenship and Difference in the American Political Imagination* (New York: Routledge, 2001); and Anthony W. Marx, *Making Race and Nation:*

A Comparison of the United States, South Africa, and Brazil (New York: Cambridge, 1998).

10. As Desmond Robinson, a black, former New York City undercover transit officer who was shot by a white male colleague says, "Everyone carries baggage subconsciously and retraining the mind takes lots of work." "On Diverse Force, Blacks Still Face Special Peril," *New York Times*, May 31, 2009 A 18.

11. Morrison, *Playing in the Dark*, 47.

12. Orlando Patterson, *Rituals of Blood: Consequences of Slavery in Two American Centuries* (New York: Basic, 1998), 240.

13. Alix de Tocqueville, Alexis, *Democracy in America*, ed. and trans. Harvey C. Mansfield and Delba Winthrop (Chicago: University of Chicago Press, 2000), 343. See William Julius Wilson and Richard P. Taub, *There Goes the Neighborhood: Racial, Ethnic, and Class Tensions in Four Chicago Neighborhoods and Their Meaning for America* (New York: Alfred A. Knopf, 2006), especially Chapter six for an example of how this repugnance persists and some of its effect.

14. Patterson, *Rituals of Blood*, 328.

15. Glenn C. Loury, *The Anatomy of Racial Inequality* (Cambridge, MA: Harvard University Press, 2002), 5.

16. Cheryl I. Harris, "Whiteness as Property," in Kimberle Crenshaw, Neil Gotanda, Gary Peller, and Kendall Thomas, eds., *Critical Race Theory: The Key Writings that Formed the Movement* (New York: The New Press, 1995), 276–291.

17. de Tocqueville, *Democracy in America*, 327.

18. Patterson, *Rituals of Blood*, 166.

19. Splitting and denial are psychoanalytic concepts. They refer to complex unconscious processes. Splitting occurs when we are unable to hold contradictory feelings about or characteristics of someone or something in mind simultaneously. For example, I may love someone but also be very angry with them. It makes me uncomfortable to have these feelings simultaneously, so unconsciously, I split my loved object into a bad one who causes anger and a good one whom I love. This splitting then enables me to deny that I am angry at all, since consciously I feel no anger toward my loved one. We can also split off aspects of our own subjectivity. For example, I may have a lot of competitive wishes, but my culture tells me women are not supposed to have these. Unconsciously, I split them off and direct their energy elsewhere, for example, to bragging about my children, a culturally acceptable behavior for mothers. In chapters two and three, I discuss in greater detail how these processes work and their effects.

20. Anne Anlin Cheng, *The Melancholy of Race* (New York: Oxford University Press, 2001), 194.

21. Writing on this subject is voluminous. The following are among the texts I have found most helpful. Lucius J. Barker, "Limits of Political

Strategy: A Systematic View of the African American Experience,"
American Political Science Review 88, 1 (1994): 1–14; Derrick Bell,
And We Are Not Saved: The Elusive Quest for Racial Justice (New York:
Basic Books, 1987); Derrick Bell, *Silent Covenants: Brown v Board of
Education and the Unfulfilled Hopes for Racial Reform* (New York:
Oxford University Press, 2004); Michael K. Brown, Martin Carnoy,
Elliot Currie, Troy Duster, David B. Oppenheimer, Marjorie M.
Shultz, and David Wellman, *Whitewashing Race: The Myth of a Color-
Blind Society* (Berkeley: University of California Press, 2003); Patricia
Hill Collins, *Black Sexual Politics: African Americans, Gender, and
the New Racism* (New York: Routledge, 2004); Kimberle Crenshaw,
Neil Gotanda, Gary Peller, and Kendall Thomas, eds., *Critical
Race Theory: The Key Writings that Formed the Movement*; Richard
Delgado and Jean Stefancic, eds., *Critical Race Theory: The Cutting
Edge*, second edition (Philadelphia: Temple University Press, 2000);
Andrew Hacker, *Two Nations: Black and White, Separate, Hostile
and Unequal* (New York: Charles Scribners, 1992); Ange-Marie
Hancock, *The Politics of Disgust: The Public Identity of the Welfare
Queen* (New York: New York University Press, 2004); Jennifer
Hochschild, *Facing Up to the American Dream: Race, Class and
the Soul of the Nation* (Princeton, NJ: Princeton University Press,
1995); Desmond King, *Separate and Unequal: African Americans
and the US Federal Government*, revised edition (New York: Oxford
University Press, 2007); Philip A. Klinkner with Rogers M. Smith,
*The Unsteady March: The Rise and Decline of Racial Equality in
America* (Chicago: University of Chicago Press: 1999); Charles R.
Lawrence, III, "The Id, the Ego, and Equal Protection: Reckoning
with Unconscious Racism." *Stanford Law Review* (vol.39, Jan.
1987): 317–388; Glenn C. Loury, *The Anatomy of Racial Inequality*;
Rogers M. Smith, *Civic Ideals: Conflicting Visions of Citizenship
in U.S. History* (New Haven, CT: Yale University Press, 1997);
Linda Faye Williams, *The Constraint of Race: Legacies of White Skin
Privilege in America* (University Park, PA: Pennsylvannia State Press,
2003); Patricia J.Williams, *The Alchemy of Race and Rights: Diary of
a Law Professor* (Cambridge, MA: Harvard University Press, 1991);
William Julius Wilson, *The Declining Significance of Race* (Chicago:
University of Chicago Press, 1980); William Julius Wilson, *The Truly
Disadvantaged* (Chicago: University of Chicago Press, 1987); and
Howard Winant, *The World Is a Ghetto: Race and Democracy Since
World War II* (New York: Basic Books, 2001). Numerous researchers
are investigating what they call "implicit racism," that is deeply held
but unconscious attitudes toward and feelings about specific racial
positions. They are also devising innovative experiments to show
how, even though they are not aware of them, these implicit biases
affect individuals' actions and choices. For a useful summary of some
of this work (and ingenious experimenting of his own), see Justin D.

Levinson, "Forgotten Racial Equality Implicit Bias, Decisionmaking, and Misremembering," *Duke Law Journal* 57 (2007): 344–421. See also the parallel research by John F. Dovidio and others on "aversive racism." Aversive racists have unconscious, negative associations to black people that are "expressed subtly, indirectly, and in rationalizable ways," John F. Dovidio and Samuel Gaertner, "On the Nature of Contemporary Prejudice: The Causes, Consequences and Challenges of Aversive Racism," in Paula S. Rothenberg, *Race, Gender and Class in the United States*, 6th edition (New York: W. H. Freeman, 2003), 137. This work overlaps with mine and supports my general contention regarding the importance of unconscious processes in enacting and sustain race/gender domination. However, the "implicit bias" and "aversive racism" research tends to focus more on unconscious cognitive structures and attitudes while I investigate unconscious fantasy. Also much of this work tends to separate race and gender while I try to understand their interweaving.

22. Thinking of subjectivity as fabricated entails understanding it as the enactment and effect of complex, historically variable, and heterogeneous practices and power relations. I discuss this approach in more detail in chapter two and return to it in chapter five.

23. For a strong argument that supports the claim that inequalities are social, not natural, see Leslie A. Jacobs, *Pursuing Equal Opportunities: The Theory and Practice of Egalitarian Justice* (New York: Cambridge University Press, 2004), especially 53–79. Jacobs develops an interesting approach to affirmative action based on this premise and defends the claim that affirmative action policies can foster, not undermine justice.

24. Loury, *The Anatomy of Racial Inequality*, 5.

25. But see Elizabeth Abel, Barbara Christian, and Helene Moglen, eds., *Female Subjects in Black and White* (Berkeley: University of California Press, 1997), especially Hortense J. Spillers, "'All the Things You Could Be by Now, If Sigmund Freud's Wife Was Your Mother': Psychoanalysis and Race," in *Female Subjects in Black and White: Race, Psychoanalysis, Feminism*, ed. Elizabeth Abel, Barbara Christian, Helene Moglen (Berkeley: University of California Press, 1997), 135–158; Elisabeth Young-Bruehl, *The Anatomy of Prejudices* (Cambridge, MA: Harvard University Press, 1996); Anne Anlin Cheng, *The Melancholy of Race* (New York: Oxford University Press, 2001) Frantz Fanon, *Black Skin, White Masks: The Experiences of a Black Man in a White World* (New York: Grove, 1967); Joel Kovel, *White Racism: A Psychohistory* (New York: Columbia University Press, 1984); Charles, R. Lawrence III, "The Id, the Ego, and Equal Protection: Reckoning with Unconscious Racism" *Stanford Law Review* (vol.39, Jan. 1987): 317–388. Kimberlyn Leary, "Race in Psychoanalytic Space," in *Gender in Psychoanalytic Space: Between Clinic and Culture*, ed. Muriel Dimen

and Virginia Goldner, 313–329 (New York: Other Press, 2002); Amina Mama, *Beyond the Masks: Race, Gender and Subjectivity* (New York: Routledge, 1995); David Marriot, "Bonding Over Phobia," in *The Psychoanalysis of Race*, ed. Christopher Lane (New York: Columbia University Press, 1998); Kalpana Seshadri-Crooks, *Desiring Whiteness: A Lacanian Analysis of Race* (New York: Routledge, 2000); Shepherdson, Charles, "Human Diversity and the Sexual Relation," in *The Psychoanalysis of Race*, ed. Christopher Lane; Claudia Tate, *Psychoanalysis and Black Novels: Desire and the Protocols of Race* (New York: Oxford, 1998); Jean Walton, *Fair Sex, Savage Dreams: Race, Psychoanalysis, Sexual Difference* (Durham, NC: Duke University Press, 2001); Eugene Victor Wolfenstein, *Victims of Democracy: Malcom X and the Black Revolution* (New York: Guilford Press, 1993); and Eugene Victor Wolfenstein, *A Gift of the Spirit: Reading the Souls of Black Folk* (Ithaca, NY: Cornell University Press, 2007).

26. Celia Brickman, *Aboriginal Populations in the Mind: Race and Primitivity in Psychoanalysis* (New York: Columbia University Press, 2003).

27. Elizabeth Abel, Barbara Christian, and Helene Moglen, "The Dream of a Common Language," in Elizabeth Abel, Barbara Christian, and Helene Moglen, eds., *Female Subjects in Black and White* (Berkeley: University of California Press, 1997), 1–18. On this point, see also Claudia Tate, *Psychoanalysis and Black Novels: Desire and the Protocols of Race* (New York: Oxford, 1998), especially 3–21.

28. Spillers, "All the Things You Could Be," 135–158. Judith Butler, in *Antigone's Claim: Kinship Between Life and Death* (New York: Columbia University Press, 2000), provides an exceptionally useful assessment of Jacques Lacan's work and its limits.

29. Anne Anlin Cheng, *The Melancholy of Race* (New York: Oxford University Press, 2001).

30. Sigmund Freud (1937), "Analysis Terminable and Interminable," in *Sigmund Freud: Collected Papers v. 5*, ed. James Strachey (New York: Basic Books, 1959), 356–357.

31. Sigmund Freud (1905), *Three Essays on The Theory of Sexuality*. In *The Penguin Freud Library v. 7*, ed. Angela Richards (London: Penguin, 1977), 33–169. On this point, see also, Jane Flax, "The Scandal of Desire: Psychoanalysis and the Disruptions of Gender: A Meditation on Freud's *Three Essays on the Theory of Sexuality*," *Contemporary Psychoanalys* 40, 1(January 2004):47–68.

32. Eldridge Cleaver, *Soul on Ice* (New York: Delta, 1969), part 4.

33. Judith Butler, *Antigone's Claim*. She might also have pointed out that until the Supreme Court ruling, *Loving vs. Virginia* (1967), interracial kinship (marriage) was subject to the Law's taboo as well.

34. Ibid., 20.

35. Cheng, *The Melancholy of Race*, 28.

36. Ibid., 220.
37. Eduardo Bonilla-Silva, Eduardo, *Racism without Racists: Color-Blind Racism and the Persistence of Racial Inequality in the United States* (Lanham, MD: Rowman and Littlefield, 2006), 7.
38. In *The Politics of Disgust*, Ange-Marie Hancock makes a parallel argument. Her notion of "public identity" captures phenomena that are simultaneously systemic, individual, fantasy and emotionally charged. She shows how a discursive construct, "the welfare queen," builds on long held beliefs and fantasies about black women. Hancock then details how, despite the fact that the majority of welfare recipients are not black women, a politics of disgust, generated in part by these fantasies, helps to shape current welfare policies. Shoshana Felman, in *The Juridical Unconscious: Trials and Traumas in the Twentieth Century* (Cambridge, MA: Harvard University Press, 2002) also explores this third dimension. She analyzes how inexpressible memories of the dead and historical trauma operate as unconscious forces in legal proceedings such as the Eichmann trial, rendering such trials necessary but also "necessary failures" (165–166).
39. I discuss social constructionist views of subjectivity in chapter five, below.
40. On the importance of collective emotional and other unconscious structures in contemporary politics, see Drew Weston, *The Political Brain: The Role of Emotion in Deciding the Fate of the Nation* (New York: Public Affairs, 2007). See also Cynthia Burack, *The Problem of the Passions: Feminism, Psychoanalysis and Social Theory* (New York: New York University Press, 1994) and Franz Fanon, *The Wretched of the Earth* (New York: Grove, 1966) for particular acute accounts of emotions' effects in politics.
41. D. W. Winnicott, *Playing and Reality* (New York. Basic Books, 1971).
42. Examples of race/gender analysis using Winnicott's "transitional space" include Muriel Dimen, "Deconstructing Difference: Gender, Splitting, and Transitional Space." In *Gender in Psychoanalytic Space: Between Clinic and Culture*, ed. Muriel Dimen and Virginia Goldner, 41–61 (New York: Other Press, 2002); Jane Flax, "Resisting Woman: On Feminine Difference in the Work of Horney, Thompson, and Moulton." *Contemporary Psychoanalysis* 38, 2 (2002): 257–276; and Leary, "Race in Psychoanalytic Space."
43. Cheng, *The Melancholy of Race*; Morrison, *Playing in the Dark*; Slavoj Zizek, "Fantasy as a Political Category: A Lacanian Approach." In *The Zizek Reader*, ed. Elizabeth Wright and Edmond Wright (Cambridge, MA: Blackwell); and Slavoj Zizek, "Enjoy Your Nation as Yourself." In *Theories of Race and Racism: A Reader*, ed. Les Back and John Solomos, 594–606 (New York: Routledge, 2000).
44. In Morrison, *Playing in the Dark*, especially 3–18.
45. Sigmund Freud (1917), "Mourning and Melancholia."

46. Fanon, *Black Skin/White Masks*, Loury, *Anatomy of Racial Inequality*, 161–162; Winant, *The World Is a Ghetto*, 16.

47. Franz Fanon, *Black Skin/White Masks*, 190. Fanon's analysis of how the political unconscious is enacted by both the colonizers and colonized remains unmatched in their insight and attention to detail.

48. Davis, *Inhuman Bondage*, 52–56; Patterson, *Rituals of Blood*, 210–215.

49. Cheng, *The Melancholy of Race*, 72.

50. See Saidiya Hartman, *Lose Your Mother: A Journey Along the Atlantic Slave Trade* (New York: Farrar, Straus and Giroux, 2007), particularly Chapter 8 for an especially poignant discussion of this form of melancholia.

51. Orlando Patterson, *Slavery and Social Death* (Cambridge, MA: Harvard University Press, 1982).

52. Davis, *Inhuman Bondage*, 3.

53. Patterson, *Slavery and Social Death*, 13.

54. For an insightful treatment of the relatedness of mirroring, see G. W. F. Hegel, *The Phenomenology of Spirit* (New York: Harper and Row, 1967), 229–240, where he delineates some dynamics of master/slave relationships. See also Paul Gilroy's reworking of Hegel's discussion of lordship and bondage in his *The Black Atlantic: Modernity and Double Consciousness* (Cambridge, MA: Harvard University Press, 1993), Chapter two.

55. Patterson, *Slavery and Social Death*, 5.

56. Ibid., 7.

57. Ibid., 94.

58. Ibid., 10.

59. Ibid., 81–89.

60. Ibid., 78.

61. But see Patterson, *Rituals of Blood*, 44–53.

62. Patterson, *Slavery and Social Death*, 95.

63. See for example, Angela Y. Davis, *Women, Race, and Class* (New York: Random House, 1981), especially Chapter one; Paula Giddings, *When and Where I Enter: The Impact of Black Women on Race and Sex in America* (New York: Bantam, 1984), especially Chapter two; Darlene Clark Hine and Kathleen Thompson, *A Shining Thread of Hope: The History of Black Women in America* (New York: Broadway Books, 1998), especially Chapter three; Jacqueline Jones, *Labor of Love, Labor of Sorrow: Black Women, Work and the Family, from Slavery to the Present* (New York: Vintage, 1986); Toni Morrison, *Beloved* (New York: Signet, 1987); and Julia S. Jordan-Zachery, *Black Women, Cultural Images, and Social Policy* (New York: Routledge, 2009), especially Chapter two.

64. Matthew Frye Jacobson, *Whiteness of a Different Color: European Immigrants and the Alchemy of Race* (Cambridge, MA: Harvard University Press, 1998), 3.

65. On the persistence of these constructs and the damage to black women caused by them and slavery more generally, see Regina Austin, "Sapphire Bound!," in Adrien Katherine Wing, ed., *Critical Race Feminism: A Reader* (New York: New York University Press, 1997); 289–296; Hazel V. Carby, *Reconstructing Womanhood: The Emergence of the Afro-American Woman Novelist* (New York: Oxford University Press, 1987); Patricia Hill Collins, *Black Sexual Politics: African Americans, Gender, and the New Racism* (New York: Routledge, 2004), especially Chapter two; Kimberle Crenshaw, "Whose Story Is It Anyway? Feminist and Antiracist Appropriations of Anita Hill," in Toni Morrison, ed. *Race-ing Justice, En-gendering Power: Essays on Anita Hill, Clarence Thomas, and the Construction of Social Reality* (New York: Pantheon, 1992), 402–440; Paula Giddings, "The Last Taboo," in Morrison, *Race-ing Justice, En-gendering Power*, 441–465; Ange-Marie Hancock, *The Politics of Disgust*, especially Chapter two; and Wahneema Lubiano, "Black Ladies, Welfare Queens, and State Minstrels: Ideological War by Narrative Means," in Morrison, *Race-ing Justice, En-gendering Power*, 323–362; Patricia Williams, *The Alchemy of Race and Rights: Diary of a Law Professor* (Cambridge, MA: Harvard University Press, 1991), Chapter twelve. Patricia Hill Collins also discusses the contemporary extensions of these constructs into new ones, including the "bitch." The bitch is "confrontational and actively aggressive." (123) I think this is one of the constructs assigned to Michelle Obama, especially early in the presidential campaign, and she has tried to combat it by using an equally historically charged one–the lady. The lady, as Carby points out was an appropriation of the good white mother/wife construct, recommended by the founders of post-civil war black women's clubs as one means to "uplift" the race.
66. Patterson, *Slavery and Social Death*, 36.
67. Ibid., 94.

CHAPTER 2

1. Julia S. Jordan Zackery, *Black Women, Cultural Images and Social Policy* (New York: Routledge, 2009), 26.
2. Evelyn Nakano Glenn, *Unequal Freedom: How Race and Gender Shaped American Citizenship and Labor* (Cambridge, MA: Harvard University Press, 2002), 12.
3. There are several other intertwining social relations that are mostly absent in my analysis. Especially important are class and sexuality. This absence is not due to any devaluation of their importance. As I discuss later in this chapter, I think access to social goods and the power to control their production and distribution are critical, both in the fabrication of race/gender and as its effects. However, I have never

been able to develop a satisfactory understanding of the meanings of class in the American context. Classic Marxist approaches, the discursive formations in which the term originated and most easily operates, evolved in and reflect the experiences of white/male European workers. Theorists have long struggled to adopt these constructs to race/gendered divisions of labor. Furthermore, in the United States, due to slavery, race/gender is so interwoven with the social construction of class as to render its enactments, permutations and effects unique. This interweaving persists into the present, as could be seen, for example, in the 2008 presidential campaign. Those positioned as white working class men were among the most resistant to Barack Obama's candidacy. Throughout this book, I try to be sensitive to the effects of differential access to social goods and economic power, but I am acutely aware that the absence of a systematic reworking of and attention to class renders my analysis inadequate and incomplete. Similarly, I do not pay sufficient attention to the effects of normative heterosexuality and how this too intertwines with race/gender. However, I recognize that it remains critical to analyze how race/ gender, class and sexuality intertwine to generate and sustain various forms of domination. I do not think it is possible to generate a grand unified theory that would specify how these social relationships and processes work in all situations. Their meanings and enactments will be context specific. In the contemporary United States, for example, they underwrite what Charles Mills calls the racial contract and Carole Pateman calls the sexual contract. Since the implicit terms of the contract presume a shared white/masculine interest in possessing women and controlling both their and black men's sexuality, homosexuality poses many threats to it and the dominant subjects it authorizes. For example, dominant subjects might fear homosexual men are unreliable allies because they feel less interest in the distribution of women, and the possibility of dominant subjects perceiving black men as objects of desire rather than objects to control is potentially disruptive of regulatory race/gender norms. Within the race/gender contract, any construal of black or white women's desire other than as objects of masculine pleasure and control is transgressive. However, there are undoubtedly more or less adequate analyses of specific contexts. A far from exhaustive list of authors who do a better job of thinking about race/gender and class include Angela Y. Davis, *Women, Race, and Class* (New York: Random House, 1981); Glenn, *Unequal Freedom*; Ange-Marie Hancock, *The Politics of Disgust: The Public Identity of the Welfare Queen* (New York: New York University Press, 2004); Evelyn Brooks Higginbotham, "African-American Women's History and the Metalanguage of Race," *Signs: Journal of Women in Culture and Society* 17, 2 (Winter 1992): 251–274; bell hooks, *Yearning: Race, Gender, and Cultural Politics* (Boston: South End Press, 1990); Deborah K. King, "Multiple Jeopardy, Multiple Consciousness: The Context of a

Black Feminist Ideology," *Signs: Journal of Women and Culture* 14, 1 (1988): 42–72; Cornel West, *Race Matters* (Boston: Beacon Press, 1993), especially 83–91; and Julia S. Jordan- Zackery, *Black Women, Cultural Images and Social Policy.* A partial list of important contributions to conceptualizing contemporary race/gender enactments would also include Kimberle Williams Crenshaw, "Mapping the Margins: Intersectionality, Identity Politics, and Violence Against Women," in Kimberle Crenshaw, Neil Gotanda, Gary Peller, and Kendall Thomas, eds., *Critical Race Theory: The Key Writings that Formed the Movement* (New York: The New Press, 1995), 357–383; Ann duCille, "The Occult of True Black Womanhood: Critical Demeanor and Black Feminist Studies." *Signs: Journal of Women in Culture and Society* 19,3 (Fall 1994): 591–629; Jane Flax, "Race/Gender and the Ethics of Difference," *Political Theory* 23, 3 (August 1995): 500–510; Ruth Frankenberg, *White Women, Race Matters: White Women and the Construction of Whiteness* (Minneapolis: University of Minnesota Press, 1993); Ange-Marie Hancock, "When Multiplication Doesn't Equal Quick Addition: Examining Intersectionality as a Research Paradigm," *Perspectives on Politics* 5, 1 (March 2007): 63–79; Angela Harris, "Race and Essentialism in Feminist Legal Theory," in Richard Delgado and Jean Stefancic, eds., *Critical Race Theory: The Cutting Edge*, 2nd ed. (Philadelphia: Temple University Press, 2000): 261–274; Mary Hawkesworth, "Congressional Enactments of Race-Gender: Toward a Theory of Raced-Gendered Institutions," *American Political Science Review* 97, 4 (November 2003): 529–550; Maria Lugones, *Pilgrimages/Peregrinajes: Theorizing Coalition Against Multiple Oppressions* (Lanham, MD: Rowman and Littlefield, 2003); Elizabeth V. Spelman, *Inessential Woman: Problems of Exclusion in Feminist Thought* (Boston: Beacon Press, 1988); and Naomi Zack, ed., *Race/Sex: Their Sameness, Difference and Interplay* (New York: Routledge, 1997). Important sources on sexuality include Patricia Hill Collins, *Black Sexual Politics: African Americans, Gender, and the New Racism* (New York: Routledge, 2004); John C. Fout and Maura Shaw Tantillo, *American Sexual Politics: Sex, Gender, and Race since the Civil War* (Chicago: University of Chicago Press, 1993); Catherine A. Holland, The Body Politic: Foundings, Citizen, and Difference in the American Political Imagination (New York: Routledge, 2001); and Orlando Patterson, *Rituals of Blood: Consequences of Slavery in Two American Centuries* (New York: Basic, 1998). On race/gender contracts in the founding of modern liberal states, see Carole Pateman and Charles Mills, *Contract and Domination* (Malden, MA: Polity Press, 2007).

4. Lugones, *Pilgrimages/Peregrinajes*, 146. For an insightful example of working with this interwoven approach, see Ellen K. Feder, *Family Bonds: Genealogies of Race and Gender* (New York: Oxford University Press, 2007). Feder suggests ways to improve its practice

by highlighting its difficulties and explaining why interwoven analysis often fails. While I find her analysis very helpful, I am not convinced by her contention that gender and race are primarily, though not exclusively, functions of different kinds of power. Using Foucault's work, she argues that gender is a function of disciplinary power while biopower is the most important producer of race. In chapter five, below, I develop my own appropriation of Foucault.

5. For excellent recent examples of this approach, see Glenn, *Unequal Freedom*; Hancock, *The Politics of Disgust*; Hawkesworth, "Congressional Enactments of Race-Gender: Toward a Theory of Raced-Gendered Institutions"; and Jordan- Zackery, *Black Women, Cultural Images and Social Policy*. On how and why to do it, see Ange-Marie Hancock, "Intersectionality as a Normative and Empirical Paradigm," *Politics and Gender* 3, 2 (June 2007): 248–263; Evelyn M. Simien, "Doing Intersectionality Research: From Conceptual Issues to Practical Examples," *Politics and Gender* 3, 2 (June 2007): 264–271; and Julia S. Jordan-Zachery, "Am I a Black Woman or a Woman Who Is Black?: A Few Thoughts on the Meaning of Intersectionality," *Politics and Gender* 3, 2 (June 2007): 254–263.

6. There is often more resistance to seeing the gendered aspects of race/gender as social artifacts than raced ones. The causal link between genitals, sexual difference, and gender seems inevitable and unquestionable. However, as is often the case, anomalies within an apparently inevitable system reveal its contingency. In regard to gendering aspects, these anomalies include cases in which people's behavior does not coincide with the social norms associated with their genitalia and ones in which children are born with "ambiguous" genitals, that is ones that do not conform to social norms. The anxieties these anomalies arouse in other subjects and their often forceful attempts to normalize the anomalies through radical interventions (behavioral or surgical) suggest that unconsciously we recognize the instability of supposedly natural facts. On this point, see Feder, *Family Bonds*, 45–68 and Judith Butler, *Bodies that Matter: On the Discursive Limits of "Sex"* (New York: Routledge, 1993), 94–119. Another interesting case is when subjects feel that they are in the "wrong" body, that is, that their felt sense of gender does not correspond to their genitals. They may attempt to remedy this misfit through a range of behaviors, including cross dressing and "sex change" procedures. An interesting account of such felt misfit is Jennifer Finney Boylan, *She's Not There: A Life in Two Genders* (New York: Broadway Books, 2003). Despite her complex introspection, there is a complete absence of conscious awareness on Boylan's part of how deeply raced her felt notions of gender (male and female) are and how her location as white and relatively well off shapes her felt gender identity. Her race/gender positions intensify her pain at misfit and provide some protection from social sanctions and resources to alter her situation. Practices of "sex selection,"

including abortion, killing of baby girls, or in vitro procedures are another way gender is made. The current race/gender asymmetries inform these practices, since the devaluation of those marked female is enacted in the marked preference for male children. Currently, in China with its "one child" policy, the result is a birth ratio of 120 males for every 100 females.

7. Glenn, *Unequal Freedom*, 12.

8. Ibid., 12–13.

9. Graham Burchell, Colin Gordon, and Peter Miller, eds. *The Foucault Effect: Studies in Governmentality* (Chicago: University of Chicago Press, 1991); Michel Foucault, *The History of Sexuality, v.1* (New York: Pantheon, 1980); Michel Foucault (1994a) *Ethics, Subjectivity and Truth*, ed. Paul Rabinow (New York: The New Press, 1994), especially 225–252; Michel Foucault, *Power*, ed. James D. Paubion (New York: The New Press, 1994), especially 201–224; Michel Foucault, "*Society Must Be Defended,*" *Lectures at the Collège de France, 1975–1976* (New York: Picador, 2003), especially 60–84. Important (and more gender sensitive) applications of Foucault's approach to the American context include Barbara Cruikshank, *The Will to Empower: Democratic Citizens and Other Subjects* (Ithaca, NY: Cornell University Press, 1999) and Feder, *Family Bonds*. In relation to Western colonalism, see Ann Laura Stoler, *Race and The Education of Desire: Foucault's History of Sexuality and the Colonial Order of Things* (Durham, NC: Duke University Press, 1997).

10. Useful genealogies include James F. Davis, *Who Is Black?: One Nation's Definition* (University Park: Pennsylvania State University Press, 1991); Matthew Pratt Guterl, *The Color of Race in America, 1900–1940* (Cambridge, MA: Harvard University Press, 2001); Matthew Frye Jacobson, *Whiteness of a Different Color: European Immigrants and the Alchemy of Race* (Cambridge, MA: Harvard University Press, 1998); Philip A. Klinkner with Rogers M. Smith, *The Unsteady March: The Rise and Decline of Racial Equality in America* (Chicago: University of Chicago Press: 1999); Anthony W. Marx, *Making Race and Nation: A Comparison of the United States, South Africa, and Brazil* (New York: Cambridge University Press, 1998); and Dvora Yanow, *Constructing "Race" and "Ethnicity" in America: Category Making in Public Policy and Administration* (Armonk, NY: M.E. Sharpe, 2003).

11. Harris, Cheryl I, "Whiteness as Property," in Kimberle Crenshaw, Neil Gotanda, Gary Peller, and Kendall Thomas, eds., *Critical Race Theory: The Key Writings that Formed the Movement* (New York: The New Press, 1995), 276–291; and Ian F. Haney Lopez, "White by Law," in Richard Delgado, and Jean Stefancic, eds., *Critical Race Theory: The Cutting Edge*, second edition (Philadelphia: Temple University Press, 2000), 626–634.

12. Winthrop D. Jordan, *White over Black: American Attitudes to the Negro, 1650–1812* (New York: W. W. Norton, 1977).
13. Jacobson, *Whiteness of a Different Color*, 43.
14. Yanow, *Constructing "Race" and "Ethnicity" in America*, 83–85.
15. In *Who Is Black?*, James F. Davis documents this process. As was evident in the 2008 presidential election, this "one drop rule" remains the dominant race/gender grammar. Despite his white mother and two white grandparents, Barack Obama was positioned as, and had to position himself as, a black/man.
16. See Richard E. Flathman, *Freedom and Its Conditions: Discipline, Autonomy, and Resistance* (New York: Routledge, 2003) for a particular helpful analysis of this dichotomy and ways to unpack it.
17. See the extensive documentation in these works: Michael K. Brown, Martin Carnoy. Elliott Currie. Troy Duster, David B. Oppenheimer, Marjorie M. Shultz, and David Wellman, *Whitewashing Race: The Myth of a Color-Blind Society* (Berkeley: University of California Press, 2003); Ira Katznelson, *When Affirmative Action Was White: An Untold History of Racial Inequality in Twentieth Century American* (New York: W. W. Norton, 2005); Desmond King, *Separate and Unequal: African Americans and the US Federal Government*, revised edition (New York: Oxford University Press, 2007); Linda Faye Williams, *The Constraint of Race: Legacies of White Skin Privilege in America* (University Park, PA: Pennsylvannia State University Press, 2003).
18. Williams, *The Constraint of Race*, 19. It is difficult to believe that born again egalitarians who rail against affirmative action, calling it reverse discrimination or racist, are acting in good faith when, as far as I can find, they have never acknowledged this long history nor have they proposed any measures to address its ongoing harms. See for example, Abigail Thernstrom's complaint about the nomination to the Supreme Court of Sonia Sotomayor, Obama "didn't pick a post-racial candidate...She's a quintessential spokesman for racial spoils," in Peter Baker, "Court Choice Pushes Issue of 'Identity Politics' Back to Forefront," *New York Times*, May 31, 2009, A 20. Evidently a distribution system only becomes improperly skewed if it potentially provides some benefits to the disadvantaged.
19. See Ira Katznelson, *When Affirmative Action Was White;* Williams, *The Constraint of Race*, 11–24 and Desmond King, *Separate and Unequal* especially chapter 6. In *Silent Covenants: Brown v Board of Education and the Unfulfilled Hopes for Racial Reform* (New York: Oxford University Press, 2004), Derrick Bell argues that racial reform is often undertaken to stabilize existing power relations rather than to fundamentally challenge them. Such reform is often more about managing domestic tensions or winning international struggles than a deep commitment on the part of those in

dominant race/gender positions to take responsibility for and remedy the harms such dominance entails.

20. Katznelson, *When Affirmative Action Was White*, 23. Some scholars disagree with Katznelson's conclusion. See, for example, Ira Katznelson and Suzanne Mettler, "On Race and Policy History: A Dialogue about the G.I. Bill," *Perspectives on Politics* 6, 3 (September 2008): 519–537.

21. Ibid., 23.

22. In David D. Kirkpatrick, "A Judge's Focus on Race Issues May Be Hurdle," *New York Times*, May 30, 2009, A 1. Among the remarkable contradictions of such statements is the evoking of "colorblind" while simultaneously not being blind at all to the color of those meant to prove the irrelevance of color. If we were truly a colorblind society, an individual's color would be irrelevant to the narratives we posit about our system. Obama's or Sotomayor's color would not transform them into generalized bearers of social meaning. Such statements employ a classic melancholic move in which the person denies their own race consciousness while making such consciousness a shortcoming of those calling attention to race/gender dynamics.

23. Neil Gotanda, "A Critique of 'Our Constitution Is Color-Blind,'" in Delgado and Stefancic, eds., *Critical Race Theory*, 37.

24. A recent example of such reversal is Newt Gingrich's calling Judge Sotomayor a "Latina racist" for suggesting that our race/gender positioning may affect the ways we think. Gingrich is quoted in Peter Baker, "Court Choice Pushes Issue of 'Identity Politics' Back to Forefront," *New York Times*, May 31, 2009, A 20. A more disturbing example is Chief Justice Roberts opinion in a 2007 case (Parents Involved in Community Schools vs. Seattle School District No. 1) in which he equated the Seattle school district's plan to insure diversity with the segregationist policies of pre-Brown vs. Board of Education Topeka, Kansas. On Chief Justice Roberts, see Jeffrey Toobin, "No More Mr. Nice Guy: The Supreme Court's Stealth Hardliner," *New Yorker*, May 25, 2009, especially 47–48. For more extended analysis of "colorblindness," see Charles R. III Lawrence and Mari J. Matsuda, *We Won't Go Back: Making the Case for Affirmative Action* (New York: Houghton Mifflin, 1997), especially Chapter three.

25. According to the Bureau of Labor Statistics, in its *Current Population Survey*, 2009, in each period of recession since 1973, unemployment among black people has been almost or more than double that of whites. The current recession is no different; in May 2009, it was 13.3 percent for blacks and 7.9 percent for whites. Reported in Applied Research Center, "Race and Recession: How Inequity Rigged the Economy and How to Change the Rules," arc.org/recession, May 2009, 4. ARC's report details the differential effects of the recession on numerous aspects of economic life, including employment, wealth, income and

housing. See also data reported by Michelle Singletary, "The Change That Hasn't Come," *Washington Post*, November 9, 2008, F 1.

26. United States Census Bureau, "Persons Below Poverty Level, by Selected Characteristics," http://www.allcountries.org/uscensus/ 757_persons_below_poverty_level_by_selected.html; and United States Census Bureau, "Money Income of Families – Number and Distribution by Race and Hispanic Origin," http://www.census. gov/compendia/statab/2010/tables/10s0679.pdf

27. Amy Joyce, "Her No. 1 Problem," *Washington Post*, Sunday, August 6, 2006, F 1.

28. Karen Donovan, "Pushed by Clients, Law Firms Step Up Diversity Efforts," *New York Times*, Friday, July 21, 2006, C 6.

29. Association of American Medical Colleges, "FACTS: Applicants, Matriculants, Graduates, and Residency Applicants – AAMC," http://www.aamc.org/data/facts/2008/gradraceeth0208.htm

30. United States Census Bureau, "Net Worth and Asset Ownership of Households, 1998 and 2000: Household Economic Studies," *http:// www.census.gov/prod/2003pubs/p70–88.pdf,* May 2003, 12.

31. Ibid., 2.

32. Anna Bernasek, "Income Inequality, and Its Costs," *New York Times*, Sunday, June 25, 2006, Business Section, 4.

33. Federal Reserve Board, Survey of Consumer Finances, *Federal Reserve Bulletin* (February 2009). http://www.federalreserve.gov/ PUBS/oss/oss2/2007/2007%20SCF%20Chartbook.pdf, 53.

34. Source: U.S. Census Bureau, Current Population Reports, P60–233; and Internet sites <http://www.census.gov/prod/2007pubs/p60– 233.pdf> (released August 2007) and <*http://www.census.gov/hhes/ www/poverty/histpov/perindex.html*> Table 689.

35. Ibid., Table 289.

36. Pew Center on the States, "One in 100: Behind Bars in America 2008," *www.pewtrusts.org,* 5.

37. United States Department of Justice, Bureau of Justice Statistics, *http://www.ojp.usdoj.gov/bjs/glance.htm#Corrections,* June 2008.

38. Center for Disease Statistics, *Health, United States, 2008. http://www. cdc.gov/nchs/data/nvsr/nvsr57/nvsr57_14.pdf,* 11.

39. Michelle Singletary, "The Change That Hasn't Come," *Washington Post*, November 9, 2008, F 1. Other important health related dispar-ities include higher rates of disease, including HIV/AIDS, cancer, diabetes, and obesity; less access to health care providers and to pre-ventative care practices including screening for breast cancer and less aggressive treatment when disease is diagnosed. See, Michael Halle, Caye B. Lewis, and Meena Sheshamani, "Healthcare Disparities: A Case for Closing the Gap," June 2009, www. Healthreform.Gov.

40. David R. Hekman, quoted in Nicholas Bakalar, "Vital Signs: A Customer Bias in Favor of White Men," *New York Times*, Tuesday, June 23, 2009, D6. This article reports on the results of several

recent studies investigating implicit race/gender bias. See also similar findings reported by John F. Dovidio and Samuel Gaertner, "On the Nature of Contemporary Prejudice: The Causes, Consequences and Challenges of Aversive Racism," in Paula S. Rothenberg, *Race, Gender and Class in the United States,* 6th edition (New York: W. H. Freeman, 2003): 132–141; and Justin L. Levinson, "Forgotten Racial Equality Implicit Bias, Decisionmaking, and Misremembering," *Duke Law Journal* 57 (2007): 344–421.

41. Steven A. Homes and Richard Morin, "Being a Black Man," *Washington Post,* Sunday, June 4, 2006, A 1.

42. Researchers associated with Project Implicit, https://implicit. harvard.edu/implicit/, report consistently finding negative associations with black people, among both black and white subjects. These associations are usually outside people's conscious awareness and often contradict their consciously felt feelings and beliefs. See also the experiments reported by Justin D, Levinson, in "Forgotten Racial Equality Implicit Bias, Decisionmaking, and Misremembering," *Duke Law Journal* 57 (2007): 344–421.

43. On the concept of microaggression, see Peggy G. Davis, "Law as Microagression," in Richard Delgado and Jean Stefancic, eds., *Critical Race Theory: The Cutting Edge,* second edition (Philadelphia: Temple University Press, 2000), 141–151.

44. This race/gendered sense of entitlement shapes views of public policy as well. As Linda Gordon and Nancy Fraser point out, social distributions of goods that favored whites such as the GI bill or social security are considered matters of equity while those that are perceived as disproportionately favoring blacks (often inaccurately) are termed "welfare." Unlike favored distributive policies welfare supposedly induces an unhealthy "dependency" that is destructive to its recipients and the larger culture. See Nancy Fraser and Linda Gordon, "The Genealogy of *Dependency," Signs* 19, 3 (1994): 309–336; and also Hancock,*The Politics of Disgust*; and Jordan-Zackery, *Black Women, Cultural Images and Social Policy.*

45. Virginia Woolf, *A Room of One's Own* (Middlesex, UK: Penguin, 1970), 37–38.

46. Williams, *The Constraints of Race,* 11–12.

47. As Danielle S. Allen, *Talking to Strangers: Anxieties of Citizenship since Brown v. Board of Education* (Chicago: University of Chicago Press, 2004) argues with particular eloquence and force. I will rely heavily on Allen's work throughout this book.

48. See Paul Gilroy, *Against Race: Imagining Political Culture Beyond the Color Line* (Cambridge, MA: Harvard University Press, 2000) for a particularly strong argument on this point.

49. The essays in Charles R. III Lawrence and Mari J. Matsuda, *We Won't Go Back: Making the Case for Affirmative Action* (New York: Houghton Mifflin, 1997) offer persuasive arguments for this claim.

50. I think these subjective investments partially generate and account for the furor around Justice Sotomayor's statement that, "I would hope that a wise Latina woman with the richness of her experiences would more often than not reach a better conclusion than a white male who hasn't lived that life." Quoted in Peter Baker, "Court Choice Pushes Issue of 'Identity Politics' Back to Forefront," *New York Times*, May 31, 2009, A 20. In the context of our dominant race/gender grids, Sotomayor's statement is transgressive, because she suggests: 1. that all subjects, not just subordinate ones, are marked by race/gender; 2. dominant race/gender positions can constrain one's knowledge; such constraints are not unique to subordinate subjects 3. subordinate subjects may have experiences that increase wisdom, not only restrict or undermine it. In our dominant narratives, phrases such as "wise Latina" and "richness of her experiences" are almost oxymoronic.

51. See, for example, Shlomo Avineri and Avner de-Shalit, eds., *Communitarianism and Individualism* (New York: Oxford University Press, 1992); Robert N. Bellah, Richard Madsen, William M. Sullivan, Ann Swidler, and Steven M. Tipton, *Habits of the Heart* (New York: Harper and Row, 1996). Michael Sandel, *Liberalism and the Limits of Justice* (Cambridge, MA: Harvard University Press, 1982).

52. David Theo Goldberg, "The Social Formation of Racist Discourse," in David Theo Goldberg, ed., *Anatomy of Racism* (Minneapolis: University of Minnesota Press, 1990), 311.

53. Such dynamics are a central theme in James Baldwin, *The Price of the Ticket* (New York: St. Martins, 1985) and Ralph Ellison, *The Collected Essays of Ralph Ellison* (New York: Modern Library, 1995).

54. Ronald W. Fairbairn, "Schizoid Factors in the Personality." In W. Ronald D. Fairbairn, *Psychoanalytic Studies of the Personality* (London: Routledge, 1992), 3–27.

55. Dawson, Michael C., *Black Visions: The Roots of Contemporary African-American Ideologies* (Chicago: University of Chicago Press, 2001), 58–59.

CHAPTER 3

1. Francine du Plessix Gray, *Them: A Memoir of Parents* (New York: Penguin, 2005), 364.

2. Jean Walton, "Re-Placing Race in (White) Psychoanalytic Discourse: Founding Narratives of Feminism." In *Female Subjects in Black and White: Race, Psychoanalysis, Feminism*, ed. Elizabeth Abel, Barbara Christian, Helene Moglen (Berkeley: University of California Press, 1997), 146.

3. United States Department of Justice, Bureau of Justice Statistics, "Criminal Offenders Statistics," *http://www.ojp.usdoj.gov/bjs/crimoff.htm*, August 2007.

4. Pew Center on the States, "One in 100: Behind Bars in America 2008," www.pewtrusts.org, 5.
5. On the centrality of protector in contemporary constructions of masculinity, see Iris Marion Young "The Logic of Masculinist Protection: Reflections on the Current Security State." *Signs: Journal of Women in Culture and Society* 29, 1 (2003): 3–6.
6. Orlando Patterson, *Rituals of Blood: Consequences of Slavery in Two American Centuries* (New York: Basic, 1998), 136.
7. Ibid., 136–137. For a race/gender sensitive and complex analysis of problems of violence within black communities, see Johnnetta Betsch Cole and Beverly Guy-Sheftall, *Gender Talk: The Struggle for Women's Equality in African American Communities* (New York: Random House, 2003), especially 128–153.
8. Data taken from United States Census Bureau, "Marriage and Divorce," *http://www.census.gov/population/www/socdemo/marr-div.html* (August 2007).
9. My analysis of these issues is deeply indebted to many years of conversation with my students at Howard University. I have also found recent published accounts of the struggles negotiating and resisting these dominant narratives of black/male and black/female entail helpful. These include Kevin Powell, *Who's Gonna Take The Weight?: Manhood, Race, and Power in America* (New York: Three Rivers Press, 2003); Cole and Guy-Sheftall, *Gender Talk*; Lonnae O'Neal Parker, *I'm Every Woman: Remixed Stories of Marriage, Motherhood, and Work* (New York; Amistad, 2005); and Tricia Rose, *Longing to Tell: Black Women Talk about Sexuality and Intimacy* (New York: Picador, 2003).
10. Sam Dillon and David M Herszenhorn, contributing, "Schools' Efforts Hinge on Justices' Ruling in Cases on Race and School Assignments," *New York Times*, Saturday, June 24, 2006, A 11.
11. Yaneer Bar-Yam, M. Klau, W. Li, J. Siow, I. Wokoma, and J. Wells, *White Flight* (New England Complex Systems Institute. MIT: 2003); Gary Orfield and Susan Eaton, *Dismantling Desegregation: The Quiet Reversal of Brown v. Board of Education* (New York: The New Press, 1996); and William Julius Wilson and Richard P. Taub, *There Goes the Neighborhood: Racial, Ethnic, and Class Tensions in Four Chicago Neighborhoods and Their Meaning for America* (New York: Alfred A. Knopf, 2006).
12. Douglas Massey and Nancy Denton, *American Apartheid: Segregation and the Making of the Underclass* (Cambridge, MA: Harvard University Press, 1993).
13. Danielle S. Allen, *Talking to Strangers: Anxieties of Citizenship since Brown v. Board of Education* (Chicago: University of Chicago Press, 2004), 164.
14. Erica Frankenberg, Chungmei Lee, and Gary Orfield, "A Multiracial Society with Segregated Schools: Are We Losing the Dream?" The Civil Rights Project, Harvard University Press, 2003.

15. David Brion Davis, *Inhuman Bondage: The Rise and Fall of Slavery in the New World* (New York: Oxford University Press, 2006), 101; see also Hazel V. Carby, Hazel V., *Reconstructing Womanhood: The Emergence of the Afro-American Woman Novelist* (New York: Oxford University Press, 1987), especially chapters one and two. On contemporary effects of this history on African American men and women and their relationships, see Cole and Guy-Sheftall, *Gender Talk*; Patricia Hill Collins, *Black Sexual Politics: African Americans, Gender, and the New Racism* (New York: Routledge, 2004); hooks, bell, *Yearning: Race, Gender, and Cultural Politics* (Boston: South End Press, 1990), 203–214; and Orlando Patterson, *Rituals of Blood: Consequences of Slavery in Two American Centuries* (New York: Basic, 1998).

16. Some of these difficulties are conveyed strongly in Ellis Cose, *The Rage of a Privileged Class* (New York: HarperCollins, 1993).

17. United States Department of Justice, Bureau of Justice Statistics, "Homicide Trends," *http://www.ojp.usdoj.gov/bjs/homicide/race.htm*, July 2007.

18. United States Department of Justice, Bureau of Justice Statistics, "Crime and Victim Statistics," *http://www.ojp.usdoj.gov/bjs/cvict.htm*, August 2008.

19. Davis, *Inhuman Bondage*, 177; Nancy Fraser and Linda Gordon, "The Genealogy of Dependence," *Signs* 19, 3 (1994): 309–336; and Ira Katznelson, *When Affirmative Action Was White: An Untold History of Racial Inequality in Twentieth Century American* (New York: W. W. Norton, 2005).

CHAPTER 4

1. Orlando Patterson, *Slavery and Social Death* (Cambridge, MA: Harvard University Press, 1982), vii–ix.

2. Evelyn Nakano Glenn, *Unequal Freedom: How Race and Gender Shaped American Citizenship and Labor* (Cambridge, MA: Harvard University Press, 2002), 263.

3. This blindness is operating, for example, in Rawls's repeated insistence that simply living under a just basic structure is sufficient to shape the "character and interests" of citizens so that they will "resist the normal tendencies to injustice." John Rawls, *Justice as Fairness: A Restatement* (Cambridge, MA: Harvard University Press, 2001), 185; on this point see also John Rawls, *A Theory of Justice* (Cambridge, MA: Harvard University Press, 1971), 534–540. It should be evident, but nonetheless to avoid misunderstanding, I will state that I am discussing the operations of the political unconscious, a set of fantasies and processes that I posit are widely shared among contemporary American subjects. The political unconscious is an interweaving of

culturally available material, power networks, and affects and processes that occur outside conscious awareness, such as projection and splitting. I am interested in these systemic phenomena. Nothing I say here addresses John Rawls's particular, idiosyncratic unconscious material nor am I concerned with how he practiced his specific subjectivity. I have no interest in speculating on such matters, nor do I think it would be appropriate. As a practicing psychotherapist, I am fully aware of how difficult it is to acquire any understanding of the idiosyncratic aspects of a subject's unconscious processes and narratives, and I would never presume to have anything to say about someone who has never been in therapy with me.

4. Patterson, *Slavery and Social Death*, ix.
5. On this point, see Catherine A. Holland, *The Body Politic: Foundings, Citizen, and Difference in the American Political Imagination* (New York: Routledge, 2001); Matthew Frye Jacobson, *Whiteness of a Different Color: European Immigrants and the Alchemy of Race* (Cambridge, MA: Harvard University Press, 1998); and Judith N. Skhlar, *American Citizenship: The Quest for Inclusion* (Cambridge, MA: Harvard University Press, 1991).
6. For a particularly eloquent defense of such investments, see Patricia J. Williams *The Alchemy of Race and Rights: Diary of a Law Professor* (Cambridge, MA: Harvard University Press, 1991).
7. Toni Morrison, *Playing in the Dark: Whiteness and the Literary Imagination* (New York: Vintage, 1992), 38.
8. Jacobson, *Whiteness of a Different Color*, 25.
9. David Brion Davis, *Inhuman Bondage: The Rise and Fall of Slavery in the New World* (New York: Oxford University Press, 2006), 377.
10. Carole Pateman, *The Sexual Contract* (Stanford: Stanford University Press, 1988). For refinement and discussion of her original argument, see Carole Pateman and Charles Mills, *Contract and Domination* (Malden, MA: Polity Press, 2007).
11. Holland, *The Body Politic: Foundings*; and Charles W. Mills, *The Racial Contract* (Ithaca, NY: Cornell University Press, 1997).
12. Holland, *The Body Politic: Foundings*, 99.
13. Ibid., 99. This history also shows why statements like, "our constitution is color blind" reveal more about our political unconscious and its wishes than they accurately portray the text. It is illuminating that those who advocate a literal, originalist, or minimalist approach to judicial decision making edit out these threads from their narratives of the founders' intent.
14. John Locke, *Two Treatises of Government* (New York: Cambridge University Press, 1965), especially chapter 5.
15. C. B. Macpherson, *The Political Theory of Possessive Individualism: Hobbes to Locke* (New York: Oxford University Press, 1962).
16. Morrison, *Playing in the Dark*, 38

17. Derrick Bell, *And We Are Not Saved: The Elusive Quest for Racial Justice* (New York: Basic Books, 1987); and Williams *The Alchemy of Race and Rights.*
18. Nancy Fraser and Linda Gordon, "The Genealogy of Dependence," *Signs* 19, 3(1994): 309–336; and Michael Omi and Howard Winant, *Racial Formations in the United States: From the 1960's to the 1980's* (New York: Routledge, 1996).
19. Morrison, *Playing in the Dark*, 44.
20. Rogers M. Smith, *Civic Ideals: Conflicting Visions of Citizenship in U.S. History* (New Haven, CT: Yale University Press, 1997), 30.
21. Desmond S. King and Rogers M. Smith, "Racial Orders in American Political Development," *American Political Science Review* 99, 1 (February 2005), 75.
22. Bonnie Honig, *Democracy and the Foreigner* (Princeton, NJ: Princeton University Press, 2001), 130.
23. This position is shared by many writers, including Derrick Bell, *Silent Covenants: Brown v Board of Education and the Unfulfilled Hopes for Racial Reform* (New York: Oxford University Press, 2004). Glenn, *Unequal Freedom*, 51–52; Holland, *The Body Politic: Foundings.* xix; xxix; Laura Janara, "Brothers and Others: Tocqueville and Beaumont, U.S. Genealogy, Democracy, and Racism." *Political Theory* 32, 6 (December 2004): 773–800; Jacobson, *Whiteness of a Different Color*, 15–38; and Joel Olson, *The Abolition of White Democracy* (Minneapolis: University of Minnesota Press, 2004).
24. Davis, *Inhuman Bondage*, 185.
25. I do not mean to imply that some other set of political beliefs and practices could perform transformative magic. As I will discuss in the next chapter, a view of subjectivity as fabricated necessarily entails different expectations of the possibilities and limits of political practices.
26. Gunnar Myrdal (1944) *An American Dilemma: The Negro Problem and American Democracy*. In *Racism: Essential Readings.*, ed. Ellis Cashmore and James Jennings (London: Sage, 2001).
27. Ibid., 91.
28. Alix de Tocqueville, *Democracy in America*, ed. and trans. Harvey C. Mansfield and Delba Winthrop (Chicago: University of Chicago Press, 2000), 343.
29. See Glenn C. Loury, *The Anatomy of Racial Inequality* (Cambridge, MA: Harvard University Press, 2002), 6–7, on the persistence of racial stigmatization.
30. Davis, *Inhuman Bondage*, 102.
31. I argue this point more fully in Jane Flax, *The American Dream in Black and White* (Ithaca, NY: Cornell University Press, 1998).
32. Julia Kristeva, *Nations Without Nationalism* (New York: Columbia University Press, 1993).

33. On these new modes of power, see particularly, Michel Foucault, *Ethics, Subjectivity and Truth*, ed. Paul Rabinow. (New York: The New Press, 1994); and Michel Foucault *Power*, ed. James D. Faubion (New York: The New Press, 1994). Particularly insightful analyses of the operation of such power networks in contemporary American politics include Wendy Brown, *States of Injury: Power and Freedom in Late Modernity* (Princeton, NJ: Princeton University Press, 1995), chapters 5–7; Barbara Cruikshank, *The Will to Empower: Democratic Citizens and Other Subjects* (Ithaca, NY: Cornell University Press, 1999); and Ellen K. Feder, *Family Bonds: Genealogies of Race and Gender* (New York: Oxford University Press, 2007).

34. Julia S. Jordan-Zachery, *Black Women, Cultural Images and Social Policy* (New York: Routledge, 2009), chapter 5, provides an excellent critique how race/gender shaped this policy approach.

35. Cruikshank, *The Will to Empower*, 20–34.

36. Danielle S. Allen, *Talking to Strangers: Anxieties of Citizenship since Brown v. Board of Education* (Chicago: University of Chicago Press, 2004), 25–49.

37. Skhlar, *American Citizenship*.

38. On this point, see also Janara, "Brothers and Others," 791–795.

39. Jennifer Hochschild, *Facing Up to the American Dream: Race, Class and the Soul of the Nation* (Princeton, NJ: Princeton University Press, 1995), 256–260.

40. Janara, "Brothers and Others," 790–793.

41. Friedrich Nietzsche, *On the Genealogy of Morals* (New York: Vintage, 1969), 127–128. See also Brown, *States of Injury*, 52–76; 96–134.

42. The "politics of disgust" that Ange-Marie Hancock discusses in her *The Politics of Disgust: The Public Identity of the Welfare Queen* (New York: New York University Press, 2004), is a good example of these dynamics.

43. Honig, *Democracy and the Foreigner*, 117.

44. Smith, *Civic Ideals*, 470–481.

45. Allen, *Talking to Strangers*. 41; Honig, *Democracy and the Foreigner*, 107–108.

46. Charles W. Mills, *The Racial Contract* (Ithaca, NY: Cornell University Press, 1997), 19.

47. The literature critiquing John Rawls's work (or written at least partially in response to it) is vast. Simply listing it, much less discussing its substance, would require more than a book itself. Therefore, I will just mention a few of the works I have found most useful in developing my own approach. These include: Ruth Abbey, "Back Toward a Comprehensive Liberalism: Justice as Fairness, Gender, and Families," *Political Theory* 35, 1 (February 2007): 3–28; Brian Barry, *The Liberal Theory of Justice* (Oxford: Oxford University Press, 1973); Seyla Benhabib, "The Generalized and the Concrete Other:

The Kohlberg-Gilligan Controversy and Feminist Theory," in Seyla Benhabib and Drucilla Cornell, eds., *Feminism as Critique* (New York: Basil Blackwell, 1987), 77–95; Bernard R. Boxill, *Blacks & Social Justice*, revised edition (Lanham, MD: Rowman and Littlefield, 1992); Romand Coles, "Traditio: Feminists of Color and the Torn Virtues of Democratic Engagement," *Political Theory* 29, 4 (August 2001): 488–516; Fred D'Agostino, "Rituals of Impartiality," *Social Theory and Practice* 27, 1 (January 2001): 65–81; Michael Dillon, "Another Justice," *Political Theory* 27, 2 (April 1999): 155–175; William A. Galston, *Liberal Purposes: Goods, Virtues, and Diversity in the Liberal State* (New York: Cambridge University Press, 1991); Kevin Graham, "The Political Significance of Social Identity: A Critique of Rawls's Theory of Agency," *Social Theory and Practice* 26, 2 (Summer 2000): 201–222; Thomas Nagel, "Rawls on Justice," *Philosophical Review* 83 (April 1973): 226–229; Robert Nozick, *Anarchy, State, and Utopia* (New York: Basic Books, 1974); Susan Moller Okin, *Justice, Gender, and the Family* (New York: Basic Books, 1989); Michael Sandel, *Liberalism and the Limits of Justice* (Cambridge, MA: Harvard University Press, 1982); Michael Walzer, *Spheres of Justice: A Defense of Pluralism and Equality* (New York: Basic Books, 1983); Sheldon Wolin, "The Liberal/Democratic Divide: On Rawls's *Political Liberalism*." *Political Theory* 24, 1 (February 1996): 97–142; and Iris Marion Young, *Justice and the Politics of Difference* (Princeton, NJ: Princeton University Press, 1990), especially 3–38.

48. See, for example, Robert D. Putnam, *Bowling Alone: The Collapse and Revival of American Community* (New York: Simon & Schuster, 2000) or Sandel, *Liberalism and the Limits of Justice*.

49. Rawls, *Justice as Fairness*, 155.

50. Ibid., 176.

51. Ibid., 66.

52. Wolin, "The Liberal/Democratic Divide," 116.

53. Anne Anlin Cheng, *The Melancholy of Race* (New York: Oxford University Press, 2001), especially 70–73. The fantasy of impossible perfection entails assigning all that is considered flawed, inferior, denigrated, disgusting, dirty, devalued, etc. onto one object (e.g., a race/gender position), thereby enabling another to be (falsely) flawless. In reality, the impossible perfection describes and is possessed by no one. However, the flaws of the dominant/superior are obscured by their splitting them off from conscious awareness and projecting them onto the denigrated/subjected other. The denigrated other has to struggle with its construction by the dominant, and may fall into the trap of believing that the dominant's fantasy of impossible perfection is actually attainable. Hence, subordinated groups may also long for such perfection, even if it is constructed at their own expense.

54. Holland, *The Body Politic*, 142.

55. John Rawls, *Political Liberalism* (New York: Columbia University Press, 1993), 25.
56. Ibid., 26.
57. Ibid., 24.
58. Ibid.
59. Rawls, *A Theory of Justice*, 255.
60. Ibid., 256.
61. Rawls, *Political Liberalism*, 26.
62. Ibid., 274.
63. Ibid., 27 and 274.
64. Ibid., 27.
65. Rawls, *A Theory of Justice*, 139.
66. Ibid., 137.
67. Ibid., 139.
68. Rawls, *Justice as Fairness*, 17.
69. Rawls, *Political Liberalism*, 28.
70. Ibid., 28.
71. Rawls, *A Theory of Justice*, 139.
72. Rawls, *Justice as Fairness*, 101.
73. Rawls, *Political Liberalism*, 23.
74. Ibid., 23.
75. Ibid.
76. Ibid., 27–28. See Kevin Graham, "The Political Significance of Social Identity," for a thorough reading of Rawls's texts that supports this point.
77. Rawls, *Political Liberalism*, 27.
78. Ibid., 25; 272.
79. Ibid., 24.
80. Rawls, *A Theory of Justice*, 137; Rawls, *Justice as Fairness*, 15.
81. Rawls, *A Theory of Justice*, 256.
82. Ibid., 256.
83. Ibid.
84. Rawls, *Political Liberalism*, 27.
85. Paul Gilroy, *The Black Atlantic: Modernity and Double Consciousness* (Cambridge, MA: Harvard University Press, 1993), 46. To hold onto a belief in a noumenal mind also requires that one disregard extensive research by contemporary neuroscientists and others regarding our psychic processes. This research supports the claim that much of our psychic processes occur outside of (and uncontrolled by) our conscious awareness. Furthermore, this research indicates that even what we experience as rational deliberation is shaped by forces of which (at best) we can have partial awareness and control. See Arnold H. Modell, "Horse and Rider Revisted: The Dynamic Unconscious and the Self as Agent," *Contemporary Psychoanalysis* 44, 3: 351–366 for an excellent integration of contemporary

neuroscience and psychoanalytic theories. For a thorough accounting of this research and some of its implications for politics, see Drew Weston, *The Political Brain: The Role of Emotion in Deciding the Fate of the Nation* (New York: Public Affairs, 2007). For its application to law and ingenious experiments that support the force of unconscious processes, see Justin D. Levinson, "Forgotten Racial Equality Implicit Bias, Decisionmaking, and Misremembering," *Duke Law Journal* 57 (2007): 344–421. In her *The Politics of Disgust*, Ange-Marie Hancock also discusses some of this research. Her research on welfare legislation demonstrates how powerfully nonrational processes shape public policy formation. This research suggests that, if humans are as risk averse as Rawls assumes, then betting on his strategy of relying on rational deliberation and calculation to derive principles that can structure and ground a stable and just set of social arrangements is unwise.

86. Rawls, *Political Liberalism*, 18.
87. Ibid., 18.
88. Bonnie Honig, *Political Theory and the Displacement of Politics* (Ithaca, NY: Cornell University Press, 1993), 155.
89. Rawls, *A Theory of Justice*, 138.
90. Ibid., 137; Rawls, *Political Liberalism*, 273.
91. Rawls, *A Theory of Justice*, 137.
92. Rawls, *Political Liberalism*, 277.
93. A recent example of this is Chief Justice Roberts's opinion in the Seattle School case. Roberts found the school district's attempt to maintain racial diversity in its schools racially discriminatory. About the integration plan, he said, "The way to stop discrimination on the basis of race is to stop discriminating on the basis of race." See Jeffrey Toobin, "No More Mr. Nice Guy: The Supreme Court's Stealth Hardliner," *New Yorker*, May 25, 2009, 48.
94. Rawls, *Justice as Fairness*, 42–43.
95. Partially in response to his many critics, Rawls repeatedly attempts to clarify his derivation and justification of the difference principle. His basic justification is that humans are risk averse and that since behind the veil of ignorance, no one knows what their actual situation might be, it would be least risky to assume that one would be among the least advantaged. See, for example, Rawls, *Justice as Fairness*, 106–111. However, this argument is far from persuasive on a number of grounds, including the problematic assumption that humans are innately rational self-interest maximizers. That people could know that the least advantaged exist but not know what their current position is, or that they are unaffected by the common American fantasy (dream) that one day they too will be among the most advantaged, is unlikely. Why give up present time advantage or belief that it will exist in the future? Only if we split off almost everything about contemporary human subjectivity is this reasoning

plausible. Furthermore, if such a principle is derived from self-interest, given Rawls's Kantian commitments, its ethical standing and relation to justice are unclear.

96. Romand Coles, "Traditio: Feminists of Color and the Torn Virtues of Democratic Engagement," 505.

97. For development of this point and proposals for supplements to public reason and reasonable discourse, see, Allen, *Talking to Strangers*; Coles, "Traditio: Feminists of Color and the Torn Virtues of Democratic Engagement"; and D'Agostino, "Rituals of Impartiality."

CHAPTER 5

1. Danielle S. Allen, *Talking to Strangers: Anxieties of Citizenship since Brown v. Board of Education* (Chicago: University of Chicago Press, 2004), 41.

2. This is a central argument in Allen, *Talking to Strangers*. See also Derrick Bell, *And We Are Not Saved: The Elusive Quest for Racial Justice* (New York: Basic Books, 1987); Evelyn Nakano Glenn, *Unequal Freedom: How Race and Gender Shaped American Citizenship and Labor* (Cambridge, MA: Harvard University Press, 2002); Catherine A. Holland, *The Body Politic: Foundings, Citizen, and Difference in the American Political Imagination* (New York: Routledge, 2001); Charles W. Mills, *The Racial Contract* (Ithaca, NY: Cornell University Press, 1997); Joel Olson, *The Abolition of White Democracy* (Minneapolis: University of Minnesota Press, 2004); and Judith N. Shklar, *American Citizenship: The Quest for Inclusion* (Cambridge, MA: Harvard University Press, 1991).

3. On this point, see also Lawrie Balfour, "Unreconstructed Democracy: W. E. B. Du Bois and the Case for Reparations," *American Political Science Review* 97, 1 (February 2003): 33–44; Thomas McCarthy, "Vergangenheitsbewaltigung in the USA: On the Politics of the Memory of Slavery," *Political Theory* 30, 5 (October 2002): 623–648; and Thomas McCarthy, "Coming to Terms with Our Past, Part II: On the Morality and Politics of Reparations for Slavery," *Political Theory* 32, 6 (December 2004): 750–772.

4. Alix de Tocqueville, *Democracy in America*, ed. and trans. Harvey C. Mansfield and Delba Winthrop (Chicago: University of Chicago Press, 2000); and Laura Janara, "Brothers and Others: Tocqueville and Beaumont, U.S. Genealogy, Democracy, and Racism." *Political Theory* 32, 6 (December 2004): 773–800.

5. Janara, "Brothers and Others," 792.

6. On the silences of political theory and political science more generally regarding race, see Hawley Fogg-Davis, "The Racial Retreat of Contemporary Political Theory," *Perspectives on Politics* 1, 3 (September 2003): 555–564; and Rogers M. Smith, "The Puzzling

Place of Race in American Political Science," *PS* (January 2004): 41–45.

7. But see, Alford, *Psychology and the Natural Law of Reparation*; Allen, *Talking to Strangers*; Zygmunt Bauman, *Life in Fragments: Essays in Postmodern Morality* (Cambridge, MA: Blackwell, 1995); James M. Glass, *Private Terror/Public Life: Psychosis and the Politics of Community* (Ithaca, NY: Cornell University Press, 1989); Cynthia Willett, *The Soul of Justice: Social Bonds and Racial Hubris* (Ithaca, NY: Cornell University Press, 2001); Slavoj Zizek, "Fantasy as a Political Category: A Lacanian Approach," in *The Zizek Reader*, ed. Elizabeth Wright and Edmond Wright (Cambridge, MA: Blackwell), 87–101; and Slavoj Zizek, "Enjoy Your Nation as Yourself," in Les Back and John Solomos, *Theories of Race and Racism: A Reader* (New York: Routledge, 2000), 594–606.

8. See John Rawls, *Justice as Fairness: A Restatement* (Cambridge, MA: Harvard University Press, 2001), especially pp. 27–31; 97–104.

9. Jurgen Habermas, *Jurgen Habermas on Society and Politics: A Reader*, ed. Steven Seidman (Boston: Beacon, 1989). On problems with Habermas's approach, see Allen, *Talking to Strangers*, especially 124–125.

10. Desmond S .King and Rogers M. Smith, "Racial Orders in American Political Development," *American Political Science Review* 99, 1(February 2005): 75–92.

11. Hannah Arendt, *The Human Condition*, 2nd edition (Chicago: University of Chicago Press, 1998), especially 175–247; Jacques Ranciere, *On The Shores of Politics* (New York: Verso, 1995); Linda M. G. Zerilli, *Feminism and the Abyss of Freedom* (Chicago: University of Chicago Press, 2005). Zerilli is aware of this problem, but her tentative solution, to posit a quasi-Kantian will operating within each subject, seems antithetical to her constructionist and Wittgensteinian approach to subjectivity.

12. We saw this horror play out in Chapter Three. The characters in all three films vigilantly policed borders between many race/gender positions, including black and white, gay and straight, Korean/white, Arab/Persian, Hispanic/white, black/Asian, foreign/native, etc.

13. Useful contributions to this project include Barbara Cruikshank, *The Will to Empower: Democratic Citizens and Other Subjects* (Ithaca, NY: Cornell University Press, 1999); and Richard E. Flathman, *Freedom and Its Conditions: Discipline, Autonomy, and Resistance* (New York: Routledge, 2003).

14. Charles, R. Lawrence, III, "The Id, the Ego, and Equal Protection: Reckoning with Unconscious Racism," *Stanford Law Review* (vol.39, Jan. 1987): 317–388; see also Philip A. Klinkner, with Rogers M. Smith, *The Unsteady March: The Rise and Decline of Racial Equality in America* (Chicago: University of Chicago Press: 1999), 328–347.

15. Michel Foucault, "Sexuality and Solitude," in *Michel Foucault: Ethics, Subjectivity and Truth*, ed. Paul Rabinow (New York: The New Press), 177.

16. It is puzzling to me that more scholars do not attend to this turn in Foucault's thinking; they often seem fixated on his earlier, less complex writings on power and reiterate criticisms based on these partial readings. I certainly do not mean to suggest that his writings are or ought to be immune from criticism. Although he does undertake a serious genealogy of race in Michel Foucault, *"Society Must Be Defended": Lectures at the College de France 1975–1976*, especially 43–85, his discussion, as is the case in his work more generally, remains uninflected by gendering practices. Furthermore, as Ann Laura Stoler argues in her *Race and The Education of Desire: Foucault's History of Sexuality and the Colonial Order of Things* (Durham, NC: Duke University Press, 1997), the absence within Foucault's investigations of any sustained consideration of practices of race/gendering and colonialism and postcoloniality is unacceptable. However, his own shortcomings do not necessarily mean that his approach is useless for developing insightful analyses of race/gender. Two particularly good examples of productively appropriating Foucault's work for such projects are Barbara Cruikshank, *The Will to Empower: Democratic Citizens and Other Subjects* (Ithaca, NY: Cornell University Press, 1999); and Ellen K. Feder, *Family Bonds: Genealogies of Race and Gender* (New York: Oxford University Press, 2007).

17. Despite Foucault's criticism of philosophies of the subject (discussed below), his work shares much with contemporary psychoanalysis. Many contemporary psychoanalysts have developed and extended Freud's distinction between psychic processes and consciousness. Subjectivity in contemporary psychoanalytic accounts is often portrayed as heterogeneous, fluid, and contextual. See, for example, Arnold H. Modell, "Horse and Rider Revisited: The Dynamic Unconscious and the Self as Agent," *Contemporary Psychoanalysis* 44, 3: 351–366. Furthermore, Foucault shares with Freud a systematic skepticism regarding the ordinary, taken for granted appearances that pass for "normalcy" in subjective constructions or social relations. Like Foucault's "care of the self," Freud sees psychoanalysis as a form of "soul service." Among the desired practices of psychoanalysis are developing the habit of dislodging certainty and comfort with dominant norms and rendering the normal puzzing and strange. From a Foucauldian perspective, part of what psychoanalysis does lack is attention to the disciplinary practices that require and inform particular modes of subjectivity. For Foucault, constraint and empowerment, inclusion and exclusion, and normalization and marginalization are aspects of the same practices, and we must always explore their intertwining. Foucault's attention to the processes of disempowerment, exclusion and constraint within socially constitutive practices

distinguishes his work from others, such as pragmatists like John
Dewey or Richard Rorty, who also stress the constituting power of
habits.

18. Foucault, "Sexuality and Solitude," 295.
19. Ibid., 290.
20. Michel Foucault, "Preface to *The History of Sexuality, Volume Two*,"
    in *Michel Foucault: Ethics, Subjectivity and Truth*, ed. Paul Rabinow
    (New York: The New Press), 201.
21. Foucault, "Sexuality and Solitude," 177.
22. Ibid.
23. Michel Foucault, "Technologies of the Self," in *Michel Foucault:
    Ethics, Subjectivity and Truth*, ed. Paul Rabinow (New York: The
    New Press), 225.
24. Ibid., 225.
25. Michel Foucault, "Subjectivity and Truth," in *Michel Foucault:
    Ethics, Subjectivity and Truth*, ed. Paul Rabinow (New York: The
    New Press), 87.
26. Foucault, "Preface to *The History of Sexuality, Volume Two*," 203.
27. Michel Foucault, *The History of Sexuality, v.1* (New York: Pantheon,
    1980), 119.
28. Nancy Leys Stepan, "Race and Gender: The Role of Analogy in
    Science," in David Theo Goldberg, *Anatomy of Racism* (Minneapolis:
    University of Minnesota Press, 1990), 38–57; Charles Shepherdson,
    "Human Diversity and the Sexual Relation," in *The Psychoanalysis of
    Race*, ed. Christopher Lane (New York: Columbia University Press,
    1998), 41–64.
29. Matthew Frye Jacobson, *Whiteness of a Different Color: European
    Immigrants and the Alchemy of Race* (Cambridge, MA: Harvard
    University Press, 1998), 95; see also Dvora Yanow, *Constructing
    "Race" and "Ethnicity" in America: Category Making in Public Policy
    and Administration* (Armonk, NY: M.E. Sharpe, 2003).
30. Nancy Fraser and Linda Gordon, "The Genealogy of Dependence,"
    Signs 19, 3 (1994): 309–336; Jacobson, *Whiteness of a Different Color*;
    and Ian F. Haney Lopez, "White by Law," in Richard Delgado and
    Jean Stefancic, eds., *Critical Race Theory: The Cutting Edge*, second
    edition (Philadelphia: Temple University Press, 2000), 626–634.
31. Michel Foucault, *Abnormal: Lectures at the College de France 1974–
    1975* (New York: Picador, 1999), 130–134; 247–258; 262–287.
32. Foucault, "Sexuality and Solitude," 177.
33. Ibid., 177–178.
34. Michel Foucault, "The Ethics of the Concern for the Self as a Practice
    of Freedom," in *Michel Foucault: Ethics, Subjectivity and Truth*, ed.
    Paul Rabinow (New York: The New Press), 291.
35. Ibid., 299.
36. Ibid., 292.

37. Michel Foucault, "Sex, Power and the Politics of Identity," in *Michel Foucault: Ethics, Subjectivity and Truth*, ed. Paul Rabinow (New York: The New Press), 167.
38. Michel Foucault, "Preface to *The History of Sexuality, Volume Two*," 203.
39. Michel Foucault, "The Ethics of the Concern," 283.
40. Ibid., 292.
41. For the most detailed presentation of what he means by "care of the self," see Michel Foucault, *The Hermeneutics of the Subject: Lectures at the College de France, 1981–1982* (New York: Picador, 2005), especially 491–505.
42. Foucault, "The Ethics of the Concern," 295.
43. On this point, see Alexander Nehamas, *The Art of Living: Socratic Reflections from Plato to Foucault* (Berkeley: University of California Press, 1998), 157–188.
44. Foucault, "The Ethics of the Concern," 294.
45. Michel Foucault, "The Hermeneutic of the Subject," in *Michel Foucault: Ethics, Subjectivity and Truth*, ed. Paul Rabinow (New York: The New Press), 96.
46. Foucault, "Technologies of the Self," 228.
47. Foucault, "The Ethics of the Concern," 295.
48. Ibid., 282.
49. Foucault, "The Hermeneutic of the Subject," 101–102.
50. Foucault, "The Ethics of the Concern," 286.
51. Foucault, "The Hermeneutic of the Subject," 99.
52. Ann duCille, "The Occult of True Black Womanhood: Critical Demeanor and Black Feminist Studies," *Signs: Journal of Women in Culture and Society* 19, 3 (Fall 1994): 591–629; and Amina Mama, *Beyond the Masks: Race, Gender and Subjectivity* (New York: Routledge, 1995) develop this point persuasively.
53. Bonnie Honig, *Democracy and the Foreigner* (Princeton, NY: Princeton University Press, 2001).
54. Paul Gilroy, *The Black Atlantic: Modernity and Double Consciousness* (Cambridge, MA: Harvard University Press, 1993), 45.
55. See Toni Morrison, *Playing in the Dark: Whiteness and the Literary Imagination* (New York: Vintage, 1992) for an example of what this sort of narrative would look like; and also Mama, *Beyond the Masks*.
56. Some are highly critical of such approaches, for example, Martha Nussbaum, "In Defense of Universal Values," in James P. Sterba, ed., *Controversies in Feminism* (Lanham, MD: Rowman and Littlefield, 2001), 3–23. However, other writers, including Allen, *Talking to Strangers*; Wendy Brown, *Politics Out of History* (Princeton, NJ: Princeton University Press, 2001); Cruikshank, *The Will to Empower*; Agnes Heller and Ferenc Feher, *The Postmodern Condition* (New York: Columbia University Press, 1988); Honig, *Democracy and*

the Foreigner; Chantal Mouffe, *The Return of the Political* (New York: Verso, 1993); Ranciere, *On The Shores of Politics* and Jacques Ranciere, *Disagreement: Politics and Philosophy* (Minneapolis: University of Minnesota Press, 1999); Tommie Shelby, *We Who Are Dark: The Philosophic Foundations of Black Solidarity* (Cambridge, MA: Harvard University Press, 2005); and Zerilli, *Feminism and the Abyss of Freedom* are pursuing a similar trajectory.

57. On the limits of discourse, especially when uncoupled with action, see Katherine Cramer Walsh, *Talking About Race: Community Dialogues and the Politics of Difference* (Chicago: University of Chicago Press, 2007).

58. For a fascinating account of how this discourse evolved, see Albert O. Hirschman, *The Passions and the Interests: Political Arguments for Capitalism before Its Triumph* (Princeton, NJ: Princeton University Press, 1997).

59. For a rich discussion of coalitions, including their necessity, discomforts and dangers, see Bernice Johnson Reagon, "Coalition Politics: Turning the Century," in Barbara Smith, ed. *Home Girls: A Black Feminist Anthology* (New York: Kitchen Table: A Woman of Color Press, 1983), 356–368.

60. I think this is where Hannah Arendt (and her followers) go wrong. Her notion of excellence (arete) has only one form, action in a strictly delimited public sphere.

61. See Richard E. Flathman, *Freedom and Its Conditions* for a particularly rich discussion of this point.

62. I am referring especially to the discussion of the social in Hannah Arendt, *The Human Condition*. For an incise critique of Arendt's construction of the social, see Hanna Pitkin, *The Attack of the Blob: Hannah Arendt's Concept of the Social* (Chicago: University of Chicago Press, 1998).

63. Jurgen Habermas, *Jurgen Habermas on Society and Politics: A Reader*, ed. Steven Seidman (Boston: Beacon, 1989), 188–299.

64. In her *The Faces of Injustice* (New Haven, CT: Yale University Press, 1990), for example, Judith N. Shklar gives a beautiful and rich account of the importance of listening to the victims of events in assessing whether such occurrences are instances of injustice and thus amenable to (and requiring) human acts of redress and remediation. Shklar's argument here also shows how we can engage in ethical action and discourse about it without assuming or relying upon universalizing principles.

65. See Sasha Roseneil, *Common Women, Uncommon Practices: The Queer Feminisms of Greenham* (London and New York: Cassell, 2000) for a wonderful case study that illustrates this point; and also Bauman, *Life in Fragments*; Ranciere, *Disagreement*; and Joan Retallack, *The Poethical Wager* (Berkeley: University of California Press, 2003).

66. Foucault, "The Ethics of the Concern," 284.

67. On the importance of conflict and disagreement for rich political spaces, see Ranciere, *Disagreement*; and Walsh, *Talking About Race*.
68. Foucault, "The Ethics of the Concern," 289.
69. Romand Coles, "Taditio: Feminists of Color and the Torn Virtues of Democratic Engagement," *Political Theory* 29, 4 (August 2001), 497–498. The failure of those such as Emmanuel Levinas to examine the complexity of our desires in relationships with "the other" limits their works' usefulness in imaginatively constructing ethical practices. Some of Levinas's most important essays are collected in Sean Hand, ed. *The Levinas Reader* (Oxford: Blackwell, 1989). For a well-argued contrary view on Levinas, ethics and politics, see C. Fred Alford, *Levinas, the Frankfurt School and Psychoanalysis* (Middletown, CT: Wesleyan University Press, 2002).

CHAPTER 6

1. Zygmunt Bauman, *Life in Fragments: Essays in Postmodern Morality* (Cambridge, MA: Blackwell, 1995), 287.
2. The documentary *Trouble the Water* (2008) provides equally important and compelling insights into the Katrina disaster. Directed by Carl Deal and Tia Lessin, it uses the video shot during the hurricane by Kimberly Rivers Roberts and Scott Roberts, who also are the film's protagonists. Graphic and gritty in conveying Katrina's force and New Orleans' suffering, the documentary is also quite moving as it charts the Rivers' transformation as subjects during and after Katrina, from lost and self-destructive to engaged citizen activists.
3. For documentation of this claim, see Thomas McCarthy, "Vergangenheitsbewaltigung in the USA: On the Politics of the Memory of Slavery," *Political Theory* 30, 5 (October 2002): 623–648; and Thomas McCarthy, "Coming to Terms with Our Past, Part II: On the Morality and Politics of Reparations for Slavery," *Political Theory* 32, 6 (December 2004): 750–772.
4. Danielle S. Allen, *Talking to Strangers: Anxieties of Citizenship since Brown v. Board of Education* (Chicago: University of Chicago Press, 2004), 183.
5. Michel Foucault, "The Ethics of the Concern for the Self as a Practice of Freedom." In *Michel Foucault: Ethics, Subjectivity and Truth*, ed. Paul Rabinow (New York: The New Press), 298.
6. Tavis Smiley (Introduction), *The Covenant with Black America* (Chicago: The Third World Press, 2006). See also the recommendations in chapter 8 of Johnnetta Betsch Cole and Beverly Guy-Sheftall, *Gender Talk: The Struggle for Women's Equality in African American Communities* (New York: Random House, 2003); and chapter six of Julia Jordan-Zachery, *Black Women, Cultural Images and Social Policy* (New York: Routledge, 2009).

7. Ira Katznelson, *When Affirmative Action Was White: An Untold History of Racial Inequality in Twentieth Century American* (New York: W. W. Norton, 2005). See also Bernard R. Boxill, *Blacks & Social Justice*, revised edition (Lanham, MD: Rowman and Littlefield, 1992), 147–172; Leslie A. Jacobs, *Pursuing Equal Opportunities: The Theory and Practice of Egalitarian Justice* (New York: Cambridge University Press, 2004), especially chapter five; the essays in Charles R. Lawrence, III and Mari J. Matsuda, *We Won't Go Back: Making the Case for Affirmative Action* (New York: Houghton Mifflin, 1997); and McCarthy, "Coming to Terms with Our Past, Part II."

8. Katznelson, *When Affirmative Action Was White*, 159.

9. Although perhaps not in the twenty-five years Justice Sandra Day O'Connor estimated her ruling in *Grutter v Bollinger* (02–241, 2003). Citing economic research, Roland G., Jr. Fryer and Glenn C. Loury, "Affirmative Action and Its Mythology," http://www.economics.harvard.edu/faculty/fryer/files/fryer_loury_jepfinal.pdf, 2005, suggest her estimate is "overly optimistic" (15).

10. Ibid., 160.

11. The essays in Charles R. Lawrence, III and Mari J. Matsuda, *We Won't Go Back* are much more attentive to the importance of this dimension of affirmative action. See also Linda Faye Williams, *The Constraint of Race: Legacies of White Skin Privilege in America* (University Park, PA: Pennsylvannia State Press, 2003), especially 1–24.

12. See, for example, John Rawls, *Justice as Fairness: A Restatement* (Cambridge, MA: Harvard University Press, 2001), 42–45.

13. I am indebted to Kennedy Turner, a Howard University undergraduate who I mentored in the McNair Program, for a thoughtful critique of an earlier version of this book. Ms. Turner's research demonstrated the need for training as an intrinsic part of any successful affirmative action program.

14. One way to interpret this incident is as an intersection of Foucauldian power/knowledge networks and the political unconscious. As both networks and the political unconscious operate in any event a mixture of contingency, power relationships, fantasy, idiosyncratic emotions, subjective and common history, knowledge, social facts, social constructions and desire interact. We cannot predict with certainty how these will play out in any one event. Yet to some degree, because (however differently we are located) the networks are familiar, events are intelligible. Interpreting it this way, it appears that Professor Gates was operating within the race/gendered history of racial profiling while Sgt. James M. Crowley, his arresting officer, enacted the fantasy of the dangerous angry black man. Like Cameron, the television producer in *Crash*, I guess that Gates finally exceeded his tolerance for the petty (or not so petty) humiliations routinely inflicted on even relatively privileged black/men and women. Despite his small size, age, and cane, Sgt. Crowley probably read Professor

Gates' anger as potentially life threatening. He stated that he feared he might not return to his wife and three children that night. It may also be that, as in the encounter between Cameron and Officer Ryan in *Crash*, Sgt. Crowley felt discomfort with Professor Gates' privileged location as a Harvard professor. Threatened with a subordinate positioning, Crowley desired respect to restore his sense of place. Instead, Gates challenged his authority, and Crowley had to arrest him to restore his own subjective order. While these histories and fantasies circulate throughout contemporary American culture, what produced an explosion was the triggering of deeply felt and intrasubjective emotion. Both parties may have been surprised by how the incident played out. According to friends of each man reporters interviewed, their actions were uncharacteristic. Professor Gates is known for his mild, even temper and Sgt. Crawley taught other police officers how to avoid racial profiling. Yet, as for all of us, other aspects of subjectivity exist outside our (and others') conscious awareness. These often shape our actions, but it is less usual for their effects to become so visible or objects of public discourse. For an account of this incident, see Don Van Natta, Jr. and Abby Goodnough, "After Call to Police, 2 Cambridge Worlds Collide in an Unlikely Meeting," *New York Times*, Monday July 27, 2009, A13.

15. For a discussion of one effective model of such training, see Laurie A. Rudman, Richard D. Ashmore, Melvin L. Gary, "'Unlearning' Automatic Biases: The Malleability of Implicit Prejudice and Stereotypes," *Journal of Personality and Social Psychology* 81, 5 (2001): 856–868. The authors insist that to be effective, programs must incorporate techniques that target implicit (unconscious) material. They identify and include such techniques in their recommended practices. Programs to confront such material may reduce a negative consequence of affirmative action programs that Glenn C. Loury's and others have found. Loury suggests that such programs may increase employers' negative feelings about disadvantaged workers; the more aggressive affirmative action programs are, the wider searches for candidates will be, and (rightly or not) employers begin to believe they are being forced to select unqualified candidates. Therefore, aggressive affirmative action programs may increase the privileged's denigration of subordinated others. See Roland G., Jr. Fryer and Glenn C. Loury, "Affirmative Action and Its Mythology," *http://www.economics.harvard.edu/faculty/fryer/files/fryer_* for a useful discussion of this issue. In this article, the authors also carefully dismantle many myths about affirmative action, including the claims that simply passing laws ensuring equal opportunity will remedy asymmetric distribution of valued social goods and that color-blind policies are as efficient as color-sighted affirmative action. The authors conclude that, while affirmative action programs entail some negative consequences, no alternative offers equal or better remedies

for the consequences of systemic inequalities. I do not mean to suggest that any training approach can eliminate all effects of our past or the political unconscious, just that there are some effective ways to better manage it. On the limits of interaction, see Katherine Cramer Walsh, *Talking About Race; Community Dialogues and the Politics of Difference* (Chicago: University of Chicago Press, 2007).

16. Katznelson, *When Affirmative Action Was White*, 172.
17. Ibid., 172.
18. Judge Gladys Kessler of Federal District Court for the District of Columbia, August 17, 2006. Quoted in Philip Shenon, "New Limits Set over Marketing for Cigarettes," *New York Times*, Friday, August 18, 2006, Washington section.
19. Sources for this information include material from the Bureau of Justice Statistics, United States Department of Justice summarized in DrugWarFacts.org., "Get the Facts," http://www.drugwarfacts.org/cms /node/64, 2009; Juan Forero, "Columbia's Coca Survives U.S. Plan to Uproot It," *New York Times*, Saturday, August 19, 2006, A 1, continued A 7; Brian O'Dea, "Lawyers, guns and money: Three Reasons to End the Drug War," *Los Angeles Times*, Opinion page, June 7, 2009; and Pew Center on the States, "One in 100: Behind Bars in America 2008," www.pewtrusts.org, 2009.
20. Forero, "Columbia's Coca Survives U.S. Plan to Uproot It," A7.
21. Pew Center on the States, "One in 100: Behind Bars in America 2008," 14.
22. Bankole, A. Johnson, "New Weapon to Curb Smoking: No More Excuses to Delay Treatment," *Archives of Internal Medicine*, 166 (2006), 1547.
23. Ali H., Mokdad, PhD, James S. Marks, MD, MPH, Donna F. Stroup, PhD, MSc, Julie L. Gerberding, MD, MPH, "Actual Causes of Death in the United States, 2000," *Journal of the American Medical Association* 291, 10 (March 10, 2004): 1238, 1241. On the other hand, according to Federal Bureau of Investigation's Uniform Crime Reports, in 2007, police arrested about 872,720 persons for cannabis violations in 2007, the highest annual total ever reported in the United States. An American is now arrested for violating these laws every 38 seconds. Reported in DrugWarFacts.org., "Get the Facts."
24. John Tierney, "Lighting Up in Amsterdam," *New York Times*, Saturday, August 26, 2006, A 25.
25. The Sentencing Project, "Young Black Americans and the Criminal Justice System: Five Years Later," *http://www.sentencing*project.org/pdfs/9070smy.pdf, April, 2001.
26. Christopher Wildeman, "Parental Imprisonment, the Prison Boom, and the Concentration of Childhood Disadvantage," *Demography* 46, 2 (May 2009): 265–280.
27. On using those positioned as black/female as scapegoats, see Ange-Marie Hancock, *The Politics of Disgust: The Public Identity of the*

Welfare Queen (New York: New York University Press, 2004); and Julia S. Jordan-Zachery, *Black Women, Cultural Images and Social Policy* (New York: Routledge, 2009).

28. Quoted in Tierney, "Lighting Up in Amsterdam," A 25.

29. Urban farming is a movement initiated by Will Allen and others to reclaim unused urban land for community farms. These movements are interested in urban farming as a means not only to address inequities in the availability of good food and environmental issues but also to change citizens' practices of subjectivity and citizenship. Public gardening requires, among other practices, patience, cooperation, and reworking our relationships to the environment and other subjects. The "edible" classroom is a movement started by Alice Waters, a Berkeley chef. Her foundation helps schools, especially in poor neighborhoods, to create gardens. Children then garden, cook, and eat together. Beyond nutrition and environmental awareness, such programs intend to facilitate different relationships among children and enlarge the scope of education. The hope is to offer children new tools to better manage themselves and their relations with others.

30. For example, Patricia Hill Collins, *Black Sexual Politics: African Americans, Gender, and the New Racism* (New York: Routledge, 2004), 149–180; and Orlando Patterson, *Rituals of Blood: Consequences of Slavery in Two American Centuries* (New York: Basic, 1998).

31. Allen, *Talking to Strangers*, 110.

32. Dan Morgan, Gilbert M. Gaul, and Sarah Cohen, "Farm Program Pays $1.3 Billion to People Who Don't Farm," *Washington Post*, Sunday, July 2, 2006, A 1.

33. Jason DeParle, Jason, "Study Finds Many Children Don't Benefit from Credits," *New York Times*, Sunday, October 2, 2005, A 16.

34. Gunnar Myrdal, *An American Dilemma: The Negro Problem and American Democracy*, in Ellis Cashmore and James Jennings, eds. *Racism: Essential Readings* (London: Sage, 2001), 35–48.

35. Barbara Cruikshank, *The Will to Empower: Democratic Citizens and Other Subjects* (Ithaca, NY: Cornell University Press, 1999).

36. Richard E. Flathman, *Freedom and Its Conditions: Discipline, Autonomy, and Resistance* (New York: Routledge, 2003), 11–35.

37. Cruikshank, *The Will to Empower*, 44.

38. Ibid., 40.

39. Glenn, *Unequal Freedom*, 52.

40. Robert D. Putnam, *Bowling Alone: The Collapse and Revival of American Community* (New York: Simon and Schuster, 2000).

41. Cruikshank, *The Will to Empower*, 91.

42. Ibid., 66.

43. Glenn C. Loury, *The Anatomy of Racial Inequality* (Cambridge, MA: Harvard University Press, 2002), 167.

44. Ibid., 168.

45. Michel Foucault, *The Hermeneutics of the Subject: Lectures at the College de France, 1981–1982.* (New York: Picador, 2005), 495–496.

46. Romand Coles, "Traditio: Feminists of Color and the Torn Virtues of Democratic Engagement," *Political Theory* 29, 4 (August 2001): 510.

47. For example, Allen, *Talking to Strangers*; Coles, "Traditio: Feminists of Color," 508–509; Michael C. Dawson, *Black Visions: The Roots of Contemporary African-American Ideologies* (Chicago: University of Chicago Press, 2001), 322; McCarthy, "Vergangenheitsbewaltigung in the USA"; and McCarthy, "Coming to Terms with Our Past, Part II."

48. Tommie Shelby, *We Who Are Dark: The Philosophic Foundations of Black Solidarity* (Cambridge, MA: Harvard University Press, 2005), 179. See also Frantz Fanon, *The Wretched of the Earth* (New York: Grove, 1966) for a classic defense of the need for self-liberation.

49. Joel Olson, *The Abolition of White Democracy* (Minneapolis: University of Minnesota Press, 2004), 142.

References

Abbey, Ruth, "Back Toward a Comprehensive Liberalism: Justice as Fairness, Gender, and Families," *Political Theory* 35, 1 (February 2007): 3–28.

Abel, Elizabeth, Barbara Christian, and Helene Moglen, eds., *Female Subjects in Black and White* (Berkeley: University of California Press, 1997).

Adams, Alice E. "Making Theoretical Space: Psychoanalysis and Lesbian Sexual Difference," *Signs: Journal of Women in Culture and Society* 27, 2 (2000): 473–499.

Alford, C. Fred, *Levinas, the Frankfurt School and Psychoanalysis* (Middletown, CT: Wesleyan University Press, 2002).

———, *Psychology and the Natural Law of Reparation* (New York: Cambridge University Press, 2006).

Allen, Danielle S., *Talking to Strangers: Anxieties of Citizenship since Brown v. Board of Education* (Chicago: University of Chicago Press, 2004).

Applied Research Center, "Race and Recession: How Inequity Rigged the Economy and How to Change the Rules," arc.org/recession, May 2009.

Arendt, Hannah, *The Human Condition*, 2nd edition (Chicago: University of Chicago Press, 1998).

Association of American Medical Colleges, "FACTS: Applicants, Matriculants, Graduates, and Residency Applicants—AAMC," http://www.aamc.org/data/facts/2008/gradraceeth0208.htm

Austin, Regina, "Sapphire Bound!," in *Critical Race Feminism: A Reader*, ed. Adrien Katherine Wing (New York: New York University Press, 1997), 289–296.

Avineri, Shlomo and Avner de-Shalit, eds., *Communitarianism and Individualism* (New York: Oxford University Press, 1992).

Bakalar, Nicholas, "Vital Signs: A Customer Bias in Favor of White Men," *New York Times*, Tuesday, June 23, 2009, D6.

Baker, Peter, "Court Choice Pushes Issue of 'Identity Politics' Back to Forefront," *New York Times*, May 31, 2009, A20.

Baldwin, James, *The Price of the Ticket* (New York: St. Martins, 1985).

Balfour, Lawrie, "Unreconstructed Democracy: W. E. B. Du Bois and the Case for Reparations," *American Political Science Review* 97, 1 (February 2003): 33–44.

Barker, Lucius J., "Limits of Political Strategy: A Systematic View of the African American Experience," *American Political Science Review* 88, 1 (1994): 1–14.

Barry, Brian, *The Liberal Theory of Justice* (Oxford: Oxford University Press, 1973).

Bar-Yam, Yaneer, M. Klau, W. Li, J. Siow, I. Wokoma, and J. Wells, *White Flight* (New England: Complex Systems Institute, MIT, 2003).

Bauman, Zygmunt, *Life in Fragments: Essays in Postmodern Morality* (Cambridge, MA: Blackwell, 1995).

Bell, Derrick, *And We Are Not Saved: The Elusive Quest for Racial Justice* (New York: Basic Books, 1987).

————, *Silent Covenants: Brown v Board of Education and the Unfulfilled Hopes for Racial Reform* (New York: Oxford University Press, 2004).

Bellah, Robert N., Richard Madsen, William M. Sullivan, Ann Swidler, and Steven M. Tipton, *Habits of the Heart* (New York: Harper and Row, 1996).

Benhabib, Seyla, "The Generalized and the Concrete Other: The Kohlberg-Gilligan Controversy and Feminist Theory," in *Feminism as Critique*, ed. Seyla Benhabib and Drucilla Cornell (New York: Basil Blackwell, 1987), 77–95.

Bernasek, Anna, "Income Inequality, and Its Costs," *New York Times*, Sunday, June 25, 2006, Business Section.

Blount, Marcellus and George P. Cunningham, ed., *Representing Black Men* (New York: Routledge, 1996).

Blow, Charles M., "A Mighty Pale Tea," *New York Times*, April 17, 2010, A15.

Bonilla-Silva, Eduardo, *Racism without Racists: Color-Blind Racism and the Persistence of Racial Inequality in the United States* (Lanham, MD: Rowman and Littlefield, 2006).

Boxill, Bernard R., *Blacks and Social Justice*, revised edition (Lanham, MD: Rowman and Littlefield, 1992).

Boylan, Jennifer Finney, *She's Not There: A Life in Two Genders* (New York: Broadway Books, 2003).

Brickman, Celia, *Aboriginal Populations in the Mind: Race and Primitivity in Psychoanalysis* (New York: Columbia University Press, 2003).

Brown, Michael K., Martin Carnoy, Elliott Currie, Troy Duster, David B. Oppenheimer, Marjorie M. Shultz, and David Wellman, *Whitewashing Race: The Myth of a Color-Blind Society* (Berkeley: University of California Press, 2003).

Brown, Wendy, *States of Injury: Power and Freedom in Late Modernity* (Princeton, NJ: Princeton University Press, 1995).

————, *Politics Out of History* (Princeton, NJ: Princeton University Press, 2001).

Burack Cynthia, *The Problem of the Passions: Feminism, Psychoanalysis and Social Theory* (New York: New York University Press, 1994).

Burchell, Graham, Colin Gordon, and Peter Miller, eds. *The Foucault Effect: Studies in Governmentality* (Chicago: University of Chicago Press, 1991).

Bureau of Labor Statistics and the Census Bureau, *Current Population Survey http://www.census.gov/cps/*

Butler, Judith, *Bodies that Matter: On the Discursive Limits of "Sex"* (New York: Routledge, 1993).

———, *Antigone's Claim: Kinship between Life and Death* (New York: Columbia University Press, 2000).

Butterfield, Fox, "Despite Drop in Crime, an Increase in Inmates," *New York Times*, November 8, 2004, 14.

Carby, Hazel V., *Reconstructing Womanhood: The Emergence of the Afro-American Woman Novelist* (New York: Oxford University Press, 1987).

Center for Disease Statistics, *Health, United States, 2008*. http://www.cdc.gov/nchs/data/nvsr/nvsr57/nvsr57_14.pdf

Cheng, Anne Anlin, *The Melancholy of Race* (New York: Oxford University Press, 2001).

Cleaver, Eldridge, *Soul on Ice* (New York: Delta, 1969).

Cole, Johnnetta Betsch and Beverly Guy-Sheftall, *Gender Talk: The Struggle for Women's Equality in African American Communities* (New York: Random House, 2003).

Coles, Romand, "Traditio: Feminists of Color and the Torn Virtues of Democratic Engagement," *Political Theory* 29, 4 (August 2001): 488–516.

Collins, Patricia Hill, *Black Sexual Politics: African Americans, Gender, and the New Racism* (New York: Routledge, 2004).

Cose, Ellis, *The Rage of a Privileged Class* (New York: HarperCollins, 1993).

Crenshaw, Kimberle Williams, "Mapping the Margins: Intersectionality, Identity Politics, and Violence Against Women," in *Critical Race Theory: The Key Writings that Formed the Movement*, ed. Kimberle Crenshaw, Neil Gotanda, Gary Peller, and Kendall Thomas (New York: The New Press, 1995), 357–383.

Cruikshank, Barbara, *The Will to Empower: Democratic Citizens and Other Subjects* (Ithaca, NY: Cornell University Press, 1999).

D'Agostino, Fred, "Rituals of Impartiality," *Social Theory and Practice* 27, 1 (January 2001): 65–81.

Davis, Angela Y., *Women, Race, and Class* (New York: Random House, 1981).

Davis, David Brion, *Inhuman Bondage: The Rise and Fall of Slavery in the New World* (New York: Oxford University Press, 2006).

Davis, James F., *Who Is Black?: One Nation's Definition* (University Park: Pennsylvania State University Press, 1991).

Davis, Peggy G., "Law as Microaggression," in *Critical Race Theory: The Cutting Edge*, second edition, ed. Richard Delgado and Jean Stefancic (Philadelphia: Temple University Press, 2000), 141–151.

Dawson, Michael C., *Black Visions: The Roots of Contemporary African-American Ideologies* (Chicago: University of Chicago Press, 2001).

Delgado, Richard, and Jean Stefancic, eds., *Critical Race Theory: The Cutting Edge*, second edition (Philadelphia: Temple University Press, 2000).

DeParle, Jason, "Study Finds Many Children Don't Benefit from Credits," *New York Times*, Sunday, October 2, 2005, A16.

de Tocqueville, Alexis, *Democracy in America*, ed. and trans. Harvey C. Mansfield and Delba Winthrop (Chicago: University of Chicago Press, 2000).

Dillon, Michael, "Another Justice," *Political Theory* 27, 2 (April 1999): 155–175.

Dillon, Sam and David M. Herszenhorn, contributing, "Schools' Efforts Hinge on Justices' Ruling in Cases on Race and School Assignments," *New York Times*, Saturday, June 24, 2006, A11.

Dimen, Muriel, "Deconstructing Difference: Gender, Splitting, and Transitional Space," in *Gender in Psychoanalytic Space: Between Clinic and Culture*, ed. Muriel Dimen and Virginia Goldner (New York: Other Press, 2002), 41–61.

Donovan, Karen, "Pushed by Clients, Law Firms Step Up Diversity Efforts," *New York Times*, Friday, July 21, 2006, C6.

Dovidio, John F. and Samuel Gaertner, "On the Nature of Contemporary Prejudice: The Causes, Consequences and Challenges of Aversive Racism," in *Race, Gender and Class in the United States*, 6th edition, ed. Paula S. Rothenberg (New York: W. H. Freeman, 2003), 132–141.

DrugWarFacts.org., "Get the Facts," http://www.drugwarfacts.org/cms/node/64, 2009.

duCille, Ann, "The Occult of True Black Womanhood: Critical Demeanor and Black Feminist Studies." *Signs: Journal of Women in Culture and Society* 19, 3 (Fall 1994): 591–629.

Ellison, Ralph, *The Collected Essays of Ralph Ellison* (New York: Modern Library, 1995).

Fairbairn, W. Ronald D., "Schizoid Factors in the Personality," in *Psychoanalytic Studies of the Personality*, ed. W. Ronald D. Fairbairn (London: Routledge, 1992): 3–27.

Fanon, Frantz, *The Wretched of the Earth* (New York: Grove, 1966).

———, *Black Skin, White Masks: The Experiences of a Black Man in a White World* (New York: Grove, 1967).

Feder, Ellen K., *Family Bonds: Genealogies of Race and Gender* (New York: Oxford University Press, 2007).

Federal Reserve Board, Survey of Consumer Finances, *Federal Reserve Bulletin* (February 2009). http://www.federalreserve.gov/PUBS/oss/oss2/2007/2007%20SCF%20Chartbook.pdf

Felman, Shoshana, *The Juridical Unconscious: Trials and Trauma in the Twentieth Century* (Cambridge, MA: Harvard University Press, 2002).

Flathman, Richard E., *Freedom and Its Conditions: Discipline, Autonomy, and Resistance* (New York: Routledge, 2003).

Flax, Jane, "Race/Gender and the Ethics of Difference," *Political Theory* 23, 3 (August 1995): 500–510.

————, *The American Dream in Black and White* (Ithaca, NY: Cornell University Press, 1998).

————, "Resisting Woman: On Feminine Difference in the Work of Horney, Thompson, and Moulton," *Contemporary Psychoanalysis* 38, 2 (2002): 257–276.

————, "The Scandal of Desire: Psychoanalysis and the Disruptions of Gender: A Meditation on Freud's *Three Essays on the Theory of Sexuality*." *Contemporary Psychoanalysis* 40, 1 (January 2004): 47–68.

Fogg-Davis, Hawley, "The Racial Retreat of Contemporary Political Theory," *Perspectives on Politics* 1, 3 (September 2003): 555–564.

Forero, Juan, "Columbia's Coca Survives U.S. Plan to Uproot It," *New York Times*, Saturday, August 19, 2006, A1, continued A7.

Foucault, Michel, *The History of Sexuality, v.1* (New York: Pantheon, 1980).

————, *Ethics, Subjectivity and Truth*, ed. Paul Rabinow (New York: The New Press, 1994).

————, *Power*, ed. James D. Faubion (New York: The New Press, 1994).

————, "Preface to *The History of Sexuality, Volume Two*," in *Michel Foucault: Ethics, Subjectivity and Truth*, ed. Paul Rabinow (New York: The New Press, 1997), 199–205.

————, "Sex, Power and the Politics of Identity," in Rabinow, *Michel Foucault*, 163–173.

————, "Sexuality and Solitude," in Rabinow, *Michel Foucault*, 175–184.

————, "Technologies of the Self," in Rabinow, *Michel Foucault*, 223–251.

————, "The Ethics of the Concern for the Self as a Practice of Freedom," in Rabinow, *Michel Foucault*, 281–301.

————, "The Hermeneutic of the Subject," in Rabinow, *Michel Foucault*, 93–106.

————, "Subjectivity and Truth," in Rabinow, *Michel Foucault*, 87–92.

————, *Abnormal: Lectures at the College de France 1974–1975* (New York: Picador, 1999).

————, *"Society Must Be Defended,"* Lectures at the College de France, 1975–1976 (New York: Picador, 2003).

————, *The Hermeneutics of the Subject: Lectures at the College de France, 1981–1982* (New York: Picador, 2005).

Fout, John C. and Maura Shaw Tantillo, *American Sexual Politics: Sex, Gender, and Race since the Civil War* (Chicago: University of Chicago Press, 1993).

Frankenberg, Erica, Chungmei Lee, and Gary Orfield, "A Multiracial Society with Segregated Schools: Are We Losing the Dream?" The Civil Rights Project, Harvard University, 2003. http://www.civilrightsproject. harvard.edu/researchreseg03/Are-We Losing the Dream.pdf

Frankenberg, Ruth, *White Women, Race Matters: The Social Construction of Whiteness* (Minneapolis: University of Minnesota Press, 1993).

Fraser, Nancy and Linda Gordon, "The Genealogy of Dependence," *Signs* 19, 3(1994): 309–336.

Freud, Sigmund (1905), *Three Essays on the Theory of Sexuality*. In *The Penguin Freud Library v. 7*, ed. Angela Richards (London: Penguin, 1977), 33–169.

——— (1917), "Mourning and Melancholia," in *Sigmund Freud: Collected Papers v.4*, ed. James Strachey (New York: Basic Books, 1959), 152–170.

——— (1923), *The Ego and the Id* (New York: W. W. Norton, 1960).

——— (1937), "Analysis Terminable and Interminable," in *Sigmund Freud: Collected Papers v. 5*, ed. James Strachey (New York: Basic Books, 1959), 316–357.

Fryer, Roland G., Jr. and Glenn C. Loury, "Affirmative Action and Its Mythology," http://www.economics.harvard.edu/faculty/fryer/files/fryer_loury_jepfinal.pdf, 2005.

Galston, William A., *Liberal Purposes: Goods, Virtues, and Diversity in the Liberal State* (New York: Cambridge University Press, 1991).

Giddings, Paula, *When and Where I Enter: The Impact of Black Women on Race and Sex in America* (New York: Bantam, 1984).

Gilroy, Paul, *The Black Atlantic: Modernity and Double Consciousness* (Cambridge, MA: Harvard University Press, 1993).

———, *Against Race: Imagining Political Culture beyond the Color Line* (Cambridge, MA: Harvard University Press, 2000).

Glass, James M., *Private Terror/Public Life: Psychosis and the Politics of Community* (Ithaca, NY: Cornell University Press, 1989).

Glenn, Evelyn Nakano, *Unequal Freedom: How Race and Gender Shaped American Citizenship and Labor* (Cambridge, MA: Harvard University Press, 2002).

Goldberg, David Theo, "The Social Formation of Racist Discourse," in David Theo Goldberg, ed., *Anatomy of Racism* (Minneapolis: University of Minnesota Press, 1990), 295–318.

Gotanda, Neil, "A Critique of 'Our Constitution Is Color-Blind,'" in Delgado and Stefancic, *Critical Race Theory*, 35–40.

Graham, Kevin, "The Political Significance of Social Identity: A Critique of Rawls's Theory of Agency," *Social Theory and Practice* 26, 2 (Summer 2000): 201–222.

Gray, Francine du Plessix, *Them: A Memoir of Parents* (New York: Penguin, 2005).

Guterl, Matthew Pratt, *The Color of Race in America, 1900–1940* (Cambridge, MA: Harvard University Press, 2001).

Habermas, Jurgen, *Jurgen Habermas on Society and Politics: A Reader*, ed. Steven Seidman (Boston: Beacon, 1989).

Hacker, Andrew, *Two Nations: Black and White, Separate, Hostile and Unequal* (New York: Charles Scribners, 1992).

Halle, Michael, Caye B. Lewis, and Meena Sheshamani, United States Department of Health and Human Services, "Healthcare Disparities: A Case for Closing the Gap," June 2009. www. Healthreform.gov

Hancock, Ange-Marie, *The Politics of Disgust: The Public Identity of the Welfare Queen* (New York: New York University Press, 2004).

———, "When Multiplication Doesn't Equal Quick Addition: Examining Intersectionality as a Research Paradigm," *Perspectives on Politics* 5, 1 (March 2007): 63–79.

———, "Intersectionality as a Normative and Empirical Paradigm," *Politics and Gender* 3, 2 (June 2007): 248–263.

Hand, Sean, ed., *The Levinas Reader* (Oxford: Blackwell, 1989).

Harris, Angela, "Race and Essentialism in Feminist Legal Theory," in Delgado and Stefancic, *Critical Race Theory*, 261–274.

Harris, Cheryl I. "Whiteness as Property," in *Critical Race Theory: The Key Writings that Formed the Movement*, ed. Kimberle Crenshaw, Neil Gotanda, Gary Peller, and Kendall Thomas (New York: The New Press, 1995), 276–291.

Hartman, Saidiya, *Lose Your Mother: A Journey Along the Atlantic Slave Trade* (New York: Farrar, Straus and Giroux, 2007).

Hawkesworth, Mary, "Congressional Enactments of Race-Gender: Toward a Theory of Raced-Gendered Institutions," *American Political Science Review* 97, 4 (November 2003): 529–550.

Hegel, G. W. F., *The Phenomenology of Spirit* (New York: Harper and Row, 1967).

Heller, Agnes and Ferenc Feher, *The Postmodern Condition* (New York: Columbia University Press, 1988).

Hero, Rodney E. "Social Capital and Racial Inequality in America," *Perspectives on Politics* 1, 1 (2003): 113–122.

Higginbotham, Evelyn Brooks, "African-American Women's History and the Metalanguage of Race," *Signs: Journal of Women in Culture and Society* 17, 2 (Winter 1992): 251–274.

Hine, Darlene Clark and Kathleen Thompson, *A Shining Thread of Hope: The History of Black Women in America* (New York: Broadway Books, 1998).

Hirschman, Albert O., *The Passions and the Interests: Political Arguments for Capitalism before Its Triumph* (Princeton, NJ: Princeton University Press, 1997).

Hochschild, Jennifer, *Facing Up to the American Dream: Race, Class and the Soul of the Nation* (Princeton, NJ: Princeton University Press, 1995).

Holland, Catherine A. *The Body Politic: Foundings, Citizen, and Difference in the American Political Imagination* (New York: Routledge, 2001).

Homes, Steven A. and Richard Morin, "Being a Black Man," *Washington Post*, Sunday, June 4, 2006, A1.

Honig, Bonnie, *Political Theory and the Displacement of Politics* (Ithaca, NY: Cornell University Press, 1993).

———, *Democracy and the Foreigner* (Princeton, NJ: Princeton University Press, 2001).

hooks, bell, *Yearning: Race, Gender, and Cultural Politics* (Boston: South End Press, 1990).

Hull, Gloria T., Patricia Bell Scott, and Barbara Smith, *All the Women Are White, All the Blacks Are Men, But Some of Us Are Brave* (New York: Feminist Press, 1982).

Jacobs, Leslie A., *Pursuing Equal Opportunities: The Theory and Practice of Egalitarian Justice* (New York: Cambridge University Press, 2004).

Jacobson, Matthew Frye, *Whiteness of a Different Color: European Immigrants and the Alchemy of Race* (Cambridge, MA: Harvard University Press, 1998).

Jameson, Fredric, *The Political Unconscious: Narrative as a Socially Symbolic Act* (Ithaca, NY: Cornell University Press, 1981).

Janara, Laura, "Brothers and Others: Tocqueville and Beaumont, U.S. Genealogy, Democracy, and Racism," *Political Theory* 32, 6 (December 2004): 773–800.

Johnson, Bankole, A. "New Weapon to Curb Smoking: No More Excuses to Delay Treatment," *Archives of Internal Medicine*, 166 (2006): 1547–1550.

Jones, Jacqueline, *Labor of Love, Labor of Sorrow: Black Women, Work and the Family, from Slavery to the Present* (New York: Vintage, 1986).

Jordan, Winthrop D., *White over Black: American Attitudes to the Negro, 1650–1812* (New York: W. W. Norton, 1977).

Joyce, Amy, "Her No. 1 Problem," *Washington Post*, Sunday, August 6, 2006, F1.

Julian, Kate, "What's the Big Idea?," *Washington Post*, January 10, 2010, B5.

Junn, Jane, "Making Room for Women of Color: Race and Gender Categories in the 2008 U.S. Presidential Election," *Politics and Gender* 5, 1 (March 2009): 105–110.

Katznelson, Ira, *When Affirmative Action Was White: An Untold History of Racial Inequality in Twentieth Century American* (New York: W. W. Norton, 2005).

Katznelson, Ira and Suzanne Mettler, "On Race and Policy History: A Dialogue about the G.I. Bill," *Perspectives on Politics* 6, 3 (September 2008): 519–537.

King, Deborah, K. "Multiple Jeopardy, Multiple Consciousness: The Context of a Black Feminist Ideology," *Signs: Journal of Women in Culture and Society* 14, 1 (Autumn, 1998): 42–72.

King, Desmond, *Separate and Unequal: African Americans and the US Federal Government*, revised edition (New York: Oxford University Press, 2007).

King, Desmond S. and Rogers M. Smith, "Racial Orders in American Political Development," *American Political Science Review* 99, 1 (February 2005): 75–92.

Kirkpatrick, David D., "A Judge's Focus on Race Issues May Be Hurdle," *New York Times*, May 30, 2009, A1.

Klinkner, Philip A. with Rogers M. Smith, *The Unsteady March: The Rise and Decline of Racial Equality in America* (Chicago: University of Chicago Press: 1999).

Kovel, Joel, *White Racism: A Psychohistory* (New York: Columbia University Press, 1984).

Kristeva, Julia, *Nations Without Nationalism* (New York: Columbia University Press, 1993).

Lawrence, Charles, R. III, "The Id, the Ego, and Equal Protection: Reckoning with Unconscious Racism." *Stanford Law Review* 39 (January 1987): 317–388.

Lawrence, Charles R. III and Mari J. Matsuda, *We Won't Go Back: Making the Case for Affirmative Action* (New York: Houghton Mifflin, 1997).

Leary, Kimberlyn, "Race in Psychoanalytic Space," in *Gender in Psychoanalytic Space: Between Clinic and Culture*, ed. Muriel Dimen and Virginia Goldner (New York: Other Press, 2002), 313–329.

Levinson Justin D., Forgotten Racial Equality Implicit Bias, Decisionmaking, and Misremembering," *Duke Law Journal* 57 (2007): 344–421.

Locke, John, *Two Treatises of Government* (New York: Cambridge University Press, 1965).

Lopez, Ian F. Haney, "White by Law," in Delgado and Stefancic, *Critical Race Theory*, 626–634.

Loury, Glenn C. *The Anatomy of Racial Inequality* (Cambridge, MA: Harvard University Press, 2002).

Lugones, Maria, *Pilgrimages/Peregrinajes: Theorizing Coalition Against Multiple Oppressions* (Lanham, MD: Rowman and Littlefield, 2003).

Macpherson, C.B., *The Political Theory of Possessive Individualism:Hobbes to Locke* (New York: Oxford University Press, 1962).

Mama, Amina, *Beyond the Masks: Race, Gender and Subjectivity* (New York: Routledge, 1995).

Marriott, David, "Bonding Over Phobia," in *The Psychoanalysis of Race*, ed. Christopher Lane (New York: Columbia University Press, 1998), 417–430.

Marx, Anthony W., *Making Race and Nation: A Comparison of the United States, South Africa, and Brazil* (New York: Cambridge University Press, 1998).

Massey, Douglas and Nancy Denton, *American Apartheid: Segregation and the Making of the Underclass* (Cambridge, MA: Harvard University Press, 1993).

McCarthy, Thomas, "Vergangenheitsbewaltigung in the USA: On the Politics of the Memory of Slavery," *Political Theory* 30, 5 (October 2002): 623–648.

———, "Coming to Terms with Our Past, Part II: On the Morality and Politics of Reparations for Slavery," *Political Theory* 32, 6 (December 2004): 750–772.

Mills, Charles W. *The Racial Contract* (Ithaca, NY: Cornell University Press, 1997).

Morrison, Toni, *Beloved* (New York: Signet, 1987).

Modell, Arnold H., "Horse and Rider Revisited: The Dynamic Unconscious and the Self as Agent," *Contemporary Psychoanalysis* 44, 3 (2008): 351–366.

200 ❖ REFERENCES

Mokdad, Ali H., PhD, James S. Marks, MD, MPH, Donna F. Stroup, PhD, MSc, Julie L. Gerberding, MD, MPH, "Actual Causes of Death in the United States, 2000," *Journal of the American Medical Association* 291, 10 (March 10, 2004): 1238, 1241.

Morgan, Dan, Gilbert M. Gaul and Sarah Cohen, "Farm Program Pays $1.3 Billion to People Who Don't Farm," *Washington Post*, Sunday, July 2, 2006, A 1.

Morrison, Toni, *Playing in the Dark: Whiteness and the Literary Imagination* (New York: Vintage, 1992).

———, ed. *Race-ing Justice, En-gendering Power: Essays on Anita Hill, Clarence Thomas, and the Construction of Social Reality* (New York: Pantheon, 1992).

Mouffe, Chantal, *The Return of the Political* (New York: Verso, 1993).

Myrdal, Gunnar, *An American Dilemma: The Negro Problem and American Democracy*, in Ellis Cashmore and James Jennings, ed. *Racism: Essential Readings* (London: Sage, 2001), 35–48.

Nagel, Thomas, "Rawls on Justice," *Philosophical Review* 83 (April 1973): 226–229.

Nietzsche, Friedrich, *On the Genealogy of Morals* (New York: Vintage, 1969).

Nozick, Robert, *Anarchy, State, and Utopia* (New York: Basic Books, 1974).

O'Dea, Brian, "Lawyers, guns and money: Three Reasons to End the Drug War," *Los Angeles Times*, Opinion page, June 7, 2009.

Olson, Joel, *The Abolition of White Democracy* (Minneapolis: University of Minnesota Press, 2004).

Nehamas, Alexander, *The Art of Living: Socratic Reflections from Plato to Foucault* (Berkeley: University of California Press, 1998).

Nussbaum, Martha, A, "In Defense of Universal Values," in *Controversies in Feminism* ed. James P. Sterba (Lanham, MD: Rowman and Littlefield, 2001), 3–23.

Obama, Barack, *Dreams from My Father: A Story of Race and Inheritance* (New York: Three Rivers Press, 1995).

———, *The Audacity of Hope: Thoughts on Reclaiming the American Dream* (New York: Vintage, 2008).

———, "A More Perfect Union," reprinted in Barack Obama, *Change We Can Believe In* (New York: Three Rivers Press, 2008), 215–232.

Omi, Michael and Howard Winant, *Racial Formations in the United States: From the 1960's to the 1980's* (New York: Routledge, 1996).

Okin, Susan Moller, *Justice, Gender, and the Family* (New York: Basic Books, 1989).

Orfield, Gary and Susan Eaton, *Dismantling Desegregation: The Quiet Reversal of Brown v. Board of Education* (New York: The New Press, 1996).

Parker, Lonnae O'Neal, *I'm Every Woman: Remixed Stories of Marriage, Motherhood, and Work* (New York: Amistad, 2005).

Pateman, Carole, *The Sexual Contract* (Stanford: Stanford University Press, 1988).

Pateman, Carole and Charles Mills, *Contract and Domination* (Malden, MA: Polity Press, 2007).

Patterson, Orlando, *Slavery and Social Death* (Cambridge, MA: Harvard University Press, 1982).

——, *Rituals of Blood: Consequences of Slavery in Two American Centuries* (New York: Basic, 1998).

Pew Center on the States, "One in 100: Behind Bars in America 2008," www.pewtrusts.org.

Peters, Gretchen, "Take the War to the Drug Lords," *New York Times*, op-ed page, May 19, 2009.

Pitkin, Hanna Fenichel, *The Attack of the Blob: Hannah Arendt's Concept of the Social* (Chicago: University of Chicago Press, 1998).

Powell, Kevin, *Who's Gonna Take the Weight?: Manhood, Race, and Power in America* (New York: Three Rivers Press, 2003).

Powell, Michael, "On Diverse Force, Blacks Still Face Special Peril," *New York Times*, May 31, 2009 A1 and 18.

Project Implicit, https://implicit.harvard.edu/implicit/.

Putnam, Robert D., *Bowling Alone: The Collapse and Revival of American Community* (New York: Simon and Schuster, 2000).

Ranciere, Jacques, *On The Shores of Politics* (New York: Verso, 1995).

——, *Disagreement: Politics and Philosophy* (Minneapolis: University of Minnesota Press, 1999).

Rawls, John, *A Theory of Justice* (Cambridge, MA: Harvard University Press, 1971).

——, *Political Liberalism* (New York: Columbia University Press, 1993).

——, *Justice as Fairness: A Restatement* (Cambridge, MA: Harvard University Press, 2001).

Reagon, Bernice Johnson, "Coalition Politics: Turning the Century," in *Home Girls: A Black Feminist Anthology*, ed. Barbara Smith (New York: Kitchen Table: A Woman of Color Press, 1983), 356–368.

Retallack, Joan, *The Poethical Wager* (Berkeley: University of California Press, 2003).

Rose, Tricia, *Longing to Tell: Black Women Talk about Sexuality and Intimacy* (New York: Picador, 2003).

Roseneil, Sasha, *Common Women, Uncommon Practices: The Queer Feminisms of Greenham* (London and New York: Cassell, 2000).

Rousseau, Jean-Jacques, *On the Social Contract*, ed. Roger D. Masters (New York: St. Martins, 1978).

Rudman, Laurie, A., Richard D. Ashmore, and Melvin L. Gary, " 'Unlearning' Automatic Biases: The Malleability of Implicit Prejudice and Stereotypes," *Journal of Personality and Social Psychology* 81, 5 (2001): 856–868.

Sandel, Michael, *Liberalism and the Limits of Justice* (Cambridge, MA: Harvard University Press, 1982).

The Sentencing Project, "Young Black Americans and the Criminal Justice System: Five Years Later," http://www.sentencingproject.org/pdfs/9070smy.pdf, April, 2001.

Seshadri-Crooks, Kalpana, *Desiring Whiteness: A Lacanian Analysis of Race* (New York: Routledge, 2000).

Shelby, Tommie, *We Who Are Dark: The Philosophic Foundations of Black Solidarity* (Cambridge, MA: Harvard University Press, 2005).

Shenon, Philip, "New Limits Set Over Marketing for Cigarettes," *New York Times*, Friday, August 18, 2006, Washington section.

Shepherdson, Charles, "Human Diversity and the Sexual Relation," in Lane, *Psychoanalysis of Race*, 41–64.

Shklar, Judith N., *American Citizenship: The Quest for Inclusion* (Cambridge, MA: Harvard University Press, 1991).

———, *The Faces of Injustice* (New Haven, CT: Yale University Press, 1990).

Simien, Evelyn M., "Doing Intersectionality Research: From Conceptual Issues to Practical Examples," *Politics and Gender* 3, 2 (June 2007): 264–271.

Singletary, Michelle, "The Change That Hasn't Come," *Washington Post*, November 9, 2008, F 1.

Smiley, Tavis (Introduction), *The Covenant with Black America* (Chicago: The Third World Press, 2006).

Smith, Rogers M., *Civic Ideals: Conflicting Visions of Citizenship in U.S. History* (New Haven, CT: Yale University Press, 1997).

———, "The Puzzling Place of Race in American Political Science," *PS* (January 2004): 41–45.

Spelman, Elizabeth V., *Inessential Woman: Problems of Exclusion in Feminist Thought* (Boston: Beacon, 1988).

Spillers, Hortense J., " 'All the Things You Could Be by Now, If Sigmund Freud's Wife Was Your Mother': Psychoanalysis and Race." In *Female Subjects in Black and White: Race, Psychoanalysis, Feminism*, ed. Elizabeth Abel, Barbara Christian, and Helene Moglen (Berkeley: University of California Press, 1997), 135–158.

Stepan, Nancy Leys, "Race and Gender: The Role of Analogy in Science," in *Anatomy of Racism*, ed. David Theo Goldberg (Minneapolis: University of Minnesota Press, 1990), 38–57.

Stoler, Ann Laura, *Race and The Education of Desire: Foucault's History of Sexuality and the Colonial Order of Things* (Durham, NC: Duke University Press, 1997).

Tate, Claudia, *Psychoanalysis and Black Novels: Desire and the Protocols of Race* (New York: Oxford University Press, 1998).

Tierney, John, "Lighting Up in Amsterdam," *New York Times*, Saturday, August 26, 2006, A26.

Toobin, Jeffrey, "No More Mr. Nice Guy: The Supreme Court's Stealth Hardliner," *New Yorker*, May 25, 2009, 42–50.

Turner, Victor, *The Ritual Process* (London: Routledge and Kegan Paul, 1969).

United States Census Bureau, "Net Worth and Asset Ownership of Households, 1998 and 2000: Household Economic Studies," http://www.census.gov/prod/2003pubs/p70–88.pdf, May 2003.

United States Census Bureau, Current Population Reports, P60–233; and Internet sites <http://www.census.gov/prod/2007pubs/p60–233.pdf> (August 2007).

United States Census Bureau, "Marriage and Divorce," http://www.census.gov/population/www/socdemo/marr-div.html (August 2007).

United States Department of Justice, Bureau of Justice Statistics, "Criminal Offenders Statistics," http://www.ojp.usdoj.gov/bjs/crimoff.htm, August 2007.

United States Department of Justice, Bureau of Justice Statistics, http://www.ojp.usdoj.gov/bjs/glance.htm#Corrections, June 2008.

United States Department of Justice, Bureau of Justice Statistics, "Crime and Victim Statistics," http://www.ojp.usdoj.gov/bjs/cvict.htm, August 2008.

United States Department of Justice, Bureau of Justice Statistics, "Homicide Trends," http://www.ojp.usdoj.gov/bjs/homicide/race.htm, July 2007.

Veyne, Paul, "The Final Foucault and His Ethics," in *Foucault and His Interlocutors*, ed. Arnold I. Davidson (Chicago: University of Chicago Press, 1997), 225–233.

Van Natta, Jr., Don and Abby Goodnough, "After Call to Police, 2 Cambridge Worlds Collide in an Unlikely Meeting," *New York Times*, Monday July 27, 2009, A13.

Walsh, Katherine Cramer, *Talking About Race; Community Dialogues and the Politics of Difference* (Chicago: University of Chicago Press, 2007).

Walton, Jean, "Re-Placing Race in (White) Psychoanalytic Discourse: Founding Narratives of Feminism," in *Female Subjects in Black and White: Race, Psychoanalysis, Feminism*, ed. Elizabeth Abel, Barbara Christian, and Helene Moglen (Berkeley: University of California Press, 1997), 223–251.

———, *Fair Sex, Savage Dreams: Race, Psychoanalysis, Sexual Difference* (Durham, NC: Duke University Press, 2001).

Walzer, Michael, *Spheres of Justice: A Defense of Pluralism and Equality* (New York: Basic Books, 1983).

West, Cornel, *Race Matters* (Boston: Beacon, 1993).

Weston, Drew, *The Political Brain: The Role of Emotion in Deciding the Fate of the Nation* (New York: Public Affairs, 2007).

Wildeman, Christopher, "Parental Imprisonment, the Prison Boom, and the Concentration of Childhood Disadvantage," *Demography* 46, 2 (May 2009): 265–280.

Willett, Cynthia, *The Soul of Justice: Social Bonds and Racial Hubris* (Ithaca, NY: Cornell University Press, 2001).

Williams, Linda Faye, *The Constraint of Race: Legacies of White Skin Privilege in America* (University Park, PA: Pennsylvannia State Press, 2003).

Williams, Patricia J. *The Alchemy of Race and Rights: Diary of a Law Professor* (Cambridge, MA: Harvard University Press, 1991).

Wilson, William Julius, *The Declining Significance of Race* (Chicago: University of Chicago Press, 1980).

———, *The Truly Disadvantaged* (Chicago: University of Chicago Press, 1987).

Wilson, William Julius and Richard P. Taub, *There Goes the Neighborhood: Racial, Ethnic, and Class Tensions in Four Chicago Neighborhoods and Their Meaning for America* (New York: Alfred A. Knopf, 2006).

Winant, Howard, *The World Is a Ghetto: Race and Democracy since World War II* (New York: Basic Books, 2001).

Wing, Adrien Katherine, ed., *Critical Race Feminism: A Reader* (New York: New York University Press, 1997).

Winnicott, D. W. 1971. *Playing and Reality* (New York. Basic Books).

Wolfenstein, Eugene Victor, *Victims of Democracy: Malcom X and the Black Revolution* (New York: Guilford Press, 1993).

———, *A Gift of the Spirit: Reading the Soulsl of Black Folk* (Ithaca, NY: Cornell University Press, 2007).

Wolin, Sheldon, "The Liberal/Democratic Divide: On Rawls's *Political Liberalism*," *Political Theory* 24, 1 (February 1996): 97–142.

Woolf, Virginia, *A Room of One's Own* (Middlesex, UK: Penguin, 1970).

Yanow, Dvora, *Constructing "Race" and "Ethnicity" in America: Category Making in Public Policy and Administration* (Armonk, NY: M.E. Sharpe, 2003).

Young-Bruehl, Elisabeth, *The Anatomy of Prejudices* (Cambridge, MA: Harvard University Press, 1996).

Young, Iris Marion, *Justice and the Politics of Difference* (Princeton, NJ: Princeton University Press, 1990).

———, "The Logic of Masculinist Protection: Reflections on the Current Security State," *Signs: Journal of Women in Culture and Society* 29, 1 (2003): 1–25.

Zack, Naomi, ed., *Race/Sex: Their Sameness, Difference and Interplay* (New York: Routledge, 1997).

Jordan-Zachery, Julia S., "Am I a Black Woman or a Woman Who Is Black?: A Few Thoughts on the Meaning of Intersectionality," *Politics and Gender* 3, 2 (June 2007): 254–263.

———, *Black Women, Cultural Images and Social Policy* (New York: Routledge, 2009).

Zerilli, Linda M. G., *Feminism and the Abyss of Freedom* (Chicago: University of Chicago Press, 2005).

Zizek, Slavoj, "Fantasy as a Political Category: A Lacanian Approach," in *The Zizek Reader*, ed. Elizabeth Wright and Edmond Wright (Cambridge, MA: Blackwell), 87–101.

————, "Enjoy Your Nation as Yourself," in *Theories of Race and Racism: A Reader*, ed. Les Back and John Solomos (New York: Routledge, 2000), 594–606.

Zernike, Kate and Megan Thee-Brenan, "Poll Finds Tea Party Backers Wealthier and More Educated," *New York Times*, April 14, 2010, A 1.

INDEX

Note: "nn" refers to multiple notes on a page

"best self," 119
Bible, 88
binaries, 100, 102
biological differences, 103
biopower, 27, 79, 80, 104, 108,
110, 138, 141, 165n4
biracial, as category, 25
"birthers," 4
"bitch" identity, 161n65
Black Atlantic, 117–118, 127,
160n54, 177n85
"black enough," not being,
62, 120
black families, 32–33, 44
Black Farmer & Agriculturalists
Association, 145
black female (women)
economic and social
disadvantages of, 32–36, 44
erasure of, 3
fantasies about, 159n38
films and, 44, 48, 53–54,
59–64, 66
marriage and, 48
motherhood and, 23, 54, 59
resisting dominant narratives of,
171n9
as scapegoats, 188n27
slavery and, 23, 161n65
voting rights and, 76
black feminists, 23, 154n14
black male (men)
Dred Scott and, 74
economic and social
disadvantages of, 28, 32–36
films and, 43–44, 60–62
as homicide victims, 63
incarceration of, 35, 43–44
out-of-group marriage and, 48
protection and, 53–54
resisting dominant narratives of,
171n9
as "thugs," 144
voting rights and, 76
white fantasies about, 54
white men's control of, 23

blackness
conflated with male, 3
"whiteness" and, 10
black power, 63
blacks (African Americans)
aggression/domesticity and, 54
Crash and, 58–64
discussion of race/gender and,
149–150
drug policy and, 142
economic and social
disadvantages of, 1, 29–30,
32–36, 74–76, 99, 145
election of Obama and, 2
Katrina and, 130–131
marking of, 10, 18–19, 25–26
mourning and, 134
slavery and, 1, 8, 11, 21–24
voting rights and, 74
white fear of, 57
Black Skin/White Masks (Fanon),
160n47
black women's clubs, 161n65
black youth, 34
blame, shifting of, 71, 81
bodies
race/gender and, 13–14, 27
as sites of power, 94
Bonilla-Silva, Eduardo, 16
Boylan, Jennifer Finney, 164n6
Braun, Carol Mosely, 34
Bruce, Blanche K., 34
Burack, Cynthia, 159n40
Butler, Judith, 14, 158nn, 164n6

cancer, 168n39
capitalism, 74
Carby, Hazel V., 161n65
care of the self, 98, 102, 104–106,
110–114, 122–124, 126,
129–130, 138, 142, 147–150,
181n17, 183n41
caretaker role, 55
Cartesian epistemology, 119
caste-based hierarchies, 56
categorical imperative, 85

election of 2008 and, 2–3
fabrication of, and movies,
41–42
fantasy and understanding of,
17–18
Glenn's categorization of, 27
Monster's Ball and, 42–49
as "natural fact," 109
object-centered practices
and, 123
Rawls and, 87–89, 92–95
recession and, 32
slavery and, 9–10, 21–24
social fabrication of, 25–29,
164–165n6
Sotomayor and, 170n50
theoretical vs. empirical approach
to, 12
race/gender impact statement, 135,
144–146
race/gender melancholia
affirmative action as "reverse
racism" and, 38
affirmative action policies to
undo, 135–138, 144
contemporary American politics
and, 2–6
defined, 10–21
democratic paradox and, 98–101
domination and, 7–24
drug policies to undo, 138–144
films and, 6, 42–67
Foucault's subjectivity and care of
self, as approach to, 102–115
genealogy of, 25–40
governmentality and, 110
importance of acting on, 15–16
individualism and, 6, 102
liberalism and, 69–95
Morrison on, 18
mourning required to overcome,
131–135
object-centered practices to undo,
118–128
paralyzing and repetitive effects
of, 6, 8, 40, 129

post-racial and colorblind society
claims and, 3–4, 29, 31,
167n22
practicing constraint to undo,
113–118
race/gender impact statements to
undo, 144–146
refabricating citizenship to undo,
146–151
remedies for, as
multidimensional, 97–98
shifting habits of thought to
undo, 24, 101
see also race/gender domination;
race/gender grids and position;
and specific issues
"race neutrality," 90, 92–93
racial profiling, 28–29, 35–36,
186–187n14
racism, 18, 31, 59, 67, 167n24
rage, 15–17, 39, 43, 45, 47, 55, 59,
63, 67, 82
"rags to riches" myth, 81
Ramsey, Charles H., 56
Ranciere, Jacques, 101, 186n67
rape, 9, 13, 60
rationality, *see* reason and rationality
Rawls, John, 6, 37, 71, 78, 83–95,
97, 100, 119–120, 123–124,
134, 136, 172–173n3,
175–176n47, 178–179nn
Reagon, Bernice Johnson, 184n59
reason and rationality, 6, 17, 82, 86,
100, 103, 97, 119, 124, 149,
179n97
fantasy of impossible perfection
and, 90–95
sadomasochistic relationships
and, 39–40
unconscious processes and,
178n85
recession of 2008–10, 32,
167–168n25
Reconstruction, 2, 34, 74
redistribution, 99, 131, 133,
135–138

social status, 80–82, 99
social welfare programs, 30, 80
"*Society Must Be Defended*"
(Foucault), 181n16
Solberg, Andy, 56
solidarity, 39, 62
Sotomayor, Justice Sonia, 31, 115,
116, 166n18, 167nn, 170n50
soul service, 102, 111–113, 147,
181n17
South, 24, 29–30, 73
South Africa, 44, 56
space, clearing or opening new,
102–104, 123–124, 135, 148,
149; *see also* public spaces;
transitional space
split, noumenal vs. phenomenal
selves and, 94, 119
splitting, 10–11, 37, 55, 67,
126, 151
ascriptive beliefs and, 76–77
defined, 19, 155n19
drug policy and, 142
fantasy of impossible perfection
and, 176n53
identity politics and, 119
liberalism and, 70
manic defenses and, 81
original position and, 87, 89–90,
94–95, 173n3, 178–179n95
overcoming, 131–134, 147
unmarked self and, 117
white women and, 55
state, 9, 109–110, 119, 154n9
Stoler, Ann Laura, 181n16
"structural/materialist" approaches,
analyzing power relations, 16
structure/subject dichotomy,
104–105, 107
subject-centered politics,
119–122, 124
subjectivity, 6, 98
deep, or unitary, 101,
119–120, 122
fabricated, *see under* fabrication of
subjectivity

Foucauldian approach to, 102,
104–110, 114–128, 135,
181–182n17
individual vs. collective
dispositions and, 16–18
liberal individualism and,
70–72, 102
metaphors of diaspora and, 117
psychoanalysis and, 12–15,
181–182n17
slavery and, 9, 21–22
urban farming and, 189n29
subject/object binary, 107
subordination, *see* denigrated
or subordinated other;
denigration; race/gender grids
and position; race/gender
domination
surveillance, 110, 138
survivalist cults, 82
Swan Lake, 51–52, 54
Swinton, Tilda, 49

taboos, 13–14, 46, 158n33
Taliban, 141
Talking to Strangers (Allen),
169n47
Taub, Richard P., 155n13
"Tea Party," 4
technologies of power, 108,
110–111, 146; *see also*
biopower; governmentality
technologies of production, 108
technologies of signification, 108
technologies of the self, 104–105,
107–108, 110–113, 115–116,
124, 126–127, 141, 144
terrorism
race/gender, 9, 30, 60, 82, 121
threat of foreign, 80, 101, 141
Thee-Brenan, Megan, 154n15
Theory of Justice, A (Rawls), 87,
172n3
There Goes the Neighborhood
(Wilson and Taub), 155n13
Thernstrom, Abigail, 166n18